MODERN TRAGEDY

MODERN TRAGEDY

Raymond Williams

1966

CHATTO AND WINDUS

LONDON

Published by
Chatto & Windus Ltd
42 William IV Street
London W.C.2

★

Clarke, Irwin & Co. Ltd
Toronto

© Raymond Williams 1966
Printed in Great Britain by
T. & A. Constable Ltd
Hopetoun Street, Edinburgh

CONTENTS

ACKNOWLEDGEMENTS

THE chapter, 'Social and Personal Tragedy', appeared as 'Tolstoy, Lawrence and Tragedy' in the *Kenyon Review*, Summer, 1963. 'From Hero to Victim' appeared in the *New Left Review*, Number 20, 1963, and in *Studies on the Left*, Spring, 1964. An early draft of Part One appeared as 'A Dialogue on Tragedy' in *New Left Review*, Numbers 13-14, 1962. 'Tragic Resignation and Sacrifice' and 'Tragic Despair and Revolt' appeared in the *Critical Quarterly*, Spring and Summer, 1963. 'Private Tragedy' is due to appear in a volume to be published by the Strindberg Society.

I have quoted, in the critical essays, from the published works of Ibsen, Arthur Miller, Strindberg, O'Neill, Tennessee Williams, Chekhov, Pirandello, Ionesco, Beckett, Tolstoy, Lawrence, Eliot, Pasternak, Camus, Sartre and Brecht, and, in my theoretical discussion, from, among others, Aristotle, Lessing, Hegel, Marx, Schopenhauer, Nietzsche and Lukács. Where these works or translations are in copyright, I am glad to acknowledge my indebtedness to their publishers.

In my general reading on tragedy I have used works by the following authors, whom I wish to acknowledge: A. Pickard-Cambridge; John Jones; J. W. H. Atkins; Israel Knox; Hannah Arendt; Frederick Copleston; Herbert Weisinger; H. D. F. Kitto; Ruth Benedict; I. A. Richards; T. R. Henn; George Steiner; Murray Krieger; Jane Harrison; Gilbert Murray; T. B. L. Webster; F. R. Leavis; Iris Murdoch; Philip Thody; Ronald Gray; J. P. Stern; T. Spencer; R. Niebuhr; Karl Jaspers; F. Fergusson; C. E. Vaughan.

I am indebted to M. I. Finley for his kindness in discussing two points with me, and to my wife for her general help with the book.

R. W.

FOREWORD

This book brings together, and tries to extend, certain kinds of work I have attempted before. The first part, a history and criticism of ideas of tragedy, follows, in some respects, the work attempted in *Culture and Society* and *The Long Revolution*. The second part follows from *Drama from Ibsen to Eliot*, though the questions being asked are different. Between that book and this I gave, over four years, a series of lectures on Modern Tragedy in the English Faculty at Cambridge, and my second part is a revised version of those lectures: revised mainly in the direction of making my own position more explicit. Meanwhile, I had been working on the play *Koba*, intermittently since 1957, before I thought of writing a book about tragedy. I include it here, with the other kinds of writing, because it seems now essentially to belong with them, although it came first.

The form of the book is, I realise, unconventional and mixed. If any reader is good enough to find one kind of work useful, but not the others, he is welcome to use the book accordingly. But I wanted to get a whole structure of feeling and thinking into one book, even where it had led to different kinds of work, and in a way just because it had led to them. For the literature of ideas and of experience is still, as I know it, a single literature. The necessary variations of matter and approach lead back, insistently, to a particular mind, but lead out, also, to a complex reality which we cannot always afford to divide. Tragedy is the most important example I know of this complex and necessary unity, as many of my predecessors have repeatedly found.

So the book is about the connections, in modern tragedy, between event and experience and idea, and its form is designed at once to explore and to emphasise these radical connections.

Cambridge, 1964   R. W.

A*

PART ONE
Tragic Ideas

TRAGIC IDEAS

I. TRAGEDY AND EXPERIENCE

We come to tragedy by many roads. It is an immediate experience, a body of literature, a conflict of theory, an academic problem. This book is written from the point where the roads cross, in a particular life.

In an ordinary life, spanning the middle years of the twentieth century, I have known what I believe to be tragedy, in several forms. It has not been the death of princes; it has been at once more personal and more general. I have been driven to try to understand this experience, and I have drawn back, baffled, at the distance between my own sense of tragedy and the conventions of the time. Thus I have known tragedy in the life of a man driven back to silence, in an unregarded working life. In his ordinary and private death, I saw a terrifying loss of connection between men, and even between father and son: a loss of connection which was, however, a particular social and historical fact: a measurable distance between his desire and his endurance, and between both and the purposes and meanings which the general life offered him. I have known this tragedy more widely since. I have seen the loss of connection built into a works and a city, and men and women broken by the pressure to accept this as normal, and by the deferment and corrosion of hope and desire. I have known also, as a whole culture has known, a tragic action framing these worlds, yet also, paradoxically and bitterly, breaking into them: an action of war and social revolution on so great a scale that it is continually and understandably reduced to the abstractions of political history, yet an action that cannot finally be held at this level and distance, by those who have known it as the history of real men and women, or by those who know, as a quite personal fact, that the action is not yet ended.

Tragedy has become, in our culture, a common name for this kind of experience. Not only the examples I have given, but many other kinds of event—a mining disaster, a burned-out family, a broken career, a smash on the road—are called tragedies. Yet tragedy is also a name derived from a particular kind of dramatic art, which over twenty-five centuries has a complicated yet arguably continuous history. The survival of many great works which we call tragedies makes this presence especially powerful. This coexistence of meanings seems to me quite natural, and there is no fundamental difficulty in both seeing their relations and distinguishing between them. Yet it is very common for men trained in what is now the academic tradition to be impatient and even contemptuous of what they regard as loose and vulgar uses of 'tragedy' in ordinary speech and in the newspapers.

To begin a discussion of modern tragedy with the modern experiences that most of us call tragic, and to try to relate these to tragic literature and theory, can provoke literal amazement, or the simpler and more conventional cry of incompetence. The word, we are given to understand, is being simply and perhaps viciously misused. And of course it is natural to hesitate, at this point. In a partly educated society, we are understandably nervous about using a word or a description wrongly. But then it becomes clear, as we listen, that what is in question is not only a word. Tragedy, we are told, is not simply death and suffering, and it is certainly not accident. Nor is it simply any response to death and suffering. It is, rather, a particular kind of event, and kind of response, which are genuinely tragic, and which the long tradition embodies. To confuse this tradition with other kinds of event and response is merely ignorant.

But again, as we listen, we see that what is in question is not only the use of 'tragedy' to describe something other than a work of dramatic literature: the extension we have already noted. What is more deeply in question is a particular kind and particular interpretation of death and suffering. Certain events and responses are tragic, and others are not. By sheer authority, and from our natural eagerness to learn, it is possible for this to be said and repeated, without real challenge. And to be half inside and half outside such a system is to be reduced to despair. For there are two questions which still need to be asked. Is it really the case that what is called the tradition carries so clear and single a meaning? And, whatever our answer to this, what actual relations are we to see and live by, between the tradition of tragedy and the kinds of experience, in our own time, that we ordinarily and perhaps mistakenly call tragic?

It takes, I believe, many years, to move from first shaping these questions, in a personal uncertainty about the implications of what is being taught, to putting them at all precisely and being in any position to try to answer them. The difficulties are in any case so severe that no time is really long enough. But the moment comes when it is necessary to make a beginning. I propose to examine the tradition, with particular reference to its actual historical development, which I see as crucial to an understanding of its present status and implications. I can then offer what I believe to be an explanation of the separation between 'tragedy' and tragedy, and try, in different ways, to describe the relations and connections which this formal separation hides.

2. TRAGEDY AND THE TRADITION

The separation of 'tragedy' and tragedy is in one sense inevitable. Our thinking about tragedy is important because it is a point of intersection between tradition and experience, and it would certainly be surprising if the intersection turned out to be a coincidence. Tragedy comes to us, as a word, from a long tradition of European civilization, and it is easy to see this tradition as a continuity in one important way: that so many of the later writers and thinkers have been conscious of the earlier, and have seen themselves as contributing to a common idea or form. Yet 'tradition' and 'continuity', as words, can lead us into a wholly wrong emphasis. When we come to study the tradition, we are immediately aware of change. All we can take quite for granted is the continuity of 'tragedy' as a word. It may well be that there are more important continuities, but we can certainly not begin by assuming them.

There is a common pressure, in the ordinary verbal contrast between traditional and modern, to compress and unify the various thinking of the past into a single tradition, 'the' tradition. In the case of tragedy, there are additional pressures of a particular kind: the assumption of a common Graeco-

Christian tradition, which has shaped Western civilization. Tragedy is at first sight one of the simplest and most powerful illustrations of this cultural continuity. Tragedy is the Greeks and the Elizabethans, in one cultural form; Hellenes and Christians, in a common activity. It is easy to see how convenient, how indispensable, an idea of tragedy this is. Most study of tragedy has been unconsciously determined by just this assumption, and indeed by a desire to teach and propagate it. At particular stages of our own history, the revival of tragedy has been a strategy determined by this consciousness of a necessary tradition. In our own century, especially, when there has been a widespread sense of that civilization being threatened, the use of the idea of tragedy, to define a major tradition threatened or destroyed by an unruly present, has been quite obvious. And then it is not a question of mere counter-assumption: that there is no such significant continuity. It is a question, rather, of realising that a tradition is not the past, but an interpretation of the past: a selection and valuation of ancestors, rather than a neutral record. And if this is so, the present, at any time, is a factor in the selection and valuation. It is not the contrast but the relationship between modern and traditional that concerns the cultural historian.

To examine the tragic tradition, that is to say, is not necessarily to expound a single body of work and thinking, or to trace variations within an assumed totality. It is to look, critically and historically, at works and ideas which have certain evident links, and which are associated in our minds by a single and powerful word. It is, above all, to see these works and ideas in their immediate contexts, as well as in their historical continuity, and to examine their place and function in relation to other works and ideas, and to the variety of actual experience.

I shall hope to show, if only in outline, an historical development of the idea of tragedy, which may enable us to escape the deadlock of the contemporary contrast between 'Tragedy, proper, so-called, as known from the tradition', and the forms and pressures of our own tragic experience. What we have really to see, in what is offered to us as a single tradition, is a tension and variation so significant, on matters continually and inevitably important to us, that we gain not only relief from a contemporary deadlock, but a positive historical insight.

Classical and Mediaeval

The uniqueness of Greek tragedy is often affirmed, but often, in the manner of its affirmation, denied. The plays survive: that is to say, thirty-two plays out of some three hundred by Aeschylus, Sophocles and Euripides, and none by the scores of other tragedians known by name. Yet what survives has an extraordinary if uneven power: some eight or ten plays are among the greatest drama of the world. The unique achievement requires emphasis, but as an *achievement*. What for us is a source (in one way rightly, for here European drama was born) was for the Greeks a fulfilment: a mature form touching at every point a mature culture. In some though not all subsequent periods, this major achievement has affected the development of tragic drama, in all degrees from general awareness to conscious imitation. Yet there has been no re-creation and in effect no reproduction of Greek tragedy, and this is not really surprising. For its uniqueness is genuine, and in important ways not transferable.

For the last century and a half (significantly during the loosening of Christian belief) many attempts have been made to systematise a Greek tragic philosophy, and to transmit it as absolute. But it is not only that the tragedies we have are extremely resistant to this kind of systematisation, with evident and intractable differences between the three major tragedians. It is also that these precise issues—of Fate, Necessity and the nature of the Gods—were not systematised by the Greeks themselves: it is a culture marked by an extraordinary network of beliefs connected to institutions, practices and feelings, but not by the systematic and abstract doctrines we would now call a theology or a tragic philosophy. The deepest inquiries and modes of understanding run back, continually, into particular myths, and this quality is of critical importance in understanding the nature of the art. For it is the nature of myth that it resists anterior explanation; its extensions are always from its particulars to these newly experienced particulars (this is the dimension of varying interpretation and emphasis in the tragedians). It is commonplace, in the modern 'Greek' system, to abstract, for example, Necessity, and to place its laws above human wills. But the character of necessity, insofar as it can be generalised in this culture and these plays, is that its limits on human action are

discovered in real actions, rather than known in advance or in
general: the precise qualities that now characterise Necessity
and are translated as determinism or fatalism. Much of the
creative vigour and tension of the tragedies is in this unique
process of remaking the real actions of the myths as particular
and presently experienced dramatic actions, yet within the
organic character of the dramatic festivals, with inescapable
general connections to contemporary experience and its social
institutions.

What is least imitable, in Greek tragedy, is the most unique
result of this process: a particular dramatic form. And this is
not an isolable aesthetic or technical achievement: it is deeply
rooted in a precise structure of feeling. This is where the
modern system most clearly misinterprets the plays. Having
abstracted a general Necessity, it sets within and against it
suffering individuals, summed up as the tragic hero. The
mainspring of the action is then seen as the isolation of this
hero. But, uniquely, this is a choral tragedy. The specific and
varying relations between chorus and actors are its true
dramatic relations. The real action is the known and grievous
history of particular ruling families, which have a representative general importance in the shared substance of myth.
The dramatic form embodies, in a unique way, both the
history and the presence, the myth and response to the myth.
The known history is enacted by the three masked actors,
who have separated out from the chorus but, as their sharing
of roles and their formal relations with the chorus make clear,
not separated out altogether. What the form then embodies
is not an isolable metaphysical stance, rooted in individual
experience, but a shared and indeed collective experience, at
once and indistinguishably metaphysical and social, which
is yet capable of great tension and subtlety, as in the dynamic
isolation of the *kommos*, or the dramatically shifting yet
formally controlling singing of the chorus. It is no accident
that as this unique culture changed, the chorus was the crucial
element of dramatic form which was weakened and eventually
discarded. The structure of feeling which, in the great period,
had developed and sustained it as the dramatised tension and
resolution of collective and individual experience, weakened
and was lost, and with it a unique meaning of tragedy. It was
remembered, but also reinterpreted, in the long centuries

that followed. The permanence of the art could be taken as the permanence of its particular meanings, which in fact were both lost and changed. We can see this clearly, in the transition from the classical to the mediaeval world.

It is now generally agreed that there was little or no tragedy in mediaeval literature, and this agreement seems to rest on two grounds: first, that tragedy was then understood as narrative, rather than as drama; second, that the general structure of mediaeval belief had little place for the genuinely tragic action. It would be easy to raise incidental objections to each of these views. The necessary relation between tragedy as an interpretation of experience and its embodiment in drama rather than in narrative can hardly be taken for granted. And if mediaeval belief was so uncongenial to tragedy, it is not easy to understand the common argument that Elizabethan tragedy was rooted in an age of faith inherited from that same mediaeval world. But the most necessary observation is not of this kind. Only an extraordinarily powerful attachment to an absolute meaning of tragedy could force us to overlook the use of the word, in a quite specific sense, in a major historical period. It is not that we lack the evidence, but that we fail to use it because it does not fit our idea of the tradition.

The most famous English mediaeval definition of tragedy is in Chaucer's *Prologue of the Monk's Tale*:

> *Tragedie is to seyn a certeyn storie,*
> *As olde bookes maken us memorie,*
> *Of hym that stood in greet prosperitee,*
> *And is yfallen out of heigh degree,*
> *Into myserie, and endeth wrecchedly.*

The emphasis here is obviously on a change of worldly condition, dramatised by the reference to 'heigh degree'. The first definition in the *Monk's Tale* itself is apparently similar:

> *I wol biwaille, in manere of tragedie,*
> *The harm of hem that stoode in heigh degree,*
> *And fillen so that ther nas no remedie*
> *To brynge hem out of hir adversitee.*
> *For certein, whan that Fortune list to flee,*
> *Ther may no man the cours of hire withholde.*
> *Lat no man truste on blynde prosperitee.*

The story of tragedy, then, is the change from prosperity to adversity, determined by the general and external fact of mutability. As such, and in spite of the differences we must later observe, it has at first sight more in common with the Greek idea of tragedy than with any later versions. Tragedy involves individuals, in this work, only in the sense of the first historical meaning of 'individual', a member of a group or kind rather than a separable and unique being.

Mediaeval tragedies are usually collected examples of the operation of a general law, and the keyword is Fortune. In the *Monk's Tale*, there is one exception, that of Nebuchadnezzar, to the wretched ending: the King is released from misery by God, and given understanding. Of the other stories, all ending in misery, three or perhaps four relate the fall to a crime: Satan (sin), Adam (misgovernance), Samson (the folly of trusting his wife), Antiochus (pride and cruelty). It is significant that these interpretations come ready-made from the Christian tradition. All the other stories illustrate a more general mutability: Nero, Holofernes, Croesus and Balthasar are seen as wrong, but there is no real distinction, in the way Fortune strikes them down, from the stories of Hercules, Zenobia, Peter of Spain, Peter of Cyprus, Bernabò, Ugolino, Alexander and Caesar, which show misfortune coming to the strong or the good.

The argument about Fortune, and about that complex of related ideas including Fate, Destiny, Chance and Providence, was important through the long centuries from the classical to the mediaeval world. No simple statement of its meaning is possible; but there were times when Fortune was clearly distinguished, in the sense of chance, from the laws of Fate or Providence; and other times when it was seen as the secondary ground, or, later, the ministering agent, of the determining laws. In the latter kind of interpretation, there was an obvious way of arguing that Fortune might appear arbitrary, but only because man's understanding was limited.

In none of the literature created within this complex, however, was the origin of a change in condition primarily assigned to what we now call individual character. At most, the individual could act by choice within limits set by the powers beyond him. The ground of tragic action, therefore, was the operation of these powers in a particular case. However powerfully or closely realised the particular case might be, it remained in this sense exemplary. In Seneca, there is an important stress on the nobility of suffering and enduring misfortune, which provided a basis for the later transfer of interest to the suffering individual, away from the general action. But in the mediaeval idea of tragedy, the general emphasis is firm to the point of extreme abstraction. There is still, within this emphasis, an apparent uncertainty, for while the orthodox Christian conception of Fortune, at this time, showed it as an agency of Providence, there was still a powerful retained stress on a much more arbitrary and incomprehensible power. The wheel of Fortune, that extraordinarily complicated and dominant image, carried arbitrariness as one of its permanent meanings. It was not easy to combine it with the essentially different idea and image of the Fall, though in the pit below the wheel the attempt was made. What was really at issue, here, was an unsettled argument about historical and arbitrary destiny.

The really new conception, in the mediaeval structure of feeling, was the putting of Fortune outside any general and common human destiny. That is to say, if you get on the wheel of Fortune, it will eventually throw you down, but you have an earlier choice, as to whether you get on it at all. The implications of this separation—a radical dualism of man and the world—are extremely important. As we saw in the definitions, the tragic action is a change in worldly condition, and is explicitly referred to high degree. We can add Lydgate:

> It begynneth in prosperite
> And endeth ever in adversite
> And it also doth the conquest trete
> Of riche kynges and of lordys grete.

There is an apparent continuity, in this emphasis on rank, from the Greek to the mediaeval conception. But, unlike the continuity of reference to a general condition beyond human powers, this apparent continuity is in fact a reversal.

In Greek tragedy the action was of ruling families, though normally these were 'heroic' in the sense of belonging to a past legendary age, intermediate between gods and men. Rank and heroic stature were then the conditions of the

general importance of the action: at once public and metaphysical. The eminence of what we would now call the tragic
hero is in this sense an involving and representative eminence;
the action embodies a whole view of life. Still, in Hellenistic
and post-classical definitions, we can feel this generic force.
The definition of tragedy by Diomedes—*est heroicae fortunae
in adversis comprehensio*—said to be based on a definition by
Theophrastus—

$$\dot\eta\rho\omega\iota\kappa\eta\hat\varsigma\ \tau\upsilon\chi\eta\varsigma\ \pi\epsilon\rho\iota\sigma\tau\alpha\sigma\iota\varsigma$$

—cannot really be given the stress on isolated greatness which
later definitions of both 'hero' and 'high rank' indicate and
assume, behind the apparent continuity of these exceptionally
complicated words. Aristotle himself, from whom these
descriptions ultimately derive, was always concerned with
the generic action rather than with the isolated hero. It is
when we come to Isidore's definition that we can feel the
change—*luctuosae res publicae et regum historiae*—and the full
change is evident when mediaeval writers take up, as tragedies,
the stories of famous men familiar in the long tradition from
Plutarch. Boccaccio's *De Casibus Virorum Illustrium* is the
type example, and Chaucer uses the same phrase as the sub-
title of the *Monk's Tale*.

The question of literary influence is immensely complicated, but what matters for the idea of tragedy is this stress
on the falls of famous men, as a whole meaning. For these
falls (already an important shift of meaning from *change* of
fortune), while still representative of a general metaphysical
assumption, are changes in the worldly condition of eminent
and therefore exposed individuals. Behind the continuity of a
change of condition, the stress has shifted from Aristotle's
'happiness and misery' to 'prosperity and adversity'.

Fortune was, then, increasingly referred to worldly
success, and, in the separation of worldly from unworldly,
the mediaeval idea of tragedy became, paradoxically, more
worldly than any before it. There might be particular sins
which led to the falls, and at times these would be examined,
in the light of the doctrine of Fortune as the ministering agent
of Providence. But behind the particular sins was a more
general sin: that of trusting to Fortune in the sense of seeking
worldly success at all. The pride of the world involved all

other vices, and the remedy was to put no trust in the world but to seek God. We see this very clearly at the end of the *Monk's Tale*:

> *Tragediës noon oother maner thyng*
> *Ne kan in syngyng crie ne biwaille*
> *But that Fortune alwey wole assaille*
> *With unwar strook the regnes that been proude;*
> *For whan men trusteth hire, thanne wol she faille,*
> *And covere hire brighte face with a clowde.*

The effect of mediaeval tragedy, then, within what was doubtless felt as a continuity, was paradoxical. It was a drastic limitation of range, and an exclusion of conflict, under the pressures of what must be seen as the alienation of feudal society. The stress on a general condition became so attached to a single particular case—the fall of princes—that the general reference became largely negative: an abstraction defining a limited action. Even more paradoxically, the exemplary element was overridden by the very stress on rank, which moved from its generic and involving quality to an isolated condition. It is in the light of this complicated development that we must see the feudal stress on the isolation and consequent exposure of 'riche kynges and lordys grete' as a factor in the emergence of the later and ultimately very different conception of the tragic hero.

The crucial change was from a culture in which the metaphysical and social categories were indistinguishable, to a culture in which they were, by the changed nature of the metaphysical, quite sharply opposed. The actual relation, for all the formulas, between the temporal power and the spiritual condition, remained unsolved. Within this deep alienation, tragedy, for all its verbal continuity, became a special case and even a ground of polemic. Tragedy was a story, an account, even at times a list, because in these terms it could not be seen as an action.

Renaissance

A main source of Renaissance tragedy was this precise emphasis on the falls of famous men. But, with the dissolution of the feudal world, the practice of tragedy made new connections. The received stories were transformed because they were increasingly seen in their whole human substance, and in ways which connected rather than separated the famous fall and the common experience. Once again, however, we find a substantial change in tragedy masked by the apparent continuity and actual complexity of definitions and terms. If we look for example at Sidney's definition of tragedy, we can observe a continuity:

> The high and excellent Tragedy, that openeth the greatest wounds, and sheweth forth the Ulcers that are covered with Tissue; that maketh Kinges feare to be Tyrants, and Tyrants manifest their tirannical humors; that, with sturring the affects of admiration and commiseration, teacheth the uncertainety of this world, and upon how weake foundations guilden roofes are builded.

The theme of mutability is still dominant, and its exemplary character. But the political distinction between King and Tyrant has replaced the simple exposure of eminence, and the emphasis of 'affects'—a rephrasing of Aristotle—provides a link to a new interest. Sidney's definition continues:

> But how much it can moove, Plutarch yeeldeth a notable testimonie of the abhominable Tyrant Alexander Pheraeus, from whose eyes a Tragedy, wel made and represented, drewe aboundance of teares, who, without all pitty, had murthered infinite nombers, and some of his owne blood, so as he, that was not ashamed to make matters for Tragedies, yet coulde not resist the sweet violence of a Tragedie.

Within the exemplary tradition, and the continuing emphasis on the affairs of Kings, there is a new interest in the actual workings of tragedy: superficially in the effect on a tyrant in the audience (though as a moral programme for tragedy this would be rather limited); more generally, in the relation of the desired effects to the tragedy 'wel made and represented'. The paradox of 'sweet violence' is a related sign of a new interest: what was to become the major question: 'how can the suffering in tragedy give pleasure?'

In his characteristic combination of different traditions— the mediaeval emphasis on the fall of princes and the new Renaissance interest in tragic methods and effects—Sidney shows quite clearly the confused way in which an idea changes, under an apparent continuity of terms. The Italian Renaissance critics on whom he drew appeared to be arguing classical doctrines of tragedy, but, as in the most famous case of Castelvetro's false ascription of the unities of time and place to Aristotle, they were mainly representing new and characteristic interests of their own period. Broadly, the idea of tragedy ceased to be metaphysical and became critical, though this development was not complete until the neo-classical critics of the seventeenth century. But Sidney already gives more attention to the methods of writing tragedy than to any moral or metaphysical idea. He assumes the exemplary effect, and then turns to construction and style, criticising *Gorboduc* 'because it might not remaine as an exact model of all Tragedies'. This distinction, while formally one of material, becomes in practice one of treatment. Over the next two centuries, until the radical Hegelian revision, the idea of tragedy comprises mainly methods and effects. But in fact, behind this critical emphasis, the assumption of the nature of a tragic action was changing radically.

Neo-classical

The key to this change is the new significance of exalted rank in tragedy, which again, at first sight, appears a continuity from Aristotle and from the mediaeval emphasis. The neo-classical rules for tragedy, while assuming that tragic themes must be historical because they must concern great matters of state, tended to argue from the necessary dignity of tragedy rather than from its general and representative quality. And if dignity was the real criterion, the discussion of method was then governed mainly by considerations of decorum.

Socially, this is an aristocratic rather than a feudal conception. Rank in tragedy became important because of its accompanying style rather than because the fate of the ruling family was the fate of a city, or because the eminence of kings was the very type of worldliness. The widespread discussion of appropriate styles for tragedy, while at one level a necessary working discussion, was quite largely determined by this habitual assumption of the nature of dignity. We find the characteristic class-metaphors, in critical terminology, of 'high' and 'low' styles. When Dryden writes of 'the noblest kind of modern verse' he is not really continuing the attention to dignity which John of Garland had given in his definition of tragedy as a poem written in what is translated as the 'grand' style but for which the actual adjective is *gravis*. Behind this kind of shift, the decisively new assumptions can be quite clearly seen.

The increasing secularisation of tragedy is again, in this first phase, related to the new understanding of dignity. Dryden could still argue that exalted rank was necessary to show that no condition was exempt from the turns of Fortune. But the moving force of tragedy was now quite clearly a matter of behaviour, rather than either a metaphysical condition or a metaphysical fault. Aristotle's description of character—'a man not pre-eminently virtuous and just, whose misfortune, however, is brought upon him not by vice and depravity but by some error (*hamartia*)'—had been contained within a description of action: the 'change of fortune', not the 'change in the hero's fortunes'. Error, that is to say, was related to the action, which was in itself a general mutability. What we find in the new emphasis is an increasingly isolated interpretation of the character of the hero: the error is moral, a weakness in an otherwise good man, who can still be pitied. This progressive internalisation of the tragic cause is still held, however, within the concept of dignity. We can see, in this respect, why the formula of 'pity and terror' was so often changed to the formula we have seen in Sidney (it had originated in Minturno): 'admiration and commiseration'. The 'nobility' of the new tragic hero, though it can be traced back in a moral sense, to Seneca, and though it could illustrate, as in the theory of Saint-Evremond, the greatness of man, still carries in its very language a conception of aristocratic decorum. The way to handle suffering is now at least as important as the way to experience it or learn from it.

This emphasis on the 'noble' way to handle suffering, and on how to conduct oneself through it, appears again, in a very subtle way, in the widespread discussion of tragic effect. This, while apparently directed to a real moral question, becomes really a discussion of how the spectator of a tragedy should conduct himself. That there is a real moral question is of course obvious. Augustine had already asked, so early, why 'a spectator desires to be made sad when he beholds doleful and tragical passages, which he himself could not endure to suffer. . . . Are tears therefore loved, and passions?' Yet any such way of putting the matter tends to abstract and predicate the spectator's response, to make it an activity in itself rather than a response to a particular action. The moral question, of the nature and therefore the effect of a tragic action, becomes a question in abstracted human nature: that is to say, not an inquiry into a specific response which must then necessarily include the action to which the response is made, but an attempt to find reasons for an assumed general form of behaviour. The intricate discussion, in Hume and Burke and others, of the status of the 'mixed feelings' of pleasure and grief, which for a time dominated and has continued to influence theoretical work on tragedy, is in this sense a radical displacement of interest. Its lack of involvement with an action, its limitation of participation to the registering and balancing of emotions, are the characteristic marks of a culture which, having separated the tragic hero by an isolation of dignity and rank, comes inevitably to see the spectator as a detached and generalised consumer of feelings. Within such an idea of tragedy, indeed, both hero and spectator are conscious consumers of feeling, and their actions are limited to occasions for displaying their modes of consumption. The comparatively limited and in effect technical concept of *katharsis*, to which this discussion of tragic effect was increasingly related, became, eventually, a substitute for tragic action. In Romantic criticism, the tragic hero was remade in the image of the tragic spectator, whose assumed division of feeling was projected as a tragic cause. The single response of pity-and-terror, within a whole action, was dissociated to pity and terror as opposed and substantive feelings, to be known and modulated within the spectator's mind. This essential detachment from the tragic action was masked only by the attempted absorption of the action, through the figure of the hero, into the conscious spectator. We tend to think of this now as a Romantic excess, but the basis for it comes earlier, in the reduction of action to shared behaviour which is the essential consequence of the idea of decorum.

Lessing and the Tradition

The most remarkable fact about the post-feudal idea of tragedy is its distance from the major creative developments in actual tragic writing. Taking its theoretical framework from received classical and mediaeval ideas, and profoundly changing while apparently codifying that formal inheritance, it failed to recognize many of the really new developments which were transforming tragedy itself. Even its secularisation of tragedy is more formal than real: an emptying of content behind a retention of terms. But the new content was already richly present, notably in the Elizabethan and Jacobean tragedians. It is significant that the major contribution of Lessing is at once a theoretical rejection of neoclassicism, a defence of Shakespeare, and an advocacy and writing of bourgeois tragedy. We have to see these positions as elements of a new structure of feeling, for which, however, the preparation had been long and deep.

Nothing is more significant and controversial, in the argument about tragedy, than the placing of Elizabethan and Jacobean tragedy in relation to the tradition. In Lessing, as so often before, the whole previous tradition was reinterpreted in terms of a pressing contemporary interest and valuation. Neo-classicism was false classicism; the real inheritor of the Greeks was Shakespeare; the real inheritor of Shakespeare was the new national bourgeois tragedy. As historical formulations only the first of these is true. Neo-classicism, as we have seen, was an aristocratic version of Greek theory and practice, rather than a revival of either. But of course Shakespeare was not the inheritor of the Greeks; he was a major instance of a new kind of tragedy. It is some indication of the weight of the persistent idea of 'the tradition' that, to pursue his argument, Lessing had to try to assimilate Greek and Elizabethan tragedy into the 'traditional' form. As we have subsequently seen, he was tactically successful, but it is wrong to see his argument as more than a tactic, by which I mean nothing discreditable but simply the normal pressure to accommodate the past to the demands of a contemporary sensibility.

To say that Shakespeare's principles of dramatic composition are fundamentally the same as those of the Greeks is meaningful only in the sense that each can be assimilated to a particular version of both. The comparable vision of human life, on which, to get past the very evident differences, this kind of argument relies, is again not the substance but the contemporary interpretation of tragedy: a mid-eighteenth century version of Sophocles and Shakespeare in which the true common factor is the mid-eighteenth century. The overthrow of neo-classicism was indeed so important, historically, that we need feel no obligation to reject Lessing's argument, but simply to recognise what kind of argument it is. And to do this adequately, we must remember the third proposition, on what, in its turn, was the inheritor of this essential Sophoclean-Shakespearian tragedy.

In the twentieth century, for reasons that we shall examine, the Greek-Elizabethan identity is still widely taken for granted, but the historical source of this identity, in the German Enlightenment and then the European Romantic movement, is, ironically, now dismissed as the very period in which the essential idea of tragedy was lost. It is the familiar case of selecting and reselecting a tradition. It is of course quite true that bourgeois and Romantic tragedy are not Shakespearian tragedy, but it is difficult to argue that they have less in common with it than Shakespearian tragedy has with the Greek. If we could admit that all these periods are in certain radical ways distinct, we might be able to go on to see what, nevertheless, they may have in common. But the pressure of 'the tradition' is so strong that there is first one assimilation and then another, and the motives for assimilation are rarely examined.

It has become commonplace, in our own century, to accept not only the Greek-Elizabethan identity, but also the major reference of Elizabethan tragedy back to the mediaeval world. And this, of course, is the key to the assimilation, for what then emerges as the essence of tragedy is a sense of order, by which is meant an order of life not only more powerful than man but specifically and consciously operating upon him. The key to the earlier assimilation, on the other hand, had been not this but humanism: a shaping spirit of aspiration and dignity and compassion. It is then easy to see why the historical position assigned to Elizabethan tragedy should be so crucial. If the element of controlling order is emphasised, the backward assimilation is assured (in spite of some difficulty with the differences between Greeks and mediaeval Christians). On the other hand, if the element of humanism is emphasised, a forward assimilation, to include Romanticism, is again assured, and the enemies are not, as in the former version, the spirit of rationalism or Romantic individualism, but the cold formalities of mediaeval or neo-classical thought.

The worst thing that can happen, if these alternatives are seen, is to suppose that we must choose between them, where we now are. The only useful way to see them is historically, as examples of the selective tradition. For the truth seems to be that the character of Elizabethan tragedy is determined by a very complicated relationship between elements of an inherited order and elements of a new humanism. And if this is so we can see the historical basis for the very different assimilations that have emerged. Lessing was able to reject neo-classicism by seeing certain real qualities in Elizabethan tragedy which indeed connected with the spirit of his own time. Correspondingly, he could not clearly see the real differences. The more recent backward assimilation depends, similarly, on qualities in Elizabethan tragedy that are undoubtedly present, and that answer to a particular kind of spiritual reaction, but again, correspondingly, is unable to recognise the new elements which connect to bourgeois tragedy and beyond it to modern tragedy.

Secular Tragedy

What has mainly to be shown, if the historical development of the idea of tragedy is to be fully understood, is the very complicated process of secularisation. In one sense all drama after the Renaissance is secular, and the only fully religious tragedy we have is the Greek. Yet the decisive factor is probably not this immediate context, in institutions, but the wider context, in beliefs. Elizabethan drama is thoroughly secular in its immediate practice, but undoubtedly retains a Christian consciousness. Neo-classicism is then the first stage of substantial secularisation, but the importance of this is lessened by the very nature of its particular emphasis: decorum is not so much a belief as a code, and the definition of tragedy, in the neo-classical period, is critical rather than moral or metaphysical. What we have now to examine is the complicated and contradictory emergence of new moral and metaphysical ideas, which exert their pressure on the whole conception of a tragic action.

The increasing emphasis on a rational morality affected the tragic action in one important way: that it insisted on relating suffering to moral error, and so required the tragic action to demonstrate a moral scheme. In the eighteenth century, this relation of suffering to moral error was, however, governed by the normal conception of a static human nature, and, less consciously, by the habitual moral and social codes which, while in fact particular, were taken as absolute. In this sense, the new bourgeois moral emphasis occurred within the concept of decorum. What it added was a belief in redemption rather than in dignified endurance. To this extent, change was possible, when error had been demonstrated. Tragedy, in this view, shows suffering as a consequence of error, and happiness as a consequence of virtue. Any tragedy which fails to do this must be reformed or even rewritten, to meet the demands of what is increasingly called 'poetic justice'. That is to say, the bad will suffer and the good will be happy; or, rather, much as in the mediaeval emphasis, the bad will do badly in the world, and the good will prosper. The moral impetus of tragedy is then the realisation of this kind of consequence. The spectator will be moved to live well by the demonstration of the consequences of good and evil. And, further, within the action itself, the characters themselves will be capable of the same recognition and change. Thus the tragic catastrophe either moves its spectators to moral recognition and resolution, or can be avoided altogether, by a change of heart.

It is customary, now, to condescend to this view, and to assume its inevitable shallowness. But what was weak in it was not the underlying demand, which is indeed inevitable, but its inability to conceive morality as other than static. What it expresses is a major tradition of Christian and humanitarian thought, but within the limited dogmas of an expanding and complacent middle-class society. The response to suffering, in this tradition, is inevitably redemption, and the response to evil is repentance and goodness. But, limited to a particular view of success and failure in the world, the moral emphasis became merely dogmatic, and even repentance and redemption took on the character of *adjustment*. As such, what was intended as a moral emphasis, of a quite traditional kind, became an ideology, to be imposed on experience and to mask the more difficult recognitions of actual living. That the scheme should have been called 'poetic justice' is, ironically,

the demonstration of this ideological character. This version
of consequence might be demonstrated in a fiction, but could
not negotiate much actual experience. The distance between
such fiction and experience was then the main fact that men
came to observe, and the consciousness of unexplained and
apparently irrational suffering provided the basis for the
eventual overthrow not only of this version of consequence
but of its whole moral emphasis.

Hegel and Hegelians

It was possible to shift the whole argument on to higher
ground. Hegel did not reject the moral scheme that had been
called poetic justice, but he described it as the triumph of
ordinary morality, and the work that embodied it as social
drama rather than tragedy. In this and other ways, the
definition of tragedy became centred on a specific kind of
spiritual action, rather than on particular events, and a
metaphysic of tragedy replaced both the critical and ordinary
moral emphases. This new emphasis, on tragedy as a specific
and even rare kind of action and response, marks the major
emergence of modern tragic ideas.

What is important in tragedy, for Hegel, is not suffering
as such—'mere suffering'—but its causes. Mere pity and fear
are not tragic pity and fear, which properly relate to a specific
kind of action, which is 'conformable with the reason and
truth of Spirit'. Just as 'ordinary morality' has been rejected,
as a tragic process, so now ordinary fear, of 'the external
power and its oppression', and ordinary compassion, for 'the
misfortunes and sufferings of another', are distinguished
from the tragic emotions. Tragedy recognises suffering as
'suspended over active characters entirely as the consequence
of their own act', and further recognises the 'ethical substance'
of this act, an involvement of the tragic character with it, as
opposed to 'occasions of wholly external contingency and
related circumstance, to which the individual does not contribute, nor for which he is responsible, such cases as ill,
loss of property, death, and the like.' (It is worth noting,
in his discussion of 'ordinary' and 'tragic' emotions, Hegel
uses language similar to the propositions of decorum: 'your
countrified cousin is ready enough with compassion of this
order' [sympathy with the misfortunes and suffering of

another]. 'The man of nobility and greatness, however, has no wish to be smothered with this sort of pity.' 'True sympathy . . . an accordant feeling with the ethical claim . . . associated with the sufferer . . . is not, of course, excited by ragamuffins and vagabonds').

Hegel's definition of tragedy is centred, then, on a conflict of ethical substance. As such, it is limited to certain cultures and periods:

> To genuine *tragic* action it is essential that the principle of *individual* freedom and independence, or at least that of self-determination, the will to find in the self the free cause and source of the personal act and its consequences, should already have been aroused.

At the same time, this conscious individuality is only the condition of tragedy. Through it, the essential tragic action can occur: an action of necessary conflict and resolution. In ancient tragedy, the ends which individuals consciously seek have a 'universal and essential content'. Our sympathy is 'evoked and claimed for the simple conflict and issue of the essential powers of life, and for the godlike manifestations of the human heart, as distinctive representatives of which the heroes of tragedy are set before us'. There are other kinds of content, which do not require the tragic resolution, because they are not ethically important and substantive, and do not represent the essential powers of life. Their resolution, as in comedy, is one merely of 'false' contradictions and oppositions which do not involve the substantive being. In tragedy, however, both the individual aims and the consequent conflict are substantive and essential. 'Despite the fact that individual characters propose that which is itself essentially valid, yet they are only able to carry it out under the tragic demand in a manner that implies contradiction and with a one-sidedness which is injurious'. This is because, as ethical forces become attached to 'the external expression of human activity, their concordancy is cancelled, and they are asserted *in contrast* to each other in interchangeable succession'. The tragic resolution of the resultant conflict, is essentially the restoration of 'ethical substance and unity in and along with the downfall of the individuality which disturbs its repose'. Though it involves the downfall and destruction of individuals, therefore, tragedy provides, 'over and above mere fear and tragic

sympathy . . . the feeling of reconciliation . . . in virtue of its
vision of eternal justice, a justice which exercises a paramount
force of absolute constringency on account of the relative
claim of all merely contracted aims and passions.'

In Hegel's version of the tragic action, valid but partial
claims come into inevitable conflict; in the tragic resolution,
they are reconciled, even at the cost of the destruction of the
characters who stand for them. In ancient tragedy, as he sees
it, the characters clearly represent the substantive ethical
ends; while in modern tragedy the ends seem more wholly
personal, and our interest is directed not to the 'ethical
vindication and necessity' but rather to 'the isolated individual and his conditions'. The modes of tragic resolution
differ correspondingly. In ancient tragedy there is not only
the downfall of conflicting persons and ends, in the achievement of eternal justice. An individual may surrender his
partial end, under a higher command, or, more interestingly,
may achieve wholeness and reconciliation within himself. In
modern tragedy, the whole question of resolution is more
difficult, because the characters are more personal. Justice
itself is more abstract, and colder, or can even appear as the
mere accident of external circumstances, and therefore
merely shocking or pitiable. Reconciliation, when it comes,
will often be within the character, and will be more complicated, and often less satisfactory, because it is the character
as such, and so the personal destiny, which is emphasised
above the ethical substance he represents.

Hegel's interpretation of tragedy is part of a general
philosophy, and is convincing or unconvincing as such,
rather than as historical criticism. Its emphasis on necessary
conflict, and on the tragic issue as a resolution, has been
widely influential, but in very different ways. Under the
influence of Bradley, the objective character of the resolution
was weakened, though the difficulty of finding such an
objective character in modern tragedy was already evident
in Hegel. Bradley shifted the emphasis to self-division and
self-restitution, and seems in the end to produce a psychological rather than an ethical theory of tragedy, though a
psychology with a decidedly ideal cast. The conflict within
the tragic hero tends to replace the conflict which is embodied
in particular men, and the isolation of the tragic hero, which

Hegel had noted as a characteristic of modern tragedy, becomes general, as the decisive spiritual assumption. The history of spirit in the world, that is to say, loses its general and objective character, and becomes a working within individuals.

Under the influence of Marx, on the other hand, the objective character of the history of spirit was at once reaffirmed and transformed. The conflict of ethical forces, and their resolution by a higher force, were seen in social and historical terms. Social development was seen as necessarily contradictory in character, and tragedy occurs at those points where the conflicting forces must, by their inner nature, take action, and carry the conflict through to a transformation. As in his more general response to Hegel, Marx took a description of a spiritual process and made it a description of a social process.

It has been left to subsequent Marxist critics to develop this idea of tragedy. Thus, Greek tragedy has been seen as the concrete embodiment of the conflict between primitive social forms and a new social order. Renaissance tragedy has been seen as the embodiment of the conflict between a dying feudalism and the new individualism. It is not eternal justice, in Hegel's sense, that is affirmed in the tragic issue, but rather the general movement of history, in a series of decisive transformations of society. Not all conflicts of this kind lead to tragedy. There is only tragedy when each side finds it necessary to act, and refuses to give way. The tragic hero, in this Marxist criticism, is similarly defined in Hegelian language, though not from Hegel's account of tragedy. He is the 'world-historical individual . . . whose own particular purposes contain the substantial, which is the will of the world-spirit'; or, in Marxist terms, the individual whose 'personal passions centre upon the content of the collision' (Lukács). This identification of the 'world-historical individual' with the 'tragic hero' is in fact doubtfully Marxist. It shifts attention from the objective conflict, which is present in the whole action, to the single and heroic personality, whom it does not seem necessary to regard as tragic if he in fact embodies 'the will of the world-spirit' or of history. In this respect, as in some others, Lukács especially is a post-Hegelian rather than a Marxist critic.

What seems to follow, from the Marxist transformation of
Hegel's theory of tragedy, is a definition of a whole and
objective action, within which the actions of conflicting
characters are at once necessary and incomplete. It is
impossible for a Marxist to retain Hegel's idea of 'reconciliation' as the tragic issue, for this is essentially a restoration of
'eternal justice' by the absolute spirit of the world. The point
of entry, if we accept the definition of these conflicts as
essentially social and historical, is Hegel's difficulty in
defining the modern tragic issue. The absolute spirit of
'eternal justice' was obviously more negotiable in ancient
tragedy, where the explicit context was metaphysical, than
in modern tragedy, with its emphasis on personal destiny. The
point is not then to elevate the isolated personal destiny to
identity with the whole action, but rather to look at types of
action which, because of their essential content, have a tragic
bearing and issue. I shall return to this point in a later section,
when I discuss tragedy and revolution.

After Hegel, though not only in these direct ways, the
theory of tragedy, which had been either enclosed within the
common beliefs of the age, or reduced to merely technical
criticism, became a system of ideas, defining a general but
often minority attitude to life and contemporary experience.
The work of Hebbel is an interesting development. For him
tragedy is the conflict between the individual, in his most
general human capacity, and the 'Idea' which through social
and religious institutions both shapes and limits him. The
individual's ideal claim grows within and yet comes into final
conflict with the embodied 'Idea', towards which his attitude
is necessarily critical. The claim is necessary and yet fatal:
'an act necessitated by the world-historical process, but at
the same time destroying the individual charged with this act
because of the partial violation of the moral law'. Tragedy is
then fundamentally associated with the great crises of human
growth: the Greek conflict 'between man and fate', and the
dualism of man in the Renaissance. Comparable crises recur,
and in modern tragedy the conflict extends to the Idea itself:
'not only shall the relations of men to moral concepts be
debated, but the validity of those moral concepts.' This is the
first theoretical formulation of a subsequently important area
of modern drama: the new form of liberal tragedy.

Schopenhauer and Nietzsche

The association of tragedy with ethical crisis, with human growth, and with history, forms only one part of the developing modern theory. Radically opposed to it, and in modern Western culture even more influential, is another kind of secularisation, which is, strangely, the secularisation of Fate. The most important voice here is that of Schopenhauer:

> Only the dull, optimistic, Protestant-Rationalistic or peculiarly Jewish view of life will make the demand for poetical justice and find satisfaction in it. The true sense of tragedy is the deeper insight, that it is not his own individual sins that the hero atones for, but original sin, i.e. the crime of existence itself.

In this formulation Schopenhauer overlooks what had happened to the idea of 'poetic justice', in its transformation from the fixed moral scheme of a particular culture to the more dynamic relations between tragedy and historical crisis. Yet, from his point of view, this radical change was bound to be secondary. The Hegelian and post-Hegelian idea of tragedy is inevitably concerned with the achievement of order through disorder, with tragic resolution as much as with tragic suffering, and thence with active and affirmed particular meanings. What Schopenhauer offers is the quite different sense of a general human fate, which is above and beyond particular causes. In this respect, he is the often unacknowledged forerunner of an idea of tragedy which seems now to be dominant: that it is an action and a suffering rooted in the nature of man, to which historical and ethical considerations are not merely irrelevant but, being 'non-tragic', hostile. What we see in tragedy, Schopenhauer insists, is

> the unspeakable pain, the wail of humanity, the triumph of evil, the scornful mastery of chance, the irretrievable fall of the just and innocent.

What we see in the tragic action is the power of evil and of blind fate; more specifically, in Schopenhauer's most characteristic contribution, an inevitable *normality* of suffering. This third kind is when we see the greatest sufferings brought about by entanglements that our fate might also partake of, and through actions that perhaps we also are capable of performing, and so could not complain of injustice; then shuddering we feel ourselves already in the midst of hell.

This is more than the ordinary recognition of the closeness of tragedy. It is the view from which much post-liberal tragedy, in our own century, has been written, in which

characters of ordinary morality, under circumstances such as often occur . . . [are] so situated with regard to each other that their position compels them, knowingly and with their eyes open, to do each other the greatest injury, without any one of them being entirely in the wrong.

Thus we can see

the greatest misfortune, not as an exception, not as something occasioned by rare circumstances or monstrous characters, but as arising easily and of itself out of the actions and characters of men, indeed almost as essential to them, and this brings it terribly near to us.

So the meaning of tragedy is this recognition of the nature of life, and the significance of the tragic hero is his resignation, the surrender not merely of life but of the will to live. The heroes of tragedy are purified by suffering in the sense that the will to live, which was formerly in them, becomes dead.

Within this negation, which seems so absolute, Nietzsche found, paradoxically, a new kind of tragic affirmation. As he writes in the *Zarathustra* comment on his *Birth of Tragedy*:

'Tragedy guides us to the final goal, which is resignation.' Dionysos had told me a very different story: his lesson, as I understood it, was anything but defeatist. It certainly is too bad that I had to obscure and spoil Dionysiac hints with formulas borrowed from Schopenhauer.

Yet the kinship is real. What Nietzsche alters is not Schopenhauer's reading of the tragic nature of life, but the consequent definition of tragedy. For Nietzsche the necessary response is active: an aesthetic of tragic delight in man's inevitable suffering, which the action of tragedy shows us in order to transcend it.

Tragedy, that is to say, in Nietzsche's view, dramatises a

tension which it resolves in a higher unity. There is a structural reminiscence of Hegel in this, but the terms are entirely altered. Tragedy is 'an Apollonian embodiment of Dionysiac insights and powers.' It creates heroes, but in order to destroy them, as a way of asserting the primal unity and joy of life. 'The hero, the highest manifestation of the will, is destroyed, and we assent, since he too is merely a phenomenon, and the eternal life of the will remains unaffected.' The metaphysical delight in tragedy is this active and communicated process:

> It makes us realise that everything that is generated must be prepared to face its painful dissolution. It forces us to gaze into the horror of individual existence, yet without being turned to stone by the vision: a metaphysical solace momentarily lifts us above the whirl of shifting phenomena. For a brief moment we become, ourselves, the primal Being, and we experience its insatiable hunger for existence. Now we see the struggle, the pain, the destruction of appearances, as necessary, because of the constant proliferation of forms pushing into life, because of the extravagant fecundity of the world will.

It is worth noting, in passing, the resemblance of this development of the idea of tragedy, in nineteenth-century thought, to the development of the idea of evolution. What had been, and was to become again, an historical process—the growth of new and higher distinguishable forms—was overridden, in the second half of the century, by a total vision of the cruel and indifferent but also immensely fertile 'law of nature and of life'. Nietzsche's imagery is clearly related to this development, and the opposed views of historical crisis and metaphysical crisis, which so deeply affected the tragic argument, are in this sense parts of the same movement of mind, of which evolutionary theory itself is perhaps only a symptom.[1]

[1] Darwin's theory of natural selection was used as a metaphor for inevitable conflict and competition, as most notably in the 'social Darwinism' which can now be seen as a rationalisation of nineteenth-century capitalist society. The 'survival of the fittest' was understood, not as the survival of the *best adapted*, but of the *strongest and most aggressive*, forms of life. Hence the continuing metaphors of 'jungle' and 'rat-race' to describe modern social life. The apparent arbitrariness of the 'selection' was in any case a powerful agent of this new fatalism: the personalisation of 'Nature', 'ruthlessly selecting', was a survival of metaphysical thinking, which could be passed off as scientific. The complicated interdependence of life-forms, which could have sustained

We hear the echo again, with a precise reference to the determining cultural crisis, when Nietzsche writes:

> The contrast between this truth of nature and the pretentious lie of civilization is quite similar to that between the eternal core of things and the entire phenomenal world.

Tragedy, in this sense, became one of the many powerful ideas through which the opposition between humanity and actual contemporary society was expressed and dramatised. But characteristically, in Nietzsche, this widespread experience was lifted at once into an absolute, and generalised into an opposition between 'life' and 'the phenomenal world'.

Yet this mere opposition is dramatised and transcended, Nietzsche argued, by tragedy:

> The truth once seen, man is aware everywhere of the ghastly absurdity of existence. . . . Then, in this supreme jeopardy of the will, art, that sorceress expert in healing, approaches him; only she can turn his fits of nausea into imaginations with which it is possible to live.

The action of tragedy is not moral, not purgative (in spite of the image of healing), but aesthetic:

> Tragedy absorbs the highest orgiastic music and in so doing consummates music. But then it puts beside it the tragic myth and the tragic hero. Like a mighty Titan, the tragic hero shoulders the whole Dionysiac world and removes the burden from us. At the same time, tragic myth, through the figure of the hero, delivers us from our avid thirst for earthly satisfaction and reminds us of another existence and a higher delight. For this delight the hero readies himself, not through his victories but through his undoing. . . . Myth shields us from music, while at the same time giving music its maximum freedom. In

---

a different general view, was overridden by an emphasis on a part of natural life—the predators and the flesh-eaters—which, however cruel, had nothing at all to do with evolution as an idea. The substantial understanding of development through inheritance and variation was of course not available until genetics was understood, yet even now the older attitudes and metaphors survive, with great emotional force: a version of the arbitrary and the brutal, drawn essentially from human social experience, and then projected and mystified as a 'natural law'.

exchange, music endows the tragic myth with a convincing metaphysical significance, which the unsupported word and image could
never achieve, and, moreover, assures the spectator of a supreme
delight—though the way passes through annihilation and negation,
so that he is made to feel that the very womb of things speaks audibly
to him.

The details of this account matter less than its important
emphasis on tragedy as a communicated action. The critical
effect is weakened, however, by the general distinction
between 'aesthetic' and 'moral' which is common in this
period, and which rests mainly on a contrast (often suppressed,
though not by Nietzsche) between 'moral' and 'metaphysical'.
It is not the use of art to bring wisdom that is questioned, but
a particular, rational kind of wisdom, as opposed to the
'wisdom of being'.

I think we have to reject the false contrast between
'aesthetic' and 'moral', and pursue the real contrast which it
masks, between 'moral' and 'metaphysical'. It is at this point
that one major element of Nietzsche's argument has become
historically important: his account of myth. 'Only a horizon
ringed about with myths can unify a culture. . . . The disappearance of tragedy also spelled disappearance of myth.'
The cause of the disappearance, in Greek culture, was,
Nietzsche argues, the rise of the 'Socratic spirit', which 'con-
siders knowledge to be the true panacea and error to be
radical evil.' Ever since Socrates, 'the dialectical drive toward
knowledge and scientific optimism has succeeded in turning
tragedy from its course'. Tragedy 'could be reborn only when
science had at last been pushed to its limits, and, faced with
these limits, been forced to renounce its claim to universal
validity'.

When he wrote *The Birth of Tragedy*, Nietzsche thought
this time had almost come: 'we . . . seem at this very moment
to be moving backward from the Alexandrian age into an age
of tragedy. And we can't help feeling that the dawn of a new
tragic age is for the German spirit only a return to itself, a
blessed recovery of its true identity'. Later, he could not
believe this: 'the German mind . . . was definitely ready to
relinquish any aspirations of this sort and to effect the transition to mediocrity, democracy, and "modern ideas" '.

B*

This powerful linking of tragedy, myth, the rejection of science, and political reaction has been of major importance. But the most evident particular consequence, in tragic theory, is the emphasis on myth as the source of tragic knowledge, and on ritual as a description of communicated action. We can note in passing Nietzsche's emphasis on the Promethean myth,

> indigenous to the entire community of Aryan races, and [attesting] to their prevailing talent for profound and tragic vision. . . . Man's highest good must be bought with a crime and paid for by the flood of grief and suffering which the offended divinities visit upon the human race in its noble ambition. . . . What distinguishes the Aryan conception (from the 'Semitic myth of the Fall') is an exalted notion of active sin as the properly Promethean virtue; this notion provides us with the ethical substratum of pessimistic tragedy, which comes to be seen as a justification of human ills, that is to say of human ills as well as the suffering purchased by that guilt.

This particular version of 'the tragedy at the heart of things' has become widely current, as the 'inevitable tragedy' of all human aspiration and, in particular, humanism.

Meanwhile, critically, Nietzsche's version of myth and ritual in tragedy was in effect repeated from a very different source. A recent translator of Nietzsche writes:

> The central thesis of *The Birth of Tragedy* anticipates, by sheer intuition, it would seem, what Frazer, Gilbert Murray, and Jane Harrison were later to establish quite irrefragably: the ritual origin of Greek tragedy, as well as the interdependence of myth and ritual in all primitive cultures.

But what we really learn from this sentence, published as late as 1956, is the 'irrefragable' character of a whole system of modern thinking about tragedy, which is now not merely the intuitive speculation of Nietzsche but, it would seem, however ironically, a science.

'Myth' and 'Ritual'

The work of what is still called 'the Cambridge School of Classical Anthropologists', whatever its intentions, has become the latest mode of an idea of tragedy which we must insist on placing in its historical and ideological context. Particularly as taken up by others, it has played a crucial interpretative role. What now needs to be said is that it is at best no more than an interpretation. It is neither established anthropology nor established classical scholarship, but a speculative system of ideas, like the many that have preceded it. It is no more and no less important than that.

The detailed and complicated argument about the origins of tragedy (made more complicated though not less detailed by the extreme scarcity of evidence) is inevitably specialised. But we can all be surprised that critics who use its conclusions and describe them as 'irrefragable' seem not even to know the powerful counter-arguments of Pickard-Cambridge, published in 1927, to say nothing of the more general methodological criticism of that kind of generalising literary anthropology. The most important effect of this slack repetition is the now widespread critical confusion of 'myth' and 'ritual', and the more radical confusion of 'ritual' and dramatic action. These terms have already been translated to Shakespearean tragedy, and indeed seem capable, in their present form, of infinite extension. What we need to clarify is the difference between 'myth' as heroic legend and 'myth' in the Nietzschean sense of a supra-rational source of spiritual wisdom. There is plenty of evidence connecting tragedy of all periods with the former, but any connection with the latter must rest on more than a verbal link. The heroic legend, in the Greeks and others, is neither rational nor irrational, in the modern sense, because it was primarily taken as history. The ways of dramatising it have, moreover, been extremely various. It is not easy to argue that because the heroic legends seem to us now to contain irrational elements, their varied dramatisation is a form of access to a supra-rational source. Similarly ritual, in the sense of a form of worship of a particular god, cannot be glibly identified with the many forms of dramatic action, in which (except perhaps in some recent plays written under the influence of this same theory) there is no properly ritual action at all. The fact is that 'myth' and 'ritual' are being used, in this modern idea of tragedy, as metaphors, but we must then ask: as metaphors of what?

The meaning of the tragic action, in this version, is a cyclic death and rebirth, linked to the seasons and centring on a sacrificial death which through lament and discovery becomes a rebirth: the death of the old is the triumph of the new. Now the essential movement described here—the making of a new order out of the death of an old order, and the release of energy in an action involving death and suffering—is indeed a common tragic meaning, though in no sense an absolute meaning. But to place this movement in a context, however rhetorically defined, of the turn of the year and the seasons, of the dying god, the tearing to pieces in sacrifice, and a spiritual rebirth, is to offer an interpretation of causes, which is not a matter of scholarship at all, but of controlling ideas of the nature of life. If it is argued, explicitly, that this interpretation of causes is valid, we can respect the interpretation among others. But what we cannot reasonably do is to identify this interpretation as 'the tragic vision', as established by the 'irrefragable' facts of tragic origins, which have somehow persisted through so many historical periods.

It is necessary to go further. What this idea of tragedy seems essentially to teach, behind the arguable details of scholarship and analogy, is that suffering is a vital and energising part of the natural order. (Evolution and the dying god came together, ironically, in many post-Christian minds.) To participate in this version of the life-process is seen as the 'tragic' response, as opposed to the 'moral' or 'optimistic' or 'rational' responses, which, having abandoned the natural order for a 'merely human' order, interpret suffering and tragedy quite differently. The whole tradition of tragic drama is then defined around a single meaning, and other kinds of drama or theory are seen as 'not really' tragic, or as at best 'mixed'.

But then an actual and complicated tradition is being described and limited by a twentieth-century version of the nature of Greek tragedy, which significantly fits very well with that other tragic idea which we have seen represented by Bradley. At the centre of this 'ritual' action, after all, is the tragic hero, whose inner conflict is the whole tragic action, and whose crisis and destruction can be seen (making allowance for the generality of myth) as the ritual tearing-to-pieces and sacrifice for life. Thus, not only do we find the use of myth in a specifically modern sense, to rationalise a post-Christian metaphysic, but the conversion of the ritual figure to a form of the modern hero: that hero who in liberal tragedy is also the victim, who is destroyed by his society but who is capable of saving it.

I believe it is to these pressures, of contemporary ideology and experience, that we must relate the idea of tragedy which is now temporarily dominant, but which is offered as at once historical and absolute. The latest point of intersection, between the experience of tragedy and the varying and complicated history of its interpretation in theory and idea, is in any case our immediate concern.

3. TRAGEDY AND CONTEMPORARY IDEAS

In the suffering and confusion of our own century, there has been great pressure to take a body of work from the past and to use it as a way of rejecting the present. That there has been tragedy (or chivalry, or community) but that lacking this belief, that rule, we are now incapable of it, is a common response of this kind. And of course it is necessary, if this position is to be maintained, to reject ordinary contemporary meanings of tragedy, and to insist that they are a mis-understanding.

Yet tragic experience, because of its central importance, commonly attracts the fundamental beliefs and tensions of a period, and tragic theory is interesting mainly in this sense, that through it the shape and set of a particular culture is often deeply realised. If, however, we think of it as a theory about a single and permanent kind of fact, we can end only with the metaphysical conclusions that are built into any such assumption. Chief among these is the assumption of a permanent, universal and essentially unchanging human nature (an assumption taken over from one kind of Christianity to 'ritual' anthropology and the general theory of psycho-analysis). Given such an assumption, we have to explain tragedy in terms of this unchanging human nature or certain of its faculties. But if we reject this assumption (following a different kind of Christianity, a different psychological theory, or the evidence of comparative anthropology) the problem is necessarily transformed. Tragedy is then not a single and permanent kind of fact, but a series of experiences and conventions and institutions. It is not a case of interpreting this series by reference to a permanent and unchanging human nature. Rather, the varieties of tragic experience are to be interpreted by reference to the changing conventions and institutions. The universalist character of most tragic theory is then at the opposite pole from our necessary interest.

The most striking fact about modern tragic theory is that it is rooted in very much the same structure of ideas as modern tragedy itself, yet one of its paradoxical effects is its denial that modern tragedy is possible, after almost a century of important and continuous and insistent tragic art. It is very difficult to explain why this should be so. Part of the explanation seems to be the incapacity to make connections which is characteristic of this whole structure. But it is also significant that the major original contributions to the theory were made in the nineteenth century, before the creative period of modern tragedy, and have since been systematised by men deeply conditioned, by their academic training, to a valuation of the past against the present, and to a separation between critical theory and creative practice.

It is in any case necessary to break the theory if we are to value the art: in the simple sense, to see it as a major period of tragic writing, directly comparable in importance with the great periods of the past; and, more crucially, to see its controlling structure of feeling, the variations within this and their connections with actual dramatic structures, and to be able to respond to them critically, in the full sense. In my second part I shall discuss modern tragedy directly, but following the historical analysis already outlined it is worth trying to engage, critically, the major points of the theory. These are, as I see them: order and accident; the destruction of the hero; the irreparable action and its connections with death; and the emphasis of evil.

Order and Accident

The argument that there is no significant tragic meaning in 'everyday tragedies' seems to rest on two related beliefs: that the event itself is not tragedy, but only becomes so through shaped response (with the implication that tragedy is a matter of art, where such responses are embodied, rather than of life where they are not); and that significant response depends on the capacity to connect the event with some more general body of facts, so that it is not mere accident but is capable of bearing a general meaning.

My doubts here are radical. I do not see how it is finally possible to distinguish between an event and response to an event, in any absolute way. It is of course possible to say that *we* have not responded to an event, but this does not mean that response is absent. We can properly see the difference between a response which has been put into a communicable form and one which has not, and this will be relevant. But, in the case of ordinary death and suffering, when we see mourning and lament, when we see men and women breaking under their actual loss, it is at least not self-evident to say that we are not in the presence of tragedy. Other responses are of course possible: indifference, justification (as so often in war), even relief or rejoicing. But where the suffering is felt, where it is taken into the person of another, we are clearly within the possible dimensions of tragedy. We can of course ourselves react to the mourning and lament of others with our own forms of indifference and justification, even relief and rejoicing. But if we do, we should be clear what we are doing. That the suffering has communicated to those most closely involved but not to us may be a statement about the suffering, about those involved, or (which we often forget) about ourselves.

Obviously the possibility of communication to ourselves, we who are not immediately involved, depends on the capacity to connect the event with some more general body of facts. This criterion, which is now quite conventional, is indeed very welcome, for it poses the issue in its most urgent form. It is evidently possible for some people to hear of a mining disaster, a burned-out family, a broken career or a smash on the road without feeling these events as tragic in the full sense. But the starkness of such a position (which I believe to be sincerely held) is of course at once qualified by the description of such events as *accidents* which, however painful or regrettable, do not connect with any general meanings. This view is made even stronger when the unavailable meanings, for a particular event, are described as universal or permanent.

The central question that needs to be asked is what kind

of general (or universal or permanent) meaning it is which
interprets events of the kind referred to as accidents. Here at
least (if not at a much earlier stage) we can see that the ordinary
academic tradition of tragedy is in fact an ideology. What is in
question is not the process of connecting an event to a general
meaning, but the character and quality of the general meaning
itself.

I once heard it said that if 'you or I' went out and got run
over by a bus, that would not be tragedy. I was not sure how
to take this: as engagingly modest; as indifferent and offensive; or as a quite alien ideology. I remembered Yeats—

> some blunderer has driven his car on to the wrong side of the road—
> that is all

—or again

> if war is necessary, or necessary in our time and place, it is best to
> forget its suffering as we do the discomfort of fever.

This has come a long way from Hegel's description of 'mere
sympathy', which he distinguished from 'true sympathy'
because it lacked 'genuine content': 'an accordant feeling
with the ethical claim at the same time associated with the
sufferer'. It is also some way from Bradley's restatement of
this: 'no mere suffering or misfortune, no suffering that does
not spring in great part from human agency, and in some
degree from the agency of the sufferer, is tragic, however
pitiful or dreadful it may be'. Here the 'ethical claim', a
positive and representative content, has been changed to the
more general concept of 'agency'. But what is really significant
is the subsequent separation of both ethical content and
human agency from a whole class of ordinary suffering.

Yeats, with his 'if war is necessary, or necessary in our
time and place', may have been simply eccentric, but the
exclusion from tragedy of certain kinds of suffering, as 'mere
suffering', is characteristic and significant. There is the
exclusion, already evident in the language of Hegel, of
ordinary suffering, and this is surely the unconscious attachment of significant suffering to (social) nobility. But there is
also the related and deeper exclusion of all that suffering which
is part of our social and political world, and its actual human
relations. The real key, to the modern separation of tragedy

from 'mere suffering', is the separation of ethical control and, more critically, human agency, from our understanding of social and political life.

What we encounter again and again in the modern distinction between tragedy and accident, and in the related distinction between tragedy and suffering, is a particular view of the world which gains much of its strength from being unconscious and habitual. The social character of this view can be seen in its ordinary examples, as well as in its deprecating language of 'you or I'. It is not as if the event chosen for argument was a death by lightning, at the far edge of the possible spectrum. The events which are not seen as tragic are deep in the pattern of our own culture: war, famine, work, traffic, politics. To see no ethical content or human agency in such events, or to say that we cannot connect them with general meanings, and especially with permanent and universal meanings, is to admit a strange and particular bankruptcy, which no rhetoric of tragedy can finally hide.

We can only distinguish between tragedy and accident if we have some conception of a law or an order to which certain events are accidental and in which certain other events are significant. Yet wherever the law or order is partial (in the sense that only certain events are relevant to it) there is an actual alienation of some part of human experience. Even in the most traditional general orders, there has been this factual alienation. The definition of tragedy as dependent on the history of a man of rank was just such an alienation: some deaths mattered more than others, and rank was the actual dividing line—the death of a slave or a retainer was no more than incidental and was certainly not tragic. Ironically, our own middle-class culture began by appearing to reject this view: the tragedy of a citizen could be as real as the tragedy of a prince. Often, in fact, this was not so much rejection of the real structure of feeling as an extension of the tragic category to a newly rising class. Yet its eventual effect was profound. As in other bourgeois revolutions, extending the categories of law or suffrage, the arguments for the limited extension became inevitable arguments for a general extension. The extension from the prince to the citizen became in practice an extension to all human beings. Yet the character of the extension largely determined its content, until the point was reached where tragic experience was theoretically conceded to all men, but the nature of this experience was drastically limited.

The important element in the earlier emphasis on rank in tragedy was always the *general* status of the man of rank. His fate was the fate of the house or kingdom which he at once ruled and embodied. In the person of Agamemnon or of Lear the fate of a house or a kingdom was literally acted out. It was of course inevitable that this definition should fail to outlast its real social circumstances, in its original form. It was in particular inevitable that bourgeois society should reject it: the individual was neither the state nor an element of the state, but an entity in himself. There was then both gain and loss: the suffering of a man of no rank could be more seriously and more directly regarded, but equally, in the stress on the fate of an individual, the general and public character of tragedy was lost. Eventually, as we shall see, new definitions of general and public interest were embodied in new kinds of tragedy. But, meanwhile, the idea of a tragic order had to co-exist with the loss of any such actual order. What happened, at the level of theory, was then the abstraction of order, and its mystification.

One practical consequence intervened. Rank in tragedy became the name-dropping, the play with titles and sonorities, of costume drama. What had formerly been a significant relationship, of the king embodying his people and embodying also the common meanings of life and the world, became an empty ceremonial: a play of bourgeois man calling himself King or Duke (as in our own twentieth-century version of honours and nobility, in which a retiring Prime Minister is called an Earl and a civil servant of a particular grade a Knight). Sometimes indeed the ceremonial was even more alienated, and the names were Agamemnon or Caesar: a social order withered to a classical education.

But the main effects were more serious. What had been a whole lived order, connecting man and state and world, became, finally, a purely abstract order. Tragic significance was made to depend on an event's relation to a supposed nature of things, yet without the specific connections which had once provided a particular relation and action of this kind.

Hegel's insistence on ethical substance, and his connection of this with a process of historical embodiment of the Idea, was a major attempt to meet the new situation. Marx pushed the connection further, into a more specific history. But, increasingly, the idea of the permanent 'nature of things' became separated from any action that could be felt as contemporary, to the point where even Nietzsche's brutal rationalisation of suffering could be welcomed as specific. The whole meaning of 'accident' changed. Fate or Providence had been beyond man's understanding, so that what he saw as accident was in fact design, or was a specifically limited kind of event outside this design. The design in any case was embodied in institutions, through which man could hope to come to terms with it. But when there is an idea of design, without specific institutions at once metaphysical and social, the alienation is such that the category of accident is stressed and enlarged until it comes to include almost all actual suffering, and especially the effects of the existing and non-metaphysical social order. This is then either newly generalised as a *blind* fate, accident taking over from design as a plan of the universe, and becoming objective rather than subjective; or significant suffering, and therefore tragedy, is pushed back in time to periods when fully connecting meanings were available, and contemporary tragedy is seen as impossible because there are now no such meanings. The living tragedies of our own world can then not be negotiated at all. They cannot be seen in the light of those former meanings, or they are, however regrettable, accidents. New kinds of relation and new kinds of law, to connect with and interpret our actual suffering, are the terms of contemporary tragedy. But to see new relations and new laws is also to change the nature of experience, and the whole complex of attitudes and relationships dependent on it. To *find* significance is to be capable of tragedy, but of course it was easier to find insignificance. Then behind the facade of the emphasis on order, the substance of tragedy withered.

The effect of this development is not only on theory; it is also on critical method. If we are to think of the relations between tragedy and order, we have to think of relations and connections substantial enough to be embodied in an action. The abstraction of order, on the other hand, emerges as a

critical procedure, corresponding to the idea that the tragic
action is a kind of putting experience to the order, for
ratification or containment. That is to say, it makes the order
exist before the action: the abstract beliefs of fifth-century
Athens are expounded as a 'background' to its tragic drama;
the abstract beliefs of the 'Elizabethan world' are expounded
as a 'background' to Marlowe and Shakespeare and Webster.
Often, in fact, these expositions are circular; the general
beliefs are derived from the works and then reapplied to them,
in an abstract and static way (the case of Greek religion is
especially to this point).

But the relations between order and tragedy are always
more dynamic than such accounts and procedures suggest.
Order, in tragedy, is the *result* of the action, even where it
entirely corresponds, in an abstract way, with a pre-existing
conventional belief. It is not so much that the order is
illustrated as that it is recreated. In any living belief, this is
always the relation between experience and conviction.
Specifically, in tragedy, the creation of order is directly related
to the fact of disorder, through which the action moves.
Whatever the character of the order that is finally affirmed,
it has been literally created in this particular action. The
relation between the order and the disorder is direct.

There is an evident variation in the nature of tragic disorder. It can be the pride of man set against the nature of
things, or it can be a more general disorder which in aspiration
man seeks to overcome. There seems to be no continuing
tragic cause, at the simple level of content. In different
cultures, disorder and order both vary, for they are parts of
varying general interpretations of life. We should see this
variation, not so much as an obstacle to discovering a single
tragic cause or tragic emotion, as an indication of the major
cultural importance of tragedy as a form of art.

The tragic meaning is always both culturally and historically conditioned, but the artistic process in which a particular
disorder is both experienced and resolved is more widely
available and important. The essence of tragedy has been
looked for in the pre-existing beliefs and in the consequent
order, but it is precisely these elements that are most narrowly
limited, culturally. Any attempt to abstract these orders, as
definitions of tragedy, either misleads or condemns us to a

merely sterile attitude towards the tragic experience of our own culture. The ideas of order matter, critically, only when they are in solution in particular works; as precipitates they are of only documentary interest.

The correlate of this, in our own time, is that our ideas of order are, while the mainstream of the culture holds, still in solution, and often unnoticed. I shall try to show, in my studies of modern tragedies, how firm and general our own ideas of order and disorder are, even though they are oriented to a pervasive individualism, and hardly seem in the same world as the definitions of tragic order and disorder which we have taken from the past and generalised as permanent tragic ideas. But tragic meanings, which differ in different cultures and are general only within particular cultures, operate in important tragedy more as actors than as background. The real action embodies the particular meaning, and all that is common, in the works we call tragedies, is the dramatisation of a particular and grievous disorder and its resolution.

When we look, then, for the historical conditions of tragedy, we shall not look for particular kinds of belief: in fate, in divine government, or in a sense of the irreparable. The action of isolating extreme suffering and then of re-integrating it within a continuing sense of life can occur in very different cultures, with very different fundamental beliefs. It is often argued that these beliefs need to be both common and stable, if tragedy is to occur. Some such argument lies behind the assertion that tragedy was dependent, in the past, on ages of faith, and is impossible now, because we have no faith. That the beliefs which are brought into action or question need to be reasonably common I would not deny. We have, as we shall see, our own beliefs of this kind, and we are surely capable of avoiding the simple trap of calling some beliefs 'faiths' and others not.

The question of stability is much more important. I would not deny the possibility of tragedy when there are stable beliefs, but it is in this direction that an historical examination seems to take us. What is commonly asserted, about the relation between tragedy and stability of belief, seems to be almost the opposite of the truth. Of course if beliefs are simply abstracted, and taken out of their context as lived behaviour and working institutions, it is possible to create the impression

of stability, the reiteration of received interpretations, even
when the real situation is quite evidently one of instability or
indeed disintegration. The most remarkable case of this kind
is the description of an Elizabethan and Jacobean sense of
order—the persistence of late mediaeval beliefs—in almost
total disregard of the extraordinary tensions of a culture
moving towards violent internal conflict and substantial
transformation. The ages of comparatively stable belief, and
of comparatively close correspondence between beliefs and
actual experience, do not seem to produce tragedy of any
intensity, though of course they enact the ordinary separations
and tensions and the socially sanctioned ways of resolving
these. The intensification of this common procedure, and the
possibility of its permanent interest, seem to depend more on
an extreme tension between belief and experience than on an
extreme correspondence. Important tragedy seems to occur,
neither in periods of real stability, nor in periods of open and
decisive conflict. Its most common historical setting is the
period preceding the substantial breakdown and transformation of an important culture. Its condition is the real tension
between old and new: between received beliefs, embodied in
institutions and responses, and newly and vividly experienced
contradictions and possibilities. If the received beliefs have
widely or wholly collapsed, this tension is obviously absent;
to that extent their real presence is necessary. But beliefs can
be both active and deeply questioned, not so much by other
beliefs as by insistent immediate experience. In such situations, the common process of dramatising and resolving disorder and suffering is intensified to the level which can be most
readily recognized as tragedy.

The Destruction of the Hero

The most common interpretation of tragedy is that it is
an action in which the hero is destroyed. This fact is seen as
irreparable. At a simple level this is so obviously true that the
formula usually gets little further examination. But it is of
course still an interpretation, and a partial one. If attention is
concentrated on the hero alone, such an interpretation
naturally follows. We have been very aware of the kind of
reading which we can describe as *Hamlet* without the Prince,
but we have been almost totally unaware of the opposite and

equally erroneous reading of the Prince of Denmark without the State of Denmark. It is this unity that we must now restore.

Not many works that we call tragedies in fact end with the destruction of the hero. Outside the undeveloped mediaeval form, most of the examples that we could offer come, significantly, from modern tragedy. Certainly in almost all tragedies the hero is destroyed, but that is not normally the end of the action. Some new distribution of forces, physical or spiritual, normally succeeds the death. In Greek tragedy this is ordinarily a religious affirmation, but in the words or presence of the chorus, which is then the ground of its social continuity. In Elizabethan tragedy it is ordinarily a change of power in the state, with the arrival of a new, uncommitted or restored Prince. There are many factual variations of this reintegrative action, but their general function is common. Of course these endings are now normally read as merely valedictory or as a kind of tidying-up. To our consciousness, the important action has ended, and the affirmation, settlement, restoration or new arrival are comparatively minor. We read the last chapters of Victorian novels, which bring the characters together and settle their future directions, with a comparable indifference or even impatience. This kind of reparation is not particularly interesting to us, because not really credible. Indeed it looks much too like a solution, which twentieth-century critics agree is a vulgar and intrusive element in any art. (It is not the business of the artist, or even the thinker, to provide answers and solutions, but simply to describe experiences and to raise questions.) Yet of course it is no more and no less a solution than its commonplace twentieth-century alternative. To conclude that there is no solution is also an answer.

When we now say that the tragic experience is of the irreparable, because the action is followed right through until the hero is dead, we are taking a part for the whole, a hero for an action. We think of tragedy as what happens to the hero, but the ordinary tragic action is what happens through the hero. When we confine our attention to the hero, we are unconsciously confining ourselves to one kind of experience which in our own culture we tend to take as the whole. We are unconsciously confining ourselves to the individual. Yet over a very wide range we see this transcended in tragedy. Life does

come back, life ends the play, again and again. And the fact
that life does come back, that its meanings are reaffirmed and
restored, after so much suffering and after so important a
death, has been, quite commonly, the tragic action.

What is involved, of course, is not a simple forgetting, or a
picking-up for the new day. The life that is continued is
informed by the death; has indeed, in a sense, been created
by it. But in a culture theoretically limited to individual
experience, there is no more to say, when a man has died, but
that others also will die. Tragedy can then be generalised not
as the response to death but as the bare irreparable fact.

'The Irreparable Action'

Human death is often the form of the deepest meanings of
a culture. When we see death, it is natural that we should draw
together—in grief, in memory, in the social duties of burial—
our sense of the values of living, as individuals and as a society.
But then, in some cultures or in their breakdown, life is
regularly read back from the fact of death, which can seem
not only the focus but also the source of our values. Death,
then, is absolute, and all our living simply relative. Death is
necessary, and all other human ends are contingent. Within
this emphasis, suffering and disorder of any kind are interpreted by reference to what is seen as the controlling reality.
Such an interpretation is now commonly described as a tragic
sense of life.

What is not usually noticed, in this familiar and now formal
procession, is precisely the element of convention. To read
back life from the fact of death is a cultural and sometimes a
personal choice. But that it is a choice, and a variable choice,
is very easily forgotten. The powerful association of a
particular rhetoric and a persistent human fact can give the
appearance of permanence to a local and temporary and even
sectional response. To tie any meaning to death is to give it a
powerful emotional charge which can at times obliterate all
other experience in its range. Death is universal, and the
meaning tied to it quickly claims universality, as it were in its
shadow. Other readings of life, other interpretations of
suffering and disorder, can be assimilated to it with great
apparent conviction. The burden of proof shifts continually
from the controversial meaning to the inescapable experience,

and we are easily exposed, by fear and loss, to the most conventional and arbitrary conclusions.

The connection between tragedy and death is of course
quite evident, but in reality the connection is variable, as the
response to death is variable. What has happened in our own
century is that a particular post-liberal and post-Christian
interpretation of death has been imposed as an absolute
meaning, and as identical with all tragedy. What is generalised
is the loneliness of man, facing a blind fate, and this is the
fundamental isolation of the tragic hero. The currency of this
experience is of course sufficiently wide to make it relevant to
much modern tragedy. But the structure of the meaning still
needs analysis. To say that man dies alone is not to state a fact
but to offer an interpretation. For indeed men die in so many
ways: in the arms and presence of family and neighbours; in
the blindness of pain, or the blankness of sedation; in the
violent disintegration of machines and in the calm of sleep.
To insist on a single meaning is already rhetorical, but to
insist on the meaning of loneliness is to interpret life as much
as death. However men die, the experience is not only the
physical dissolution and ending; it is also a change in the lives
and relationships of others, for we know death as much in the
experience of others as in our own expectations and endings.
And just as death enters, continually, our common life, so any
statement about death is in a common language and depends
on common experience. The paradox of 'we die alone' or 'man
dies alone' is then important and remarkable: the maximum
substance that can be given to the plural 'we', or to the group-
name 'man', is the singular loneliness. The common fact, in a
common language, is offered as a proof of the loss of connection.

But then, as we become aware of this structure of feeling,
we can look through it at the experience which it has offered
to interpret. It is using the names of death and tragedy, but
it has very little really to do with the tragedies of the past, or
with death as a universal experience. Rather, it has correctly
identified, and then blurred, the crisis around which one main
kind of contemporary tragic experience moves. It blurs it
because it offers as absolutes the very experiences which are
now most unresolved and most moving. Our most common
received interpretations of life put the highest value and

significance on the individual and his development, but it is
indeed inescapable that the individual dies. What is most
valuable and what is most irreparable are then set in an
inevitable relation and tension. But to generalise this
particular contradiction as an absolute fact of human existence is to fix and finally suppress the relation and tension, so
that tragedy becomes not an action but a deadlock. And then
to claim this deadlock as the whole meaning of tragedy is to
project into history a local structure that is both culturally and
historically determined.

It is characteristic of such structures that they cannot even
recognise as possible any experience beyond their own
structural limits; that such varying and possible statements as
'I die but I shall live', 'I die but we shall live', or 'I die but we
do not die' become meaningless, and can even be contemptuously dismissed as evasions. The whole fact of community is
reduced to the singular recognition, and it is angrily denied
that there can be any other. Yet what seems to me most
significant about the current isolation of death, is not what it
has to say about tragedy or about dying, but what it is saying,
through this, about loneliness and the loss of human connection, and about the consequent blindness of human
destiny. It is, that is to say, a theoretical formulation of liberal
tragedy, rather than any kind of universal principle.

The tragic action is about death, but it need not end in
death, unless this is enforced by a particular structure of
feeling. Death, once again, is a necessary actor but not the
necessary action. We encounter this alteration of pattern
again and again in contemporary tragic argument. The most
spectacular example, perhaps, is the resurgence of the concept
of evil.

The Emphasis of Evil

Evil, of course, is a traditional name, but, like other names,
it has been appropriated by a particular ideology which then
offers itself as the whole tragic tradition. In recent years
especially, we have been continually rebuked by what is
called the fact of transcendent evil, and the immense social
crisis of our century is specifically interpreted in this light or
darkness. The true nature of man, it is argued, is now dramatically revealed, against all the former illusions of civilisation and

progress. The concentration camp, especially, is used as an image of an absolute condition, in which man is reduced, by men, to a thing. The record of the camps is indeed black enough, and many other examples could be added. But to use the camp as an image of an absolute condition is, in its turn, a blasphemy. For while men created the camps, other men died, at conscious risk, to destroy them. While some men imprisoned, other men liberated. There is no evil which men have created, of this or any other kind, which other men have not struggled to end. To take one part of this action, and call it absolute or transcendent, is in its turn a suppression of other facts of human life on so vast a scale that its indifference can only be explained by its role in an ideology.

The appropriation of evil to the theory of tragedy is then especially significant. What tragedy shows us, it is argued, is the fact of evil as inescapable and irreparable. Mere optimists and humanists deny the fact of transcendent evil, and so are incapable of tragic experience. Tragedy is then a salutary reminder, indeed a theory, against the illusions of humanism.

But this can only be maintained if the tragic action can be reduced and simplified, in ways very similar to the simplifications of tragic order and the tragic individual and the irreparable death. Evil, as it is now widely used, is a deeply complacent idea. For it ends, and is meant to end, any actual experience. It ends, among other things, the normal action of tragedy. It is not that any of us can deny, or wish to deny, the description, as evil, of particular actions. But when we abstract and generalise it, we remove ourselves from any continuing action, and deliberately break both response and connection.

The current emphasis of Evil is not, we must remind ourselves, the Christian emphasis. Within that structure, evil was certainly generalised, but so also was good, and the struggle of good and evil in our souls and in the world could be seen as a real action. Evil was the common disorder which was yet overcome in Christ. As such, for all the magnitude of its name, it has commonly operated within the terms of the tragic action.

Culturally, evil is a name for many kinds of disorder which corrode or destroy actual life. As such, it is common in tragedy, though in many particular and variable forms:

vengeance or ambition or pride or coldness or lust or jealousy
or disobedience or rebellion. In every case it is only fully
comprehensible within the valuations of a particular culture
or tradition. It may indeed be possible, in any particular
ideology, to generalise it until it appears as an absolute and
even singular force. As a common name, also, it appears to
take on a general character. But we cannot then say that
tragedy is the recognition of transcendent evil. Tragedy
commonly dramatises evil, in many particular forms. We
move away from actual tragedies, and not towards them,
when we abstract and generalise the very specific forces that
are so variously dramatised. We move away, even more
decisively, from a common tragic action, when we interpret
tragedy as only the dramatisation and recognition of evil. A
particular evil, in a tragic action, can be at once experienced
and lived through. In the process of living through it, and in a
real action seeing its moving relations with other capacities
and other men, we come not so much to the recognition of
evil as transcendent but to its recognition as actual and indeed
negotiable.

This is of course far from its simple abolition, which is the
opposite and yet complementary error to its recognition as
transcendent, just as the proposition that man is naturally
good is the complementary error to the proposition that man
is naturally evil. Within a religious culture, man is seen as
naturally limited, but within a liberal culture man is seen as
naturally absolute, and good and evil are then alternative
absolute names. They are not, however, the only alternatives.
It is equally possible to say that man is not 'naturally' anything: that we both create and transcend our limits, and that
we are good or evil in particular ways and in particular
situations, defined by pressures we at once receive and can
alter and can create again. This continuing and varying
activity is the real source of the names, which can only in
fantasy be abstracted to explain the activity itself.

Tragedy, as such, teaches nothing about evil, because it
teaches many things about many kinds of action. Yet it can
at least be said, against the modern emphasis on transcendent
evil, that most of the great tragedies of the world end not with
evil absolute, but with evil both experienced and lived
through. A particular tragic hero may put out his eyes when

he sees the evil that he has committed, but we see him do this, in a continuing action. Yet that blindness, which was part of the action, is now abstracted and generalised, as an absolute blindness: a rejection of particulars, a refusal to look into sources and causes and versions of consequence. The affirmation of absolute Evil, which is now so current, is, under pressure, a self-blinding; the self-blinding of a culture which, lacking the nerve to inquire into its own nature, would have not only actors but also spectators put out their eyes. What is offered as tragic significance is here, as elsewhere, a significant denial of the possibility of *any* meaning.

If I am right in seeing this fundamental pattern in the orthodox modern idea of tragedy, both negative and positive conclusions follow. Negatively, we must say that what is now offered as a total meaning of tragedy is in fact a particular meaning, to be understood and valued historically. Some would go further and dispense with tragedy as an idea at all. There is a certain attraction in accepting the consequences of historical criticism, and cutting out all general considerations because they have been shown to be variable. A sophisticated and mainly technical criticism will then supervene: the meanings do not matter, but we can look at how they are expressed, in particular arrangements of words. It is in fact doubtful if in any case this can be done. If the words matter, the meanings will matter, and to ignore them formally is usually to accept some of them informally.

I believe that the meanings matter as such; in tragedy especially, because the experience is so central and we can hardly avoid thinking about it. If we find a particular idea of tragedy, in our own time, we find also a way of interpreting a very wide area of our experience; relevant certainly to literary criticism but relevant also to very much else. And then the negative analysis is only part of our need. We must try also, positively, to understand and describe not only the tragic theory but also the tragic experience of our own time.

4. TRAGEDY AND REVOLUTION

The most complex effect of any really powerful ideology is that it directs us, even when we think we have rejected it, to the same kind of fact. Thus, when we try to identify the disorder which is at the root of our tragic experiences, we tend to find elements analogous to former tragic systems, as the ideology has interpreted them. We look, almost unconsciously, for a crisis of personal belief: matching a lost belief in immortality with a new conviction of mortality, or a lost belief in fate with a new conviction of indifference. We look for tragic experience in our attitudes to God or to death or to individual will, and of course we often find tragic experience cast in these familiar forms. Having separated earlier tragic systems from their actual societies, we can achieve a similar separation in our own time, and can take it for granted that modern tragedy can be discussed without reference to the deep social crisis, of war and revolution, through which we have all been living. That kind of interest is commonly relegated to politics, or, to use the cant word, sociology. Tragedy, we say, belongs to deeper and closer experience, to man not to society. Even the general disorders, which can hardly escape the most limited attention, and which equally can hardly be said to involve only societies and not men, can be reduced to symptoms of the only kind of disorder we are prepared to recognize: the fault in the soul. War, revolution, poverty, hunger; men reduced to objects and killed from lists; persecution and torture; the many kinds of contemporary martyrdom: however close and insistent the facts, we are not to be moved, in a context of tragedy. Tragedy, we know, is about something else.

Yet the break comes, in some minds. In experience, suddenly, the new connections are made, and the familiar world shifts, as the new relations are seen. We are not looking for a new universal meaning of tragedy. We are looking for the structure of tragedy in our own culture. Once we begin to doubt, in experience and then in analysis, the ordinary twentieth-century idea, other directions seem open.

Tragedy and Social Disorder

Since the time of the French Revolution, the idea of tragedy can be seen as in different ways a response to a culture in conscious change and movement. The action of tragedy and the action of history have been consciously connected, and in the connection have been seen in new ways. The reaction against this, from the mid-nineteenth century, has been equally evident: the movement of spirit has been separated from the movement of civilisation. Yet even this negative reaction seems, in its context, a response to the same kind of crisis. The academic tradition, on the whole, has followed the negative reaction, but it is difficult to hear its ordinary propositions and feel that they are only about a set of academic facts. They sound, insistently, like propositions about contemporary life, even when they are most negative and most consciously asocial. The other nineteenth-century tradition, in which tragedy and history were consciously connected, seems then deeply relevant. In experience and in theory we have to look again at this relation.

We must ask whether tragedy, in our own time, is a response to social disorder. If it is so, we shall not expect the response to be always direct. The disorder will appear in very many forms, and to articulate these will be very complex and difficult. A more immediate difficulty is the ordinary separation of social thinking and tragic thinking. The most influential kinds of explicitly social thinking have often rejected tragedy as in itself defeatist. Against what they have known as the idea of tragedy, they have stressed man's powers to change his condition and to end a major part of the suffering which the tragic ideology seems to ratify. The idea of tragedy, that is to say, has been explicitly opposed by the idea of revolution: there has been as much confidence on the one side as on the other. And then to describe tragedy as a response to social disorder, and to value it as such, is to break, apparently, from both major traditions.

The immediate disturbance is radical, for the fault in the soul was a recognition of a kind; it was close to the experience, even when it added its ordinary formulas. From the other position, from the recognition of social disorder, there is a habit of easy abstraction which the scale of the disorder almost inevitably supports. As we recognise history, we are referred to history, and find it difficult to acknowledge men like ourselves. Before, we could not recognise tragedy as social crisis; now, commonly, we cannot recognise social crisis as tragedy. The facts of disorder are caught up in a new ideology, which cancels suffering as it finds the name of a period or a phase. From day to day we can make everything past, because we

believe in the future. Our actual present, in which the disorder is radical, is as effectively hidden as when it was merely
politics, for it is now only politics. It seems that we have
jumped from one blindness to another, and with the same
visionary confidence. The new connections harden, and no
longer connect.

What seems to matter, against every difficulty, is that the
received ideas no longer describe our experience. The most
common idea of revolution excludes too much of our social
experience. But it is more than this. The idea of tragedy, in
its ordinary form, excludes especially that tragic experience
which is social, and the idea of revolution, again in its ordinary
form, excludes especially that social experience which is tragic.
And if this is so, the contradiction is significant. It is not a
merely formal opposition, of two ways of reading experience,
between which we can choose. In our own time, especially, it
is the connections between revolution and tragedy—
connections lived and known but not acknowledged as ideas
—which seem most clear and significant.

The most evident connection is in the actual events of
history, as we all quite simply observe them. A time of
revolution is so evidently a time of violence, dislocation and
extended suffering that it is natural to feel it as tragedy, in the
everyday sense. Yet, as the event becomes history, it is often
quite differently regarded. Very many nations look back to
the revolutions of their own history as to the era of creation
of the life which is now most precious. The successful
revolution, we might say, becomes not tragedy but epic: it
is the origin of a people, and of its valued way of life. When
the suffering is remembered, it is at once either honoured or
justified. That particular revolution, we say, was a necessary
condition of life.

Contemporary revolution is of course very different. Only
a post-revolutionary generation is capable of that epic
composition. In contemporary revolution, the detail of
suffering is insistent, whether as violence or as the reshaping
of lives by a new power in the state. But further, in a contemporary revolution, we inevitably take sides, though with
different degrees of engagement. And a time of revolution
is ordinarily a time of lies and of suppressions of truths. The
suffering of the whole action, even when its full weight is

acknowledged, is commonly projected as the responsibility of this party or that, until its very description becomes a revolutionary or counter-revolutionary act. There is a kind of indifference which comes early whenever the action is at a distance. But there is also an exposure to the scale of suffering, and to the lies and campaigns that are made from it, which in the end is also indifference. Revolution is a dimension of action from which, for initially honourable reasons, we feel we have to keep clear.

Thus the social fact becomes a structure of feeling. Revolution as such is in a common sense tragedy, a time of chaos and suffering. It is almost inevitable that we should try to go beyond it. I do not rely on what is almost certain to happen: that this tragedy, in its turn, will become epic. However true this may be, it cannot closely move us; only heirs can inherit. Allegiance to even a probable law of history, which has not, however, in the particular case, been lived through, becomes quite quickly an alienation. We are not truly responding to this action but, by projection, to its probable composition.

The living alternative is quite different in character. It is neither the rejection of revolution, by its simple characterisation as chaos and suffering, nor yet the calculation of revolution, by laws and probabilities not yet experienced. It is, rather, a recognition; the recognition of revolution as a whole action of living men. Both the wholeness of the action, and in this sense its humanity, are then inescapable. It is this recognition against which we ordinarily struggle.

Revolution and Disorder

As we have reduced tragedy to the death of the hero, so we have reduced revolution to its crisis of violence and disorder. In simple observation, these are often the most evident effects, but in the whole action they are both preceded and succeeded, and much of their meaning depends on this fact of continuity. Thus it is strange that from our whole modern history revolution should be selected as the example of violence and disorder: revolution, that is, as the critical conflict and resolution of forces. To limit violence and disorder to the decisive conflict is to make nonsense of that conflict itself. The violence and disorder are in the whole

c

action, of which what we commonly call revolution is the
crisis.

The essential point is that violence and disorder are
institutions as well as acts. When a revolutionary change has
been lived through, we can usually see this quite clearly. The
old institutions, now dead, take on their real quality as
systematic violence and disorder; in that quality, the source
of the revolutionary action is seen. But while such institutions
are still effective, they can seem, to an extraordinary extent,
both settled and innocent. Indeed they constitute, commonly,
an order, against which the very protest, of the injured and
oppressed, seems the source of disturbance and violence.
Here, most urgently, in our own time, we need to return the
idea of revolution, in its ordinary sense of the crisis of a society,
to its necessary context as part of a whole action, within which
alone it can be understood.

Order and disorder are relative terms, although each is
experienced as an absolute. We are aware of this relativism,
through history and comparative studies: intellectually
aware, though that is often not much use to us, under the
pressure of fear or interest or in the simple immediacy of our
local and actual world. In the ideas of both tragedy and
revolution, this dimension and yet also these difficulties are
at once encountered. I have already argued that the relation
between tragedy and order is dynamic. The tragic action is
rooted in a disorder, which indeed, at a particular stage, can
seem to have its own stability. But the whole body of real
forces is engaged by the action, often in such a way that the
underlying disorder becomes apparent and terrible in overtly
tragic ways. From the whole experience of this disorder, and
through its specific action, order is recreated. The process of
this action is at times remarkably similar to the real action of
revolution.

Yet revolution, at least in its feudal form as rebellion, is
often, in many valued tragedies, the disorder itself. The
restoration of 'lawful' authority is there literally the restoration
of order. But the essential consideration lies deeper than this,
below the false consciousness of feudal attitudes to rebellion.
It is not difficult to see that the feudal definitions of lawful
authority and rebellion are, at the political level, at worst
timeserving, at best partisan. The majesty of kings is usually

the political façade of successful usurpers and their descendants. What challenges it, as an action, is of the same human kind as what established it. Yet the investment of political power with religious or magical sanctions is also, in its most important examples, a vehicle for the expression of a fundamental conception of order, and indeed of the nature of life and of man. Characteristically, this is a conception of a static order, and of a permanent human condition and nature. Around such conceptions, real values are formed, and the threat to them overrides the temporary and arbitrary association of them with a particular figure or system. When connections of this kind are a living reality, the tragic action, whatever its local form, can have the widest human reference.

In its actual course, the tragic action often undercuts the ordinary association between fundamental human values and the acknowledged social system: the claims of actual love contradict the duties of family; the awakened individual consciousness contradicts the assigned social role. In the transition from a feudal to a liberal world, such contradictions are common and are lived out as tragedy. Yet the identification between a permanent order and a social system is still not really challenged. The contradictions and disorders are normally seen in terms of the identification, which has been blurred by human error but which the tragic action essentially restores. The figures of the true and false kings, of the lawful authority and his erring deputy, are dramatic modes of just this structure of feeling. There is a close relation between such dramatic modes and the type of argument common to political reformers and even political revolutionaries, in England in the seventeenth century, in which it was claimed that nothing new was being proposed or fought for, but only the restoration of the true and ancient constitution. This consciousness contained the most radical and even revolutionary actions. In tragedy, the stage was at last reached when there was scepticism about the possibility of any social order, and then resolution was seen as altogether outside the terms of civil society. A religious or quasi-religious withdrawal restored order by supernatural or magical intervention, and the tragic action came full circle.

Liberalism

Liberal tragedy inherited this separation between ultimate human values and the social system, but in a mode which it finally transformed. Slowly, in the development of liberal consciousness, the point of reference became not a general order but the individual, who as such embodied all ultimate values, including (in the ordinary emphasis of Protestantism) divine values. I shall trace the course of liberal tragedy to the point where new contradictions, in this absolute conception of the individual, led to deadlock and then to final breakdown (a breakdown of which I expect to see many further examples).

But the great current of liberalism had other effects, and is especially responsible for the sharp opposition between the idea of tragedy and the idea of revolution which we find so clearly in our own time. Liberalism steadily eroded the conceptions of a permanent human nature and of a static social order with connections to a divine order. From these erosions, and from the alternative conception of the possibility of human and social transformation, the early idea of revolution, in the modern sense, took its origins. Rebellion became revolution, and the most important human values became associated not with the received order but with development, progress and change. The contrast between the ordinary ideas of tragedy and of revolution seemed then quite stark. Revolution asserted the possibility of man altering his condition; tragedy showed its impossibility, and the consequent spiritual effects. On that opposition, we are still trying to rest.

Yet the essential history has already changed. The liberal idea of revolution and the feudal idea of tragedy are no longer the only alternatives, and to go on offering to choose between them is to be merely stranded in time. To understand this we must see what happened to the liberal idea of revolution.

It is at first sight surprising that so open and positive a movement as liberalism should ever have produced tragedy at all. Yet each of the literary movements which took their origins from liberalism came to a point where the most decisive choices were necessary, and where, while some chose, others merely divided. The nature of these choices is in the end essentially a matter of attitudes toward revolution. It is in this process that we are still engaged.

Naturalism

The literature of naturalism is the most obvious example. It seems now the true child of the liberal enlightenment, in which the traditional ideas of a fate, an absolute order, a design beyond human powers, were replaced by a confidence in reason and in the possibility of a continually expanding capacity for explanation and control. In politics this produced a new social consciousness of human destiny; in philosophy, analysis of the ideologies of religion and of social custom, together with new schemes of rational explanation; in literature, a new emphasis on the exact observation and description of the contemporary social world. But the literature of naturalism, finally, is a bastard of the enlightenment. Characteristically, it detached the techniques of observation and description from the purposes which these were intended to serve. What became naturalism, and what distinguished it from the more important movement of realism, was a mechanical description of men as the creatures of their environment, which literature recorded as if man and thing were of the same nature. The tragedy of naturalism is the tragedy of passive suffering, and the suffering is passive because man can only endure and can never really change his world. The endurance is given no moral or religious valuation; it is wholly mechanical, because both man and his world, in what is now understood as rational explanation, are the products of an impersonal and material process which though it changes through time has no ends. The impulse to describe and so change a human condition has narrowed to the simple impulse to describe a condition in which there can be no intervention by God or man, the human act of will being tiny and insignificant within the vast material process, universal or social, which at once determines and is indifferent to human destiny.

This naturalism, at once the most common theory and the most ordinary practice of our literature, began in liberalism but ends, ironically, as a grotesque version of the system originally challenged by liberalism, just as atheism ends as a grotesque version of faith. A living design became a mechanical fate, and the latter is even further from man than the former; more decisively alienated from any image of himself.

But then this development had real causes. It is, essentially, a deliberate arrest of the process of enlightenment, at the point of critical involvement. As such it corresponds to the deliberate arrest and subsequent decadence of liberalism, at the point where its universal principles required the transformation of its social programme, and where men could either go on or must go back. Everywhere in the nineteenth century we see men running for cover from the consequences of their own beliefs. In our own century, they do not even have to run; the temporary covers have become solid settlements. The universal principles of human liberation have become an embarrassment to men who, benefiting themselves from change of this kind, see before them an infinitely extending demand, of other classes and other peoples, which threatens to submerge and destroy their own newly-won identity. A few men hold to their principles, and make their commitment to a general social revolution. But the majority compromise, evade, or seek to delay, and the most destructive form of this breakdown—for simple reaction is easily recognised—is the characteristic substitution of evolution for revolution as a social model.[1]

The whole point of the new theories of social evolution, most evident in the theory of administered reform, was the separation of historical development from the actions of the majority of men, or even, in its extreme forms, from all men. Society, in this view, was an impersonal process, a machine with certain built-in properties. The machine might be described or regulated, but was not, ultimately, within human control. Social change, at its maximum, was the sub-

[1] Evolution in this Fabian sense is different again from both Darwinism and the competitive struggle for life. Yet it shares with the latter a metaphorical quality, still essentially unrelated to the scientific theory. For behind the idea of social evolution was an unconscious attachment to the development of a *single* form. Social development was unconsciously based on the experience of one type of Western society, and its imperialist contacts with more 'primitive' societies. The real social and cultural variation of human history was thus reduced to a single model: unilinear and predictable. Even Marxists took over this limited model, and its rigidity has been widely experienced in some twentieth-century communist practice. A more adequate understanding of both natural and cultural evolution would have made so mechanical and unilinear a model untenable, for it would have emphasised both variation and creativity and thus a more genuinely open and (in the full sense) revolutionary future.

stitution of one group of fitters for another. Social description, at its best, was neutral and mechanical. The process, so to say, would build up, would evolve, and we must watch it, go with it, not get in its modernising way. Any attempt to assert a general human priority, over the process as a whole, is then of course seen as childish: the mere fantasy of revolution.

The extent to which almost all our politics has been re-shaped to this mechanical materialism hardly needs emphasis. But what has to be said is that this movement of mind, claiming its origins in reason, was theoretically and factually a mystification of real social activity, and as such discredited reason itself. It thus worked, finally, to the same effect as the other major movement which sought to express the values of liberalism but which seemed for so long to have so different a direction: the whole current of subjectivism and romanticism.

Romanticism

Utilitarianism, the most common English form of mechanical materialism, had sought liberal values in the reform of civil society. Romanticism, on the other hand, sought liberal values in the development of the individual. In its early stages, Romanticism was profoundly liberating, but, partly because of the inadequacy of any corresponding social theory, and partly because of the consequent decline from individualism to subjectivism, it ended by denying its own deepest impulses, and even reversing them. Almost all our revolutionary language in fact comes from the Romantics, and this has been a real hindrance as well as an incidental embarrassment. Romanticism is the most important expression in modern literature of the first impulse of revolution: a new and absolute image of man. Characteristically, it relates this transcendence to an ideal world and an ideal human society; it is in Romantic literature that man is first seen as making himself.

But of course when this is particularised, to social criticism and construction, it encounters fundamental obstacles. It is easier to visualise the ideal in an exotic or fabled community (or an historical community transformed by these elements). The existing social world is seen as so hostile to what is most deeply human that even what begins as social criticism tends to pass into nihilism. For more than a century, the fate of this

Romantic tradition was uncertain. Some part of its force inspired the developing idea of total social revolution. A related part, while moving in this direction, got no further, finally, than the images of revolution: the flag, the barricade, the death of martyr or prisoner. But perhaps the major part went in a quite different direction, towards the final separation of revolution from society.

The decisive element, here, was the Romantic attitude to reason. In form, Romanticism can seem a negative reaction to the Enlightenment: its stress on the irrational and the strange seems an absolute contradiction of the stress on reason. But there is, here, a curious dialectic. Romanticism was not proposing what the Enlightenment had opposed; the one version of man was as new as the other. Yet, because this was not seen, the essential unity of these movements, as programmes for human liberation, was disastrously narrowed and confused. What the Romantics criticised as reason was not the reasoning activity, but the abstraction and final alienation of this activity, into what was called a rational but was in fact a mechanical system. Such criticism, and notably the English Romantic critique of utilitarianism, was not only humane; it was also on the side of man as a creative and active being. The eventual collapse to irrationalism can be understood only in terms of the earlier collapse to rationalism. The alienation of reason, from all the other activities of man, changed reason from an activity to a mechanism, and society from a human process to a machine. The protest against this was inevitable, but to stay with society as a human process involved commitments to social action which were indeed difficult to make. Under the pressure of difficulty and the disillusion of failure, the Romantic vision of man became in its turn alienated. The alienation of the rational, into a system of mechanical materialism, was matched by an alienation of the irrational, which has become complete only in our own century.

Thus, while one major part of the liberal idea of revolution had run into the mechanics of social evolution and administered reform, another major part had run into the parody of revolution, in nihilism and its many derivatives. To the former society was a machine, which would go its own predestined way in its own time. To the latter, society was the enemy of human liberation: man could free himself only by rejecting or escaping from society, and by seeing his own deepest activities, in love, in art, in nature, as essentially asocial and even anti-social. Ironically, just as mechanical materialism had produced a new kind of fate, the 'evolutionary' society from which man's activity and aspiration were shut out, so nihilism, also, produced a version of fate: the separation of humanity from society, but also the internalisation of what had once been an external design. In its later variants, especially, nihilism emphasised and generalised the irrational as more powerful than social man. From its assumption of hostility between personal liberation and the social fact, it rationalised an irrationality, more dark and destructive than any known gods. In its last stages, the dream of human liberation was the nightmare of an ineradicable destructive instinct and the death-wish.

The End of Liberalism

The liberal idea of revolution was finally hemmed in on both sides: by its reduction to a mechanical and impersonal process, and by the channelling of personal revolt into an ideology which made social construction seem hopeless, because man as such was deeply irrational and destructive. In Western societies, the contrast of these positions is now normally offered as total, so that we see ourselves as having to choose between them. In politics we are offered not revolution, or even substantial change, but what is widely called modernisation: that is, a separation of change from value. We are asked to go along with what is supposed to be an inevitable evolutionary process, or to bend, whatever its direction, to the 'wind of change' (which is an exact expression of just this alienation in that it blows from elsewhere and is rationalised as a natural force). Or, alternatively, we reject politics, and see the reality of human liberation as internal, private and apolitical, even under the shadow of politically willed war or politically willed poverty or politically willed ugliness and cruelty.

Yet in fact, since 1917, we have been living in a world of successful social revolutions. In this sense it is true to say that our attitude to the revolutionary societies of our own time is central and probably decisive in all our thinking. What our

c*

own ideology, in its many variants, has theoretically excluded, has happened or seems to have happened elsewhere. And then there are not really many choices left. We can actively oppose or seek to contain revolution elsewhere, as in national practice we have been continually doing. Militancy and indifference serve this tactic almost equally well. Or we can support revolution elsewhere, in a familiar kind of romanticism, for which the images lie ready in the mind. Or, finally—I am stating my own position—we can work to understand and participate in revolution as a social reality: that is to say, not only as an action now in progress among real men, but also, and therefore, as an activity immediately involving ourselves.

It is here that the relation between revolution and tragedy is inescapable and urgent. It may still be possible, for some thinkers, to interpret actual revolution in the received ideology of rationalism. We can all see the constructive activity of the successful revolutionary societies, and we can take this as evidence of the simple act of human liberation by the energy of reason. I know nothing I welcome more than this actual construction, but I know also that the revolutionary societies have been tragic societies, at a depth and on a scale that go beyond any ordinary pity and fear. At the point of this recognition, however, where the received ideology of revolution, its simple quality as liberation, seems most to fail, there is waiting the received ideology of tragedy, in either of its common forms: the old tragic lesson, that man cannot change his condition, but can only drown his world in blood in the vain attempt; or the contemporary reflex, that the taking of rational control over our social destiny is defeated or at best deeply stained by our inevitable irrationality, and by the violence and cruelty that are so quickly released when habitual forms break down. I do not find, in the end, that either of these interpretations covers enough of the facts, but also I do not see how anyone can still hold to that idea of revolution which simply denied tragedy, as an experience and as an idea.

Socialism and Revolution

Socialism, I believe, is the true and active inheritor of the impulse to human liberation which has previously taken so many different forms. But in practice, I also believe, it is an idea still forming, and much that passes under its name is only a residue of old positions. I do not mean only such a movement as Fabianism, with its cast of utilitarianism and its mechanical conceptions of change. I mean also a main current in Marxism, which though Marx may at times have opposed it is also profoundly mechanical, in its determinism, in its social materialism, and in its characteristic abstraction of social classes from human beings. I can see that it is possible, with such habits of mind, to interpret revolution as only constructive and liberating. Real suffering is then at once non-human: is a class swept away by history, is an error in the working of the machine, or is the blood that is not and never can be rose water. The more general and abstract, the more truly mechanical, the process of human liberation is ordinarily conceived to be, the less any actual suffering really counts, until even death is a paper currency.

But then I do not believe, as so many disillusioned or broken by actual revolution have come to believe, that the suffering can be laid to the charge of the revolution alone, and that we must avoid revolution if we are to avoid suffering. On the contrary, I see revolution as the inevitable working through of a deep and tragic disorder, to which we can respond in varying ways but which will in any case, in one way or another, work its way through our world, as a consequence of any of our actions. I see revolution, that is to say, in a tragic perspective, and it is this I now seek to define.

Marx's early idea of revolution seems to me to be tragic in this sense:

> A class must be formed which has *radical chains*, a class in civil society which is not a class of civil society, a class which is the dissolution of all classes, a sphere of society which has a universal character because its sufferings are universal, and which does not claim a *particular redress* because the wrong which is done to it is not a *particular wrong* but *wrong in general*. There must be formed a sphere of society which claims no *traditional* status but only a *human* status . . . a sphere finally which cannot emancipate itself without emancipating itself from all the other spheres of society, without therefore emancipating all these other spheres; which is, in short, a *total loss* of humanity and which can only redeem itself by a *total redemption of humanity*.
>
> (*Zur Kritik der Hegelschen Rechts-Philosophie: Einleitung*)

So absolute a conception distinguishes revolution from rebellion, or, to put it another way, makes political revolution into a general human revolution:

> In all former revolutions the form of activity was always left unaltered, and it was only a question of redistributing this activity among different people, of introducing a new division of labour. The communist revolution, however, is directed against the former *mode* of activity, does away with *labour*, and abolishes all class rule along with the classes themselves. . . .   (*Die Deutsche Ideologie*)

> The *social life* from which the worker is shut out . . . is *life* itself, physical and cultural life, human morality, human activity, human enjoyment, real human existence. . . . As the irremediable exclusion from this life is much more complete, more unbearable, dreadful, and contradictory, than the exclusion from political life, so is the ending of this exclusion, and even a limited reaction, a *revolt* against it, more fundamental, as *man* is more fundamental than the *citizen*, *human life* more than *political life*.   (*Vorwärts* (1844))

This way of seeing revolution seems to me to stand. Whatever we have learned, since Marx wrote, about actual historical development, and thence about the agencies and tactics of revolution, does not affect the idea itself. We need not identify revolution with violence or with a sudden capture of power. Even where such events occur, the essential transformation is indeed a long revolution. But the absolute test, by which revolution can be distinguished, is the change in the *form* of activity of a society, in its deepest structure of relationships and feelings. The incorporation of new groups of men into the pre-existing form and structure is something quite different, even when it is accompanied by an evident improvement of material conditions and by the ordinary changes of period and local colour. In fact the test of a pre-revolutionary society, or of a society in which the revolution is still incomplete, is in just this matter of incorporation. A society in which revolution is necessary is a society in which the incorporation of all its people, *as whole human beings*, is in practice impossible without a change in its fundamental form of relationships. The many kinds of partial 'incorporation'—as voters, as employees, or as persons entitled to education, legal protection, social services and so on—are real human gains, but do not in themselves amount to that full membership of society which is the end of classes. The reality of full membership is the capacity to direct a particular society, by active mutual responsibility and co-operation, on a basis of full social equality. And while this is the purpose of revolution, it remains necessary in all societies in which there are, for example, subordinate racial groups, landless landworkers, hired hands, the unemployed, and suppressed or discriminate minorities of any kind. Revolution remains necessary, in these circumstances, not only because some men desire it, but because there can be no acceptable human order while the full humanity of any class of men is in practice denied.

The Tragedy of Revolution

This idea of 'the total redemption of humanity' has the ultimate cast of resolution and order, but in the real world its perspective is inescapably tragic. It is born in pity and terror: in the perception of a radical disorder in which the humanity of some men is denied and by that fact the idea of humanity itself is denied. It is born in the actual suffering of real men thus exposed, and in all the consequences of this suffering: degeneration, brutalisation, fear, hatred, envy. It is born in an experience of evil made the more intolerable by the conviction that it is not inevitable, but is the result of particular actions and choices.

And if it is thus tragic in its origins—in the existence of a disorder that cannot but move and involve—it is equally tragic in its action, in that it is not against gods or inanimate things that its impulse struggles, nor against mere institutions and social forms, but against other men. This, throughout, has been the area of silence, in the development of the idea. What is properly called utopianism, or revolutionary romanticism, is the suppression or dilution of this quite inevitable fact.

There are many reasons why men will oppose such a revolution. There are the obvious reasons of interest or privilege, for which we have seen men willing to die. There is the deep fear that recognition of the humanity of others is a denial of our own humanity, as our whole lives have known it. There is the flight in the mind from disturbance of a familiar world, however inadequate. There is the terror, often justified, of what will happen when men who have been treated as less than men gain the power to act. For there will of course be revenge and senseless destruction, after the bitterness and deformity of oppression. And then, more subtly, there are all the learned positions, from an experience of disorder that is as old as human history and yet also is continually re-enacted: the conviction that any absolute purpose is delusion and folly, to be corrected by training, by some social ease where we are, or by an outright opposition to this madness which would destroy the world.

From all these positions, revolution is practically opposed, in every form from brutal suppression and massive indoctrination to genuine attempts to construct alternative futures. And all our experience tells us that this immensely complicated action between real men will continue as far ahead as we can foresee, and that the suffering in this continuing struggle will go on being terrible. It is very difficult for the mind to accept this, and we all erect our defences against so tragic a recognition. But I believe that it is inevitable, and that we must speak of it if it is not to overwhelm us.

In some Western societies we are engaged in the attempt to make this total revolution without violence, by a process of argument and consensus. It is impossible to say if we shall succeed. The arrest of humanity, in many groups and individuals, is still severe and seems often intractable. At the same time, while the process has any chance of success, nobody in his senses would wish to alter its nature. The real difficulty, however, is that we have become introverted on this process, in a familiar kind of North Atlantic thinking, and the illusions this breeds are already of a tragic kind.

Thus we seek to project the result of particular historical circumstances as universal, and to identify all other forms of revolution as hostile. The only consistent common position is that of the enemies of revolution everywhere, yet even they, at times, speak a liberal rhetoric. It is a very deep irony that, in ideology, the major conflict in the world is between different versions of the absolute rights of man. Again and again, men in Western societies act as counter-revolutionaries, but in the name of an absolute liberation. There are real complexities here, for revolutionary regimes have also acted, repeatedly and brutally, against every kind of human freedom and dignity. But there are also deep and habitual forms of false consciousness. Only a very few of us, in any Western society, have in fact renounced violence, in the way that our theory claims. If we believe that social change should be peaceful, it is difficult to know what we are doing in military alliances, with immense armament and weapons of indiscriminate destruction. The customary pretence that this organised violence is defensive, and that it is wholly dedicated to human freedom, is literally a tragic illusion. It is easy to move about in our own comparatively peaceful society, repeating such phrases as 'a revolution by due course of law', and simply failing to notice that in our name, and endorsed by repeated majorities, other peoples have been violently opposed in the very act of their own liberation. The bloody tale of the past is always conveniently discounted, but I am writing on a day when British military power is being used against 'dissident tribesmen' in South Arabia, and I know this pattern and its covering too well, from repeated examples through my lifetime, to be able to acquiesce in the ordinary illusion. Many of my countrymen have opposed these policies, and in many particular cases have ended them. But it is impossible to believe that as a society we have yet dedicated ourselves to human liberation, or even to that simple recognition of the absolute humanity of all other men which is the impulse of any genuine revolution. To say that in our own affairs we have made this recognition would also be too much, in a society powered by great economic inequality and by organised manipulation. But even if we had made this recognition, among ourselves, it would still be a travesty of any real revolutionary belief. It is only when the recognition is general that it can be authentic, for in practice every reservation, in a widely communicating world, tends to degenerate into actual opposition.

Our interpretation of revolution as a slow and peaceful growth of consensus is at best a local experience and hope, at worst a sustained false consciousness. In a world determined by the struggle against poverty and against the many forms of colonial and neo-colonial domination, revolution continually and inescapably enters our society, in the form of our own role in those critical areas. And here it is not only that we have made persistent errors, and that we comfort ourselves with the illusion of steady progress when the gap between wealth and poverty is actually increasing in the world, and when the consciousness of exploitation is rapidly rising. It is also that the revolutionary process has become, in our generation, the ordinary starting point of war. It is very remarkable, in recent years, how the struggles for national liberation and for social change, in many different parts of the world, have involved the major powers in real and repeated dangers of general war. What are still, obtusely, called 'local upheavals', or even 'brushfires', put all our lives in question, again and again. Korea, Suez, the Congo, Cuba, Vietnam, are names of our own crisis. It is impossible to look at this real and still active history without a general sense of tragedy: not only because the disorder is so widespread and intolerable that in action and reaction it must work its way through our lives, wherever we may be; but also because, on any probable estimate, we understand the process so little that we continually contribute to the disorder. It is not simply that we become involved in this general crisis, but that we are already, by what we do and fail to do, participating in it.

There is, here, a strange contradiction. The two great wars we have known in Europe, and the widespread if still limited awareness of the nature of nuclear war, have induced a kind of inert pacifism which is too often self-regarding and dangerous. We say, understandably, that we must avoid war at all costs, but what we commonly mean is that we will avoid war at any cost but our own. Relatively appeased in our own situation, we interpret disturbance elsewhere as a threat to peace, and seek either to suppress it (the 'police action' to preserve what we call law and order; the fire brigade to put out the 'brushfire'), or to smother it with money or political manoeuvres. So deep is this contradiction that we regard such activities, even actual suppression, as morally virtuous; we even call it peacemaking. But what we are asking is what, in a limited consciousness, we have ourselves succeeded in doing: to acquiesce in a disorder and call it order; to say peace where there is no peace. We expect men brutally exploited and intolerably poor to rest and be patient in their misery, because if they act to end their condition it will involve the rest of us, and threaten our convenience or our lives.

In these ways, we have identified war and revolution as the

tragic dangers, when the real tragic danger, underlying war and revolution, is a disorder which we continually re-enact. So false a peacemaking, so false an appeal to order, is common in the action of tragedy, in which, nevertheless, all the real forces of the whole situation eventually work themselves out. Even if we were willing to change, in our attitudes to others and even more in our real social relations with them, we might still not, so late in the day, avoid actual tragedy. But the only relevant response, to the tragedy of this kind that we have already experienced, is that quite different peacemaking which is the attempt to resolve rather than to cover the determining tragic disorder. Any such resolution would mean changing ourselves, in fundamental ways, and our unwillingness to do this, the certainty of disturbance, the probability of secondary and unforeseen disorder, put the question, inevitably, into a tragic form.

The only consciousness that seems adequate in our world is then an exposure to the actual disorder. The only action that seems adequate is, really, a participation in the disorder, as a way of ending it. But at this point another tragic perspective opens. I find that I still agree with Carlyle, when he wrote in *Chartism*:

> Men who discern in the misery of the toiling complaining millions not misery, but only a raw material which can be wrought upon and traded in, for one's own poor hide-bound theories and egoisms; to whom millions of living fellow-creatures, with beating hearts in their bosoms, beating, suffering, hoping, are 'masses', mere 'explosive masses for blowing-down Bastilles with', for voting at hustings for *us*: such men are of the questionable species.

I have already argued the questionable nature of our many kinds of failure to commit ourselves to revolution. I would now repeat, with Carlyle, and with much real experience since he wrote, the questionable nature of a common kind of commitment. It is undoubtedly true that a commitment to revolution can produce a kind of hardening which even ends by negating the revolutionary purpose. Some people make the false commitment—the use of the misery of others—from the beginning. The most evident example is in Fascism, which is false revolution in just this sense. But, under real historical pressures, this hardening and negation occur again and again in authentic revolutionary activity, especially in isolation, under fire, and in scarcity so extreme as to threaten survival. The enemies of the revolutionary purpose then seize on the evidence of hardening and negation: either to oppose revolution as such, or to restore the convenient belief that man cannot change his condition, and that aspiration brings terror as a logical companion.

But this tragic aspect of revolution, which we are bound to acknowledge, cannot be understood in such ways. We have still to attend to the whole action, and to see actual liberation as part of the same process as the terror which appals us. I do not mean that the liberation cancels the terror; I mean only that they are connected, and that this connection is tragic. The final truth in this matter seems to be that revolution—the long revolution against human alienation—produces, in real historical circumstances, its own new kinds of alienation, which it must struggle to understand and which it must overcome, if it is to remain revolutionary.

I see this revolutionary alienation in several forms. There is the simple and yet bloody paradox that in the act of revolution its open enemies are easily seen as 'not men'. The tyrant, as he is killed, seems not a man but an object, and his brutality draws an answering brutality, which can become falsely associated with liberation itself. But it is not only a matter of the open enemies. Under severe pressure, the revolutionary purpose can become itself abstracted and can be set as an idea above real men. The decisive connection between present and future, which can only be a connection in experience and in continuing specific relations, is at once suppressed and replaced. There is then the conversion of actual misery and actual hope into a merely tactical 'revolutionary situation'. There is the related imposition of an idea of the revolution on the real men and women in whose name it is being made. The old unilinear model, by which revolution is abstractly known, is imposed on experience, including revolutionary experience. Often only this abstracted idea can sustain men, at the limits of their strength, but the need to impose it, in just such a crisis, converts friends into enemies, and actual life into the ruthlessly moulded material of an idea. The revolutionary purpose, born in what is most human and therefore most various, is negated by the single and often heroic image of revolutionary man, arrested at a stage in the very process of liberation and, persistent, becoming its most inward enemy.

In such ways, the most active agents of revolution can become its factual enemies, even while to others, and even to themselves, they seem its most perfect embodiment. But while we see this merely as accident, as the random appearance of particular evil men, we can understand nothing, for we are evading the nature of the whole action, and projecting its general meaning on to individuals whom we idealise or execrate. Elevating ourselves to spectators and judges, we suppress our own real role in any such action, or conclude, in a kind of indifference, that what has happened was inevitable and that there is even a law of inevitability. We see indeed a certain inevitability, of a tragic kind, as we see the struggle to end alienation producing its own new kinds of alienation. But, while we attend to the whole action, we see also, working through it, a new struggle against the new alienation: the comprehension of disorder producing a new image of order; the revolution against the fixed consciousness of revolution, and the authentic activity reborn and newly lived. What we then know is no simple action: the heroic liberation. But we know more also than simple reaction, for if we accept alienation, in ourselves or in others, as a permanent condition, we must know that other men, by the very act of living, will reject this, making us their involuntary enemies, and the radical disorder is then most bitterly confirmed.

The tragic action, in its deepest sense, is not the confirmation of disorder, but its experience, its comprehension and its resolution. In our own time, this action is general, and its common name is revolution. We have to see the evil and the suffering, in the factual disorder that makes revolution necessary, and in the disordered struggle against the disorder. We have to recognize this suffering in a close and immediate experience, and not cover it with names. But we follow the whole action: not only the evil, but the men who have fought against evil; not only the crisis, but the energy released by it, the spirit learned in it. We make the connections, because that is the action of tragedy, and what we learn in suffering is again revolution, because we acknowledge others as men and any such acknowledgement is the beginning of struggle, as the continuing reality of our lives. Then to see revolution in this tragic perspective is the only way to maintain it.

5. CONTINUITY

I began from the gap between tragic theory and tragic experience, and went on to inquire into the history of the idea of tragedy, and to criticise what I see as a dominant contemporary ideology. I then argued the relationship between tragedy and history, and in particular the contemporary relationship between tragedy and revolution. In the rest of the book my emphasis will be different. What I have written about tragedy and revolution is in a sense a preface to my third part. What I have written more generally, on tragic ideas and experiences, needs another kind of discussion, of modern tragic literature, and this is the substance of my second part. The test of what I have argued will come again there, in a quite different form.

PART TWO
Modern Tragic Literature

FROM HERO TO VICTIM

THE MAKING OF LIBERAL TRAGEDY, TO IBSEN AND MILLER

We have seen, in our own time, the climax and the decline of liberal tragedy. To understand its structure of feeling is now a central problem. For we are all to some extent still governed by it, even now when we can see that it is failing to hold.

At the centre of liberal tragedy is a single situation: that of a man at the height of his powers and the limits of his strength, at once aspiring and being defeated, releasing and destroyed by his own energies. The structure is liberal in its emphasis on the surpassing individual, and tragic in its ultimate recognition of defeat or the limits of victory. We have known, for nearly four centuries, a tension between this thrust of the individual and an absolute resistance, but the tension has passed through many forms, which we must try to distinguish. What we must trace, finally, is the transformation of the tragic hero into the tragic victim.

Tragedy, for us, has been mainly the conflict between an individual and the forces that destroy him. When any feeling is as strong as this, it can shape the mind so closely that the past itself is absorbed and transmuted, and the art of others lives only in its light. Our reading of Greek tragedy is perhaps the clearest example. Until very recently, against the evidence, we have remade Greek tragic drama in this image of our own: the tragic hero, at the centre of the play, magnificently exposed to a crushing external design. We have tried to take psychology, because that is our science, into the heart of an action to which it can never, critically, be relevant. We have looked for a tragic flaw, capable of starting such an action, in the character of an individual man. Yet it is now becoming clear (at a time, significantly, when our own governing structure of feeling is beginning to disintegrate) that the Greek tragic action was not rooted in individuals, or in individual psychology, in any of our senses. It was rooted in history, and not a human history alone. Its thrust came, not from the personality of an individual but from a man's inheritance and relationships, within a world that ultimately transcended him. What we then see is a general action specified, not an individual action generalised. What we learn is not character but the mutability of the world. Human life as such, always and everywhere, is subject to these exigencies. The exemplary case, reminding us, reliving this knowledge, brings pity and fear, in the general human condition.

It is said that Christianity altered this view of the world, putting a new emphasis on the individual. But this seems doubtful, especially in its assumption of a single Christian tradition. There is no important tragedy, within the Christian world, until there is also humanism and indeed individualism. In our own literature, there is no important tragedy before the release of personal energy, the emphasis of personal destiny, which we can see, looking back, in the complex process of Renaissance and Reformation. By the time of Marlowe and Shakespeare, the structure we now know was being actively shaped: an individual man, from his own aspirations, from his own nature, set out on an action that led him to tragedy.

We are bound to recognise this new spirit, even when we have properly remembered how strong a hold a different and traditional interpretation of life still had. Certainly we cannot understand Elizabethan tragedy if we fail to notice the elements that persisted from a mediaeval view of the world. The old conceptions of order and hierarchy, the intricate connections between man and nature, are there not only in active speech but in some of the essential conventions of the dramatic form. It is comparatively easy to demonstrate such continuities, in particular the continuation of the morality tradition, with all this implied for the relationship between individual and type and a common condition. But the continuities were within a very active process of change. We have only to go back a hundred years from Marlowe, to the morality *Everyman*, to see what these fundamental ideas and conventions produced on their own. Death comes to Everyman, in the midst of life, and of course is feared; the attempt made to avert it. But the action, confidently, takes Everyman forward to the edge of that dark room in which he must disappear, and the most remarkable aspect of this confidence is

that physically, on a scaffold above the dark room, God himself is waiting for Everyman to come. The hesitation in
entering is still strong; the room itself can not be seen into.
But to pass through it is not only inevitable; it is also the only
way in which Everyman can come to his Father. While that
dimension holds, there is aversion and fear, but the later
tragic voice cannot come. When it does come, it is unmistake-
able: a man alone in his extremity. It is not only, dramatically,
that God has gone from the scaffold. It is also that life, before
this extremity, is quite differently experienced. Where there
had been, in *Everyman*, a gathering of life into common and
formal categories, there is now a particularity, a momentari-
ness, an active awareness of process. Much of the new drama,
even when its reference points are familiar categories, takes
its most active life from a consciousness of the self in a passing
moment of experience: a self-consciousness which is now in
itself dramatic, and which new dramatic resources are
employed to express. The common process of life is seen at
its most intense in an individual experience.

The action changes accordingly. Again and again it is
rooted in the nature of a particular man. It is true that this
man, this hero, ends by finding his limits: tragic limits,
including the absolute limit of death. But it is also true that
again and again, if not invariably, he has *reached* for these
limits: set his whole energy on an aspiring course which yet
finally reveals them. Much of the extraordinary richness of
this drama, beyond its incomparable celebration of the
particularity of life, is precisely in the discovery and exploration of these limits, which can never be only death. Here,
indeed, the persistence of orders and hierarchies, the familiar
categories of man, exerts its necessary pressures. There is
confusion, an exciting confusion, as the pressures are taken
and tested, in the living act.

But the limits men reach, in their challenge to order, are
not only of this kind. There are also new limits, within man
himself. Order can break there, within the personality, as
decisively and as tragically. Breakdown and madness, as
private experiences, are quite newly realised and explored.
The emphasis, as we take the full weight, is not on the naming
of limits, but on their intense and confused discovery and
exploration. The traditional categories are affirmed, but

everything is questioned, in an outburst of energy so great that it seems, at times, to be shaking the whole body of man to pieces. Here, decisively, is one of the origins of the structure of feeling we are tracing: the thrust of living energy, in individual men, against limits which had once been composed into a confident order but which now, though still present and active, are questioned, fragmented, newly known and named, and are also confused by new experiences, new sources, of tragedy. The tragic voice, of our own immediate tradition, is then first heard: the aspiration for a meaning, at the very limits of a man's strength; the known meanings and answers, affirmed and yet also questioned, broken down, by contradictory experience.

The most important persistence, for the subsequent history of drama, was that of a public order, at the centre of what is otherwise personal tragedy. The hero is still, normally, the man of rank, the prince. An order can rise or fall with him, be affirmed or broken by him, even when what is driving him is a personal energy. The tragic hero is still marked by a social status, which defines his general importance, even when, in this new exploration of life, the hero becomes other than his status, or at least can be otherwise seen. Where in Greek tragedy the hero's status, with all it implied of inheritance, kinship and duty, enclosed the personality, which was developed only so far as the general action required, we find now, in Elizabethan tragedy, a personality within and beyond the similarly defining status, and the conflict that can result from this coexistence is often one of the sources of the tragedy. Thus the tension of the general action, between the exploring energies of life and all that is known of order, is repeated in the hero himself, between the individual man and the social role. In these tensions, this particular tragedy was formed.

At this stage of development, we can properly speak of humanist tragedy, but not yet, in a precise way, of liberal tragedy. The next stage was indeed a collapse of the tensions which had produced this remarkable drama. In the early eighteenth century, a determined attempt was made in England to adapt tragedy to the habits of thinking of middle-class life. This necessary and understandable attempt had little immediate success, though the imitation of its example in France and Germany provided one of the elements for the emergence of serious modern tragedy. It is easy, looking back, to fix attention on the change most often discussed: that of the status of the hero.

> *Stripp'd of Regal Pomp, and glaring Show*
> *His Muse reports a tale of Private Woe*
> *Works up Distress from Common Scenes in Life*
> *A Treach'rous Brother, and an Injur'd Wife.*

But something else is happening, beyond the change of rank:

> *Long has the Fate of Kings and Empires been*
> *The common business of the Tragick Scene,*
> *As if Misfortune made the Throne her Seat,*
> *And none could be unhappy but the Great . . .*
> *Stories like this with Wonder we may hear,*
> *But far remote, and in a higher Sphere,*
> *We ne'er can pity what we ne'er can share.*

Or again:

> *The Tragic Muse, sublime, delights to show*
> *Princes distrest and scenes of royal woe;*
> *In awful pomp, majestic, to relate*
> *The fall of nations or some hero's fate:*
> *That sceptered chiefs may by example know*
> *The strange vicissitude of things below;*
> *What dangers on security attend,*
> *How pride and cruelty in ruin end;*
> *Hence Providence supreme to know, and own*
> *Humanity adds glory to a throne.*
> *In ev'ry former age and foreign tongue*
> *With native grandeur thus the goddess sung.*
> *Upon our stage. indeed with wished success*
> *You've sometimes seen her in a humbler dress . . .*
> *The brilliant drops that fall from each bright eye*
> *The absent pomp with brighter gems supply.*
> *Forgive us then, if we attempt to show,*
> *In artless strains, a tale of private woe.*
> *A London 'prentice ruined, is our theme . . .*

And finally:

> *From lower Life we draw our Scene's Distress:*
> *—Let not your Equals move your Pity less.*

What we notice here is the new and single emphasis on pity: pity as sympathy. This is the mark of a growing humanitarianism, at least as aspiration. But what is then interesting is the contrast of pity with pomp, and the extent to which previous tragedy is interpreted as if rank as such were the decisive factor. It was inevitable, of course, in an age of bourgeois revolutions, that feudal and post-feudal connections between princely power and the order of the universe should be rejected. But what happens in practice, in this rejection, is an evident loss of dimension, which we can define as the loss of human connection at anything more than a private level. Humanitarianism, as an ideology, is the exact expression of this reduction. It expresses sympathy and pity between private persons, but tacitly excludes any positive conception of society, and thence any clear view of order or justice.

It is of course easy to blame the bourgeois for this, as so many historians of the drama have done. But simple blame conveniently omits the actual intermediate stage, in which the feudal order, as expressed in drama, collapsed from within. The vigorous exploration of the tensions between individuality and order had in fact ended abruptly in the early seventeenth century, so far as the drama was concerned. The decisive social challenge of the English Revolution might have produced new kinds of drama, but did not; the Puritan distrust of the drama was probably decisive. What in fact happened was a separation of drama from the mainstream of the society, and the reduction of the great tensions of Elizabethan tragedy to 'pomp' and 'show' took place within the continuing minority drama itself. The energy of the hero, reaching out to the human limits, was conventionalised and frozen into the fixed postures of 'heroic tragedy'. Pope might describe Addison's Cato as

> *A brave man struggling in the storms of fate,*
> *And greatly falling with a falling State*

but the truer description, of what had become tragedy, is Cotes's:

> *What pen but yours could draw the doubtful strife*
> *Of honour struggling with the love of life?*

The conflict of fixed and formal passions with the fixed and formal duties of rank and honour had decisively replaced the earlier and more creative tensions. When the bourgeois tragedians rejected 'pomp' they were hitting an already empty shell.

Rank, that is to say, became class, and once it did so a new definition of tragedy was inevitable. Rank implied order and connection; class was only separation, within an amorphous society. The attempt at human connection was then necessarily a matter of humanitarian sympathy, in 'private woe' and 'private distress'. The growth of active pity was accompanied by a belief in what was called redemption: in fact, repentance and the change of heart. It is not only that this structure of feeling made the writing of tragedy difficult; such a loss would be small, if the structure really held. Nor is it only that the attempt to combine disparate structures produced a sentimental tragedy, which is now valueless. The important loss is one of dimension and reference. There is an evident gap between private sympathy and the public order. The bourgeois tragedians, moved by pity and sympathy, and struggling for realism, were in fact betrayed by this gap, where no realism was possible. For the sources of tragedy were not, even in their experience, *only* private. The best known play of the period, Lillo's *The London Merchant*, is even explicitly social. And what we must then notice is that pity and sympathy have little chance, except as gestures, against the actual and affirmed imperatives of the new society. Where property is in question, as in this story of the thieving apprentice, the judgement is sharp and certain. Thieving is connected with murder as systematically, and as mystically, as once rebellion with disturbing the universe. Then the gallows is erected, with its own kind of inevitability, and the humanitarian feelings of pity and sympathy have to stand in its shadow. Distress accompanies execution, and humanitarianism is at its limits.

What we then see, behind the loss of dimension, is a complacent affirmation of the existing social framework. Crime does not pay, and crime is about property. The arbitrariness of power had been experienced in the blood; its pretensions could be dismissed as pomp. But the arbitrariness of property is a human datum, which the bourgeois tragedians

lack the nerve to test. Obliquely, confusedly, the recognition
is made, that the struggle for money has replaced the struggle
for power as a human motive and as a tragic motive. The disruption of the family by greed for money is obliquely present
in Lillo's *Fatal Curiosity*. But the imperative is not seriously
questioned, and certainly cannot be connected with the whole
body of human desire. Bourgeois tragedy has been blamed
for being too social, for excluding the universal reference of
Renaissance and humanist tragedy. Another way of putting
the matter is that it is not social enough, for with its private
ethic of pity and sympathy it could not negotiate the real
contradictions of its own time, between human desire and the
now social limits set on it. Through its double voice, of pity
and certainty, we hear the first weak accents of man the
victim: the old far-reaching heroism gone, the limits known
but not named. When at last, in fact, the limits were known
and named, as a false society, the hero could re-emerge, as a
rebel against it. But this, effectively, was still a century ahead,
in the period of liberal tragedy.

Bourgeois tragedy, as a creative force, faded quickly, in its
original forms. In a sense it went underground, was driven
there by its own contradictions. The exploring energy re-
emerged, in strange ways, in Romantic tragedy. What is quite
evident, through all the failures of Romantic drama, is a
renewal and a renewed assertion of individual energy. The
desires of man are again intense and imperative; they reach
out and test the universe itself. Society is identified as convention, and convention as the enemy of desire. The individual rebellion is humanist, at a conscious level. Prometheus
and Faust, characteristically, are its heroes. But the condition
of desire, unconsciously, is that it is always forbidden. What
then happens is that the forms of desire become devious and
often perverse, and what looks like revolt is more properly a
desperate defiance of heaven and hell. There is a related preoccupation with remorse: deep, pervasive, and beyond all its
nominal causes. For in Romantic tragedy man is guilty of the
ultimate and nameless crime of being himself.

The impossibility of finding a home in the world, the con-
demnation to a guilty wandering, the dissolution of self and
others in a desire that is beyond all relationships: these
Romantic themes are an important source of nearly all

modern tragedy. Aspiration is absolute, but occurs, paradoxically, within a situation of man on the run from himself.
Within this paradox, one dramatist of genius was eventually
to work. But also, by the time of Ibsen's maturity, the last
source of liberal tragedy had appeared: the increasingly confident identification of a false society as man's real enemy; the
naming, in social terms, of the formerly nameless alienation.
This body of social thinking had many kinds of influence. In
one direction, it led to the denial of tragedy. Man had not only
made but could remake himself. The Romantic desire for
redemption and regeneration was given, in this tendency, a
more or less precise social definition: when man was at the
limits which ordinarily produced tragedy he became conscious of their nature and could begin to abolish them. When
this abolition was seen as a social process, it did not, at least
in the nineteenth century, lead to tragedy at all. The idea of
tragedy, indeed, was dismissed as mystification and fatalism:
an irony that still haunts us now that collective tragedy, and
the tragic society, have been widely and deeply experienced.
But this was not, in any case, the liberal path. What emerged
there, as a controlling image, was not revolution, but the
individual liberator. Acting on his own, and for his own
reasons, a single man could change the human limits and
transform his world. Looking back to Romantic tragedy, and
forward to existentialist tragedy, this conception was still in
its purest form in the late nineteenth century. By an act of
choice, by an act of will, the individual refused the role of
victim and became a new kind of hero. The heroism was not
in the nobility of suffering, as the limits were reached. It was
now, unambiguously, in the aspiration itself. What was
demanded was self-fulfilment, and any such process was a
general liberation. The singular man, as a matter of speech,
became plural and capital: Man.

Liberal tragedy, at its full development, drew from all the
sources that have been named, but in a new form and pressure
created a new and specific structure of feeling. It is important,
at this stage, not to try to fragment it, when it appears in
Ibsen. The humanist exploration of the unknown reaches of
life; the bourgeois preoccupation with humanitarianism and
with money; the romantic intensities of alienation, remorse
and perverted desire; the social recognition of dead institu-

tions and limiting beliefs: all these are present in Ibsen, but in active combination, not as separate influences. To try to resolve his work into one of these lines has been a common practice in criticism: Ibsen the social critic; Ibsen the romantic or existentialist: each has been plausibly presented. But the real interest lies, where the work lies, in the struggle of these forces and in their composition into a particular drama.

Ibsen creates again and again in his plays, with an extraordinary richness of detail, false relationships, a false society, a false condition of man. The marks along this scale are often difficult to discern. The immediate lie is almost always present, but there is great variation in its ultimate reference: sometimes to an alterable condition; sometimes to an absolute condition; often, ambiguously, between these. Yet the generalising reference, in whatever kind, is persistent; the lie is never merely local, for it is seen as a symptom of a general condition. Characteristically, for liberal tragedy, the fight against the lie is individual; a man fights for his own life. Brand's vocation is 'All or Nothing', and compromise is personally impossible:

> One thing is yours you may not spend,
> Your very inmost self of all,
> You may not bind it, may not bend,
> Nor stem the river of your call.

Or again:

> Self completely to fulfil,
> That's a valid right of man,
> And no more than that I will.

At the same time, the 'right' is also the 'call':

> A great one gave me charge. I must.

The call to wholeness is seen as self-fulfilment, and yet also as necessary. The right and the duty coincide in self-fulfilment, as in the classic liberal statements.

Yet the whole point about self-fulfilment is that it challenges, to the death, the existing compromise order. For here the lie is actual: men are afraid of wholeness and of self-fulfilment. As the Provost argues:

> The surest way to destroy a man
> Is to turn him into an individual.

Men have settled for a fragmentary life, as the easiest way, but this settlement is the sickness of their own personal lives and of their society. Routine is destructive, but so also are the wild breaks from routine, the simple refusals. What is needed is a new and total assent, for

> *Our time, our generation, that is sick*
> *And must be cured.*

Thus the individual, fulfilling himself absolutely, becomes, or offers himself as, the liberator. This position is reached again and again in Ibsen, but the resolution varies. In *Pillars of Society*, *A Doll's House*, *Enemy of the People*, the refusal of compromise is unambiguously carried through, if not to liberation, at least to positive individual defiance. In *Peer Gynt*, what looks like the quest for self-fulfilment is shown in the end to be simple evasion: the self alone, detached from the reality of world and relationships, withers and is wasted, to be redeemed only by return. More commonly, in varying degrees of emphasis, the individual's struggle is seen as both necessary and tragic. The evasion of fulfilment, by compromise, breeds false relationships and a sick society, but the attempt at fulfilment ends again and again in tragedy: the individual is destroyed in his attempt to climb out of his partial world.

This is the crux of liberal tragedy, and it is in many ways difficult to understand. The simple position is that of the heroic liberator opposed and destroyed by a false society: the liberal martyr. It is clear that Ibsen knew this feeling; it finds memorable expression in Stockmann. But it is not in this pattern that Ibsen takes his heroes to their deaths. Stockmann, faced only by this, is stronger and survives:

The strongest man in the world is he who stands most alone.

Nor is it merely by accident and complication that the hero dies. The tragedy, in fact, is built into the form of the aspiration, in the significant concept of *debt*.

In the action and imagery of the plays, the nature of debt is persistently explored. Just as aspiration cannot be reduced simply to social reform, to a religious calling, or to self-expression, but remains obstinately general—the liberation of human spirit and energy—so debt cannot be reduced to inherited obligations, to a society burdened by compromises,

D

or to original sin. These are often the forms in which aspiration and debt appear, but the actual works are more often explorations of the conflicting forces than definitions of them. Thus while in *Brand* there is a simple fatalism—

> *Blood of children must be spilt*
> *To atone for parents' guilt*

—it is also clear that new debts are contracted in the act of refusal of compromise; it is Brand himself, and not merely Brand the son or the human being, who is eventually guilty. The position would be simpler if this guilt were then condemned, if the voice through the final avalanche—'He is the God of love'—were a verdict. But this is not the case. Brand had to do what he did, and yet had to come to this point. This is not ethical tragedy, where a different choice would have brought safety. The choice and the fate admit no real alternatives.

What happens, again and again in Ibsen, is that the hero defines an opposing world, full of lies and compromises and dead positions, only to find, as he struggles against it, that as a man he belongs to this world, and has its destructive inheritance in himself. Ibsen turned this way and that, looking for a way out of this tragic deadlock, but normally he returned to it, and confessed its terrible power:

> Ghosts!... I almost believe we are all ghosts, Pastor Manders. It is not only what we have inherited from our fathers and mothers that walks in us. It is every kind of dead idea, lifeless old beliefs and so on. They are not alive, but they cling to us for all that, and we can never rid ourselves of them. Whenever I read a newspaper I seem to see ghosts stealing between the lines. There must be ghosts the whole country over, as thick as the sands of the sea. And then we are all of us so wretchedly afraid of the light.

This position, so often stated, is not a gloss for surrender to the darkness. The cry for light, the desire to climb out of such a world, is persistent and emphatic:

> Give me air and the blaze of day ...
> Through darkness to light ...
> A summer night on the uplands ...
> The joy of life ... always, always the joy of life—light and sunshine and glorious air ...
> Mother, give me the sun.

But as the last phrase, the dying cry of Osvald, reminds us, the light is only a breaking aspiration, at the limits of human endurance. The death of Julian the Apostate, not the death of Christ, is the significant ending:

> Beautiful earth, beautiful life . . . O, Helios, Helios, why hast thou betrayed me?

There is no turning away from life to death, no tragic resignation. Ibsen's heroes, characteristically, die fighting and struggling and climbing: the aspiration to light is confirmed, not contradicted, by their deaths. In this sense, they are still heroes, but also they are tragic heroes. The ghosts

> cling to us . . . we can never rid ourselves of them.

Or as the liberal Rosmer puts it:

> We can never escape them, we of this house.

Ibsen seems to depend, as some of his language certainly depends, on a traditional idea of original sin. But the effect of his whole work is in fact a transformation of this. He never gives up the idea of the false society, even when he has realised that its complications eat into the lives of those opposing it. Nor, truly, does he ever mean 'sin' by 'debt'. The debts that count, in bringing his heroes down, are incurred in the struggle for life and light, however wayward this is often shown to be. When we have said 'sin', of Adam's desire, we have discounted human life, in any aspiring sense. But this desire, in Ibsen, is deep and valid. This is most clearly shown in *Emperor and Galilean*, where the false world of power and the false doctrine of resignation are alike rejected, in the struggle for the 'third empire', in which 'the spirit of men shall re-enter on its heritage'. It is the false condition of spirit against flesh that Julian fights, because

> all that is human has become unlawful since the day when the seer of Galilee became ruler of the world. Through him, life has become death.

The desire fails, or is broken, but is never denied. Ibsen's world, from his historical dramas to his domestic plays, is recognisable always by this fact: the struggle of individual desire, in a false and compromising situation, to break free and know itself. This is why we must not render him back to a dramatic tradition which would show the desire as false or unlawful. In the best sense, this is still a liberal world.

It is also, however, the world of liberal tragedy. Implacably, in most of his plays, the affirmed desire is brought to a breaking-point

> —a tight place where you stick fast. There is no going forward or backward—

and the hero, if not the desire itself, is broken. Why should this be so? Why, repeatedly, should so powerful a struggle of human desire fail to break through? It is not any force outside man that breaks him. As Rosmer says, going to his death:

> There is no judge over us, and therefore we must do justice upon ourselves.

But the justice, still, is death. The conviction of guilt, and of necessary retribution, is as strong as ever it was when imposed by an external design.

And this is the heart of liberal tragedy, for we have moved from the heroic position of the individual liberator, the aspiring self against society, to a tragic position, of the self against the self. Guilt, that is to say, has become internal and personal, just as aspiration was internal and personal. The internal and personal fact is the only general fact, in the end. Liberalism, in its heroic phase, begins to pass into its twentieth-century breakdown: the self-enclosed, guilty and isolated world; the time of man his own victim.

We are still in this world, and it is doubtful if we can clearly name all its pressures. A characteristic ideology has presented it as truth and even as science, until argument against it has come to seem hopeless. A structure of feeling as deep as this enacts a world, as well as interpreting it, so that we learn it from experience as well as from ideology. All we can say, reflecting on Ibsen's tragedy, is that the deadlock reached there, the heroic deadlock in which men die still struggling to climb, was indeed necessary. For there is no way out, there is only an inevitable tragic consciousness, while desire is seen as essentially individual. We have to push past Ibsen's undoubted social consciousness to discover, at its roots, this same individual consciousness. Certainly there is to be reform, the 'sick earth' is to be 'made whole', but this is to happen, always, by an individual act: the liberal conscience, *against* society. Change is never to be *with* people; if others come, they can at most be led. But also change, significantly often, is against people; it is against their wills that the liberator is thrown, and disillusion is then rapid. He speaks for human desire, as a general fact, but he knows this only as individual fulfilment. The self then makes its most terrible discovery: that there is not only a world outside it, resisting it, but other selves, capable of similar suffering and desire. It is possible then for fulfilment to be re-defined: a getting away from the world and from others; the loneliness of the high mountains. But desire had included the joy of life: the life of earth, and of men and women, which the hero is still governed by, even while he drives himself to reject it. The conflict is then indeed internal: a desire for relationship when all that is known of relationship is restricting; desire narrowing to an image in the mind, until it is realised that the search for warmth and light has ended in cold and darkness. Every move towards relationship ends in guilt. It is significant that no-where in Ibsen is there a loving, active, lasting relationship; the image of it, at the end of *Peer Gynt*, is as much a relapse from effort, a return to the mother, as a discovery of a loving equal. More often, the tie to the parent is not even relapse. There is a kind of terror in natural inheritance itself. As later in Freudian psychology, the parent-child relationship is guilty as such, and the revelation of the face or feeling of father and mother, behind the adult self, is in itself horrifying. That inescapable connection haunts, quite literally, the liberal idea of the self. In this sense, to be born is to be guilty, and inheritance is inevitably 'debt'. For the identity of the 'free' self is limited and impugned by the necessary physical inheritance. That connection to others is involuntary, and is in the blood. To the liberal self this is not connection but tainting.

Then, driven by individual desire, which cannot admit any final connection, Ibsen's adult persons simply involve and damage each other, beyond the possibility of fulfilment. Freedom is defined as getting away from this net, or exposing it, in the name of truth. But there is nowhere to get away to, except by renunciation of the individual life and desire which are still active and compelling. Desire, consistently, betrays desire. The most active search to fulfil the self leads away from the persons in whom fulfilment is desired. It was this that Ibsen recognised, in his last plays; most notably in the Dramatic Epilogue:

> We see the irretrievable only when . . .
> When? . . .
> When we dead awaken.
> What do we really see then?
> We see that we have never lived.

The search for self-fulfilment has ended in the denial of life:

> It was self-murder, a deadly sin against myself. And that sin I can never expiate.

It is the final tragic recognition: that the self, which is all that is known as desire, leads away from fulfilment, and to its own breakdown.

From this recognition, there is no way out, within the liberal consciousness. There is either the movement to common desire, common aspiration, which politically is socialism, or there is the acceptance, reluctant at first but strengthening and darkening, of failure and breakdown as common and inevitable. In one way or the other, a total condition is asserted, and the differentiated self becomes dramatically rare. It is true that Shaw, in *Saint Joan* and elsewhere, could retain the simpler pattern, of the heroic and liberating individual destroyed by a false society. Numerically, many other plays have repeated this, but, at least in European drama, this pattern has commonly failed to include any of the deepest human energies and problems. The heroic individual, as in Shaw, survives only as a romantic portrait, emptied of personality so that the positive role can be played without complications. The act of liberation, correspondingly, is in the narrow sense historical or political; it is not an absolute human demand, but a limited cause here and there. The problem of the frustrated individual is masked by his theatrical transformation into a movement, leaving all the deeper problems, of history and personality, untouched.

The mainstream of tragedy has gone elsewhere: into the self-enclosed, guilty and isolated world of the breakdown of liberalism. We shall need to trace this through its complicated particular phases. But, with Ibsen in mind, it is worth looking briefly at the plays of Arthur Miller, who represents, essentially, a late revival of liberal tragedy, on the edge (but only on the edge) of its transformation into socialism. What distinguishes Miller from the majority contemporary drama of guilt and breakdown is the retained consciousness of a false society, an alterable condition. In *All My Sons* we are in many ways back in the world of Ibsen: a particular lie becomes the demonstration of a general lie. Joe Keller, a small manufacturer, has committed a social crime for which he has escaped responsibility. He acquiesced in the sending of defective parts to the Air Force in wartime, and allowed another man to take the consequences and imprisonment. The action of the play is that the social crime is made personal (by the fact of the death of Keller's own pilot son), and from this realisation made social again, in a new understanding of what society is. This is, in fact, the overcoming of alienation:

> Joe Keller's trouble . . . is not that he cannot tell right from wrong but that his cast of mind cannot admit that he, personally, has any viable connection with his world, his universe, or his society.

This is

> the concept of a man's becoming a function of production or distribution to the point where his personality becomes divorced from the actions it propels.

By seeing a particular case, to which he has a father's connection, he is forced to recognise the general fact of human connection:

> I think to him they were all my sons. And I guess they were, I guess they were.

However, this new positive consciousness cannot go beyond the level of statement; it is a new feeling, of collective responsibility and of collective guilt, personally affirmed, but the tragedy is in the fact that it is retrospective. Keller, and those he has killed, can only be victims.

This sense of the victim is very deep in Miller. *The Crucible* may remind us, dramatically, of *Enemy of the People*, but there is a wholly new sense of the terrible power of collective persecution. Individuals suffer for what they are and naturally desire, rather than for what they try to do, and the innocent are swept up with the guilty, with epidemic force. The social consciousness has now changed, decisively. Society is not merely a false system, which the liberator can challenge. It is actively destructive and evil, claiming its victims merely because they are alive. It is still seen as a false and alterable society, but merely to live in it, now, is enough to become its victim. In *Death of a Salesman* the victim is not the nonconformist, the heroic but defeated liberator; he is, rather, the conformist, the type of the society itself. Willy Loman is a man who from selling things has passed to selling himself, and has become, in effect, a commodity which like other commodities will at a certain point be discarded by the laws of the economy. He brings tragedy down on himself, not by opposing the lie, but by living it. Ironically, the form of his aspiration is again the form of his defeat, but now for no liberating end; simply to get by, to see himself and his sons all right. The connection between parents and children, seen as necessarily contradictory, is again tragically decisive. A new consciousness is then shaped: that of the victim who has no living way out, but who can try, in death, to affirm his lost identity and his lost will.

Proctor, in *The Crucible*, had died as an act of self-preservation: preservation of the truth of himself and of others, in opposition to the lies of the persecuting authority.

How may I live without my name?

This sense of personal verification by death is the last stage of liberal tragedy. In *The Crucible* it is virtually the position of the liberal martyr, though characteristically complicated by Proctor's personal guilt. But in *Death of a Salesman* and *A View from the Bridge* this wider implication is absent. It is not now the martyr but the victim; the disconnected individual. In Willy Loman's death the disconnection confirmed a general fact about the society; in Eddie Carbone's death, Miller has moved further back, and the death of the victim illustrates a total condition. Here, once again, at the end of a development, is the self against the self. Desire is quickened, releasing energies which destroy. As Eddie moves out of routine and into desire, there is rapid disintegration: the known sexual rhythms break down into their perverse variations, which now alone have energy. He rejects his wife, as his desire transfers to the girl they have brought up. And as his most vital energy drives him towards both incest and homosexuality, guilt becomes so much a part of desire that his identity and his normal connections are simply burned out. In the terror of his complicated jealousies, he betrays the human connection by which he has lived, surrenders immigrants of his wife's kin to the inhuman and alien society. When desire and guilt are thus inextricable, there is no way to live, and he provokes his death shouting 'I want my name'.

It is a last tragic cry, in a disintegrating world. Human desire destroys itself, under intolerable pressures, and the figure of the individual hero, who would remake his life and his world, is now quite forgotten, is one of the old stories, while isolated contemporary man, wanting no more than to be himself, fails even in this and transfers significance to his name and his death. To preserve one's life, as things are, is 'to settle for half', as Miller puts it at the end of *A View from the Bridge*. And if this is so, in a false society which the individual alone cannot change, then the original liberal impulse, of complete self-fulfilment, becomes inevitably tragic. The self that wills and desires destroys the self that lives, yet the rejection of will and desire is also tragedy: a corroding insignificance, as the self is cut down.

The final step, made clear in *After the Fall*, is the acceptance and generalisation of just this insignificance: the personally urgent yet finally complacent acknowledgement that desire and guilt are inextricable; the identification of the false society —torture, betrayal—as part of one's own desires, so that it can no longer be meaningfully opposed, or even bitterly challenged by death, but has simply to be confirmed, forgiven, and lived with, in our separate and isolated suffering. And then at this point the deadlock is absolute, and we are all victims: aspiration itself is only a disguise for cruelty. But when this has happened, in the mind of a whole culture, liberal tragedy has ended, in its own deadlock.

D*

2

PRIVATE TRAGEDY

STRINDBERG, O'NEILL, TENNESSEE WILLIAMS

There is a kind of tragedy which ends with man bare and unaccommodated, exposed to the storm he has himself raised. This exposure in struggle has been a common deadlock of humanism and liberalism. But there is another kind of tragedy, superficially much like this, which in fact begins with bare and unaccommodated man. All primary energy is centred in this isolated creature, who desires and eats and fights alone. Society is at best an arbitrary institution, to prevent this horde of creatures destroying each other. And when these isolated persons meet, in what are called relationships, their exchanges are forms of struggle, inevitably.

Tragedy, in this view, is inherent. It is not only that man is frustrated, by others and by society, in his deepest and primary desires. It is also that these desires include destruction and self-destruction. What is called the death-wish is given the status of a general instinct, and its derivatives, in destructiveness and aggression, are seen as essentially normal. The process of living is then a continual struggle and adjustment of the powerful energies making for satisfaction or death. It is possible to give great emphasis to the state of satisfaction, but within the form of this isolate thinking it is inevitable that satisfaction, however intense, is temporary, and that it involves the subjugation or defeat of another. The desire for death may be less strong, or more deeply disguised, but of course, when achieved, is permanent. Then, within this form, life and death have been transvalued. The storm of living does not have to be raised, by any personal action; it begins when we are born, and our exposure to it is absolute. Death, by contrast, is a kind of achievement, a comparative settlement and peace.

The work of August Strindberg is the most challenging single example, within this range of tragedy. Argued schematically, even in its many orthodox textbooks, such a version of man can seem indifferent or absurd. But when charged with experience, and with dramatic power, it is often a very different matter. We can see that in many ways the schematic version is remarkably exclusive, of many real kinds of action and feeling. Yet historically the emergence of this version seemed most remarkable for its inclusiveness: bringing many kinds of known action and feeling into a new and powerful light. The tragedy of destructive relationships, when taken into newly described areas of living and persuasively communicated and generalised, had for many the force of a revelation.

Strindberg wrote in his Preface to *Lady Julie*:

> Personally, I find the joy of life in its tense and cruel struggles, and my enjoyment lies in getting to know something, in getting to learn something.

The centre of interest is characteristic: the 'tense and cruel struggles' are indeed an epitome. But the attention is modulated, in this early phase of Strindberg's work, by the spirit of inquiry, the desire for knowledge and understanding. Similarly, the inhuman assumptions of Freud were heroically modulated, throughout his life, by the long effort to understand and to heal. The final development of the pattern, when the 'tense and cruel struggles' are assumed as a whole truth, and are then merely demonstrated, comes later and in other hands.

When the bourgeois tragedians spoke of private tragedy, they were directing attention towards the family, as an alternative to the state. Society, characteristically, was a lost term. Personal life was a family matter. Already, so early, the possible disintegration of a family, by separate personal desires, was seen as a tragic theme. But the kind of disintegration which was eventually to dominate the bourgeois imagination was much more than this. We have seen how, in liberal tragedy, the fact of inheritance became tainted and terrifying. The world of Strindberg, and of many writers since him, is a stage beyond even this. Within the primary relationships, which are intensely valued, the fact of tainting is taken for granted, and is minor by comparison with the association of love and destruction: an association so deep that it is not, as the liberal writers assumed, the product of a particular history; it is, rather, general and natural, in all relationships. Men and women seek to destroy each other in the act of loving and of creating new life, and the new life is itself always guilty, not so much by inheritance as by the relationships it is inevitably born into. For it is used as weapon and prize in the parents' continuing struggle, and is itself unwanted, not only as itself, in its own right, but continually unwanted, since there is no final place for it where it was born, and yet the loss of this place is an absolute exposure, haunted by the desires of an impossible return. Thus the creation of life and the condition of life are alike tragic: a deep and terrible pain which the active desires of loving and growing only in the end accentuate and confirm: accentuate, because their joys will be brief; confirm, because by their nature they lead back into the same struggle and wounding. Love and loss, love and destruction, are two sides of the same coin.

> CAPTAIN: ... My father and mother didn't *want* me, and thus I was born without a will. So I thought I was completing myself when you and I became one, and that is why you got the upper hand. ...
>
> LAURA: ... That is why I loved you as if you were my child. But whenever you showed yourself instead as my lover, you must have seen my shame. Your embraces were a delight followed by aches of conscience, as if my very blood felt shame. The mother became mistress! That is where the mistake lay. The mother, you see, was your friend, but the woman was your enemy, and love between the sexes is strife. And don't imagine that I gave myself to you. I didn't give, I took—what I wanted. ...

This is the central statement in what Strindberg called 'my tragedy, *The Father*'. The captain is driven into insanity by a wife determined at any cost to control the child. The man's share in creating the child was no more than suffered, and now his role is over and he can be driven out. Yet it is not merely Laura's cruelty, backed by the other women, which drives the captain to breakdown. It is also the loss of the will to live, as he discovers what he takes to be the truth about being a father:

> For me, not believing in a life after death, the child was my idea of immortality, perhaps the only idea that has any real expression. Take that away and you cut off my life.

Yet the taking away comes to be seen as inevitable:

Have you never felt ridiculous in your role as father? I know nothing
so ludicrous as to see a father leading his child by the hand along the
street, or to hear him talking about his children. 'My wife's children',
he should say . . . My child! A man has no children. It is women who
get children, and that's why the future is theirs, while we die
childless.

In the power of *The Father*, and of *The Dance of Death*,
Strindberg enacts this at once terrible and absurd vision. This
combination of qualities explains the tone of the plays, which
are without pity only because of the simultaneous presence
of exasperation and disgust. Suffering is known, and deeply
respected, but there is the energy also of a protest against the
impossible and yet the permanent.

It is especially relevant to Strindberg that the vision of
destructive relationships is still, at this stage, connected with
other energies and faculties. The desire for knowledge, as in
the captain's experiments, is real and seemingly absolute, until
the generated hatred of the marriage overwhelms it. And, in
the speech about the meaning of the child, reference is
explicitly made to ideas of will, purpose and immortality. This
is part of the tragedy: that these human impulses are cut off
by the terror at the roots of life.

Strindberg described himself as a naturalist, and this was
much more than a description of method:

Naturalism is not a dramatic method like that of Becque, a simple
photography which includes everything, even the speck of dust on
the lens of the camera. That is realism; a method, lately exalted to
art, a tiny art which cannot see the wood for the trees. That is the
false naturalism, which believes that art consists simply of sketching a
piece of nature in a natural manner; but it is not the true naturalism,
which seeks out those points in life where the great conflicts occur,
which rejoices in seeing what cannot be seen every day.

It is perhaps a pity that subsequent uses of 'naturalism' and
'realism' have been directly opposite, in each case, to the
definitions given by Strindberg. But the essential point is not
difficult. For Strindberg, naturalism was primarily an
attitude to experience, which determined the substance of his
art. Dramatic method followed from the nature of this
experience. The principle of selection was quite fairly called

'naturalism', in line with the philosophical rather than the critical uses of this term. Strindberg wrote, for example:

> The naturalist has abolished guilt by abolishing God.

In his own early work, this standpoint is evident. It is the main reason why the tragedy is of a new kind. The sentence quoted comes in the middle of an explanation of why Lady Julie is tragic:

> She is a victim of the discord which a mother's 'crime' has produced in a family; a victim, too, of the delusions of the day, of circumstances, of her own defective constitution—all of which together are the equivalents of the old-fashioned Fate or Universal Law. The naturalist has abolished guilt by abolishing God; but the consequences of an action—punishment, imprisonment or the fear of it—these he cannot abolish, for the simple reason that they remain, whether his verdict be acquittal or not; for an injured fellow-creature is not so complaisant as an outsider, who has not been injured, can well afford to be.

Thus there is no justice and no external law, but there is hurt and revenge, exposure and hatred: a simply human struggle. This is sufficient ground for human beings to destroy each other, and indeed to destroy themselves, as Strindberg goes on to argue, driven by their own ideas and illusions.

Yet still, while the outward connection is made, an alternative standpoint is available. In *Lady Julie*, particularly, Strindberg connects the destructive passions with a struggle of social classes:

> So the valet, Jean, continues to live, while Lady Julie cannot live without honour.

He suggests, even, that Jean is a stronger and higher type, and that we ought to see the struggle in this way:

> There is no such thing as absolute evil; the ruin of one family means the good fortune of another, which is thereby enabled to rise.

This, certainly, is a kind of naturalism, of the type popularised by the false analogy of biological evolution to the struggles of classes and individuals. The 'survival of the fittest' was translated as the victory of the stronger type; thus even violent conflict made for general happiness. Strindberg tried hard and brilliantly to retain this conception, though in retrospect it is equivocal:

> Lady Julie is a modern character; not that the half-woman, the man-hater, has not existed in all ages, but because she has now been discovered, has stepped to the front and made herself heard. The half-woman is a type that is thrusting itself forward, that sells itself nowadays for power, for titles, for distinctions, for diplomas, as it used to sell itself for money. And it points to degeneration. It is not a good type—for it does not last—but unfortunately it transmits its own misery to another generation; moreover, degenerate men seem unconsciously to make their choice from among them, so that they multiply and produce offspring of indeterminate sex, to whom life is a torture. Fortunately, these women perish, either through lack of harmony with reality, or through the uncontrolled mutiny of their own suppressed instinct, or through the shattering of their hopes of catching up with the men. The type is tragic, offering, as it does, the spectacle of a desperate fight with nature; tragic, too, as a romantic inheritance now being dispersed by naturalism, whose sole desire is happiness; and for happiness strong and good types are required.

The portrait is vigorous, and the analysis is social. But in practice Strindberg could not sustain this alternative view. The class element in the affair of Julie and Jean is important, certainly, but behind it and through it rages a different pattern. It is not only that Jean himself is far from the 'strong and good type' of the intellectual commentary. It is that the sex is either indifferent, as with Kristina, or the fever in the blood of Julie, carrying its own violence. Within the particular situation, which has its own importance, the supposedly universal pattern recurs, and it is very much like fate. Between man and women there is only taking, and in reaction there is hatred. Nowhere, in modern literature, has this rhythm been more powerfully heard. The dance of sexual excitement is again the dance of death.

Strindberg's power as a dramatist is his emphasis on process:

> The psychological process is what chiefly interests the newer generation; our inquisitive souls are not content with seeing a thing happen; they must also know how it happens.

In this sense Strindberg is pre-eminently the dramatist of a dynamic psychology. He is extraordinarily creative in a purely technical way: in the capacity to find new and dynamic forms through which psychological process can be enacted. The merit of this kind of commitment is in any case its particularity: the convincing detail of an actually destructive relationship. Yet it is true of Strindberg, as of so much psychology in our century, that behind the particularity of detail there is a very firm and even rigid body of generalisation and assumption. To show that a particular relationship is destructive can be empirical and dynamic, but the effect is lessened, in any final analysis, when we realise that the relationship follows from an assumed general condition. Nothing whatever has been shown about relationship, and the particularity of detail can be mere embellishment, if the finally governing assumption is a personal isolation in a meaningless world. Relationship is then by definition destructive: not only because isolated beings cannot combine, can only collide and damage each other; but also because the brief experiences of physical union, whether in sexual love or in infancy, are inevitably destructive, breaking or threatening the isolation which is all that is known of individuality:

> We, like the rest of mankind, lived our lives, unconscious as children, filled with fancies, ideals and illusions. And then we woke. Yes, but we woke with our feet on the pillow, and the man who woke us was himself a sleepwalker. . . . It was nothing but a little morning sleep, with wild dreams, and there was no awakening.

This is the feeling of the captain in *The Father*, as his marriage breaks down, but the generalisation is characteristic. This world of the sleepwalker, the dreamer, the stranger, becomes, in Strindberg's later work, total. The covering of particular relationships is dropped, and a single consciousness takes over. The human struggle, at this extreme of pain, becomes wholly internal. Other people are simply images within a private agony.

The Road to Damascus is a search for an end to this agony, and it is significant that the search, ultimately, is for death, as the only conceivable end. Characteristically, however, in a world without God, it is

> death without the need to die—mortification of the flesh, of the old self.

It is not only that all experience is seen as destructive, with
other people and all past relationships combining into a
macabre and cursing pattern. It is also that in this agony the
self fragments and is finally alienated. The central character
is the Stranger, who is primarily a stranger to himself:

> STRANGER: It's whispered in the family that I'm a changeling. . . . A
> child substituted by the elves for the baby that was born. . . . Are
> these elves the souls of the unhappy, who still await redemption?
> If so, I am the child of an evil spirit. Once I believed I was near
> redemption, through a woman. But no mistake could have been
> greater. My tragedy is I cannot grow old; that's what happens to
> the children of the elves. . . .
> LADY: We must see if you can't become a child again.
> STRANGER: We should have to start with the cradle; and this time
> with the right child.

In this conviction of malign forces which have robbed him
of his identity, the Stranger transforms everyone he sees into
his own pattern of guilt and aggression. Even his own search
for self-knowledge, and his desire to liberate himself and
others, are transformed into destructive acts. Every relationship becomes destructive, not so much in its substance as in
these inchoate and malignant forces working through it. The
Stranger longs for redemption through a woman, but this is
only achieved by the transfer of evil:

> The evil in him was too strong; you had to draw it out of him into
> yourself to free him.

This profoundly sexual image records the destruction of the
most living impulse of man. It is paralleled by the destruction
of the Stranger's hope of salvation in the new life of a child:

> What is loveliest, brightest? The first, the only, the last that ever
> gave life meaning. I too once sat in the sunlight on a veranda, in the
> Spring, beneath the first tree to show new green, and a small crown
> crowned a head, and a white veil lay like morning mist over a face—
> that was not that of a human being. Then came darkness.

Far beyond the detail of particular relationships, this powerful imagery reaches to the roots of life and destroys them. And
the paradox is that only the most intense love of life, the most
burning desire, the clearest perception of beauty, could pro-

duce, by reversal, this ultimate terror. It is not only man the inquirer, man the liberator, who is reduced to blind agony and the desperate wandering search. It is human life as such, spiralling down towards the inhuman and the willed lapse into death. The play ends in the forms of conversion and redemption, but these are without connection and without hope. The phrases of peace cover a simple lapse, when the agony is at last unbearable. This is not a tragedy of man and the universe, or of man and society. It is a tragedy that has got into the bloodstream: the final and lonely tragedy that is beyond relationships and is in the living process itself.

Strindberg's work after *The Road to Damascus* achieves the kind of stability available after such a recognition. It is the fixed world of collective and overwhelming guilt. As in *Ghost Sonata*:

> MUMMY: Oh God, if we might die! If we might die!
>
> OLD MAN: But why do you keep together then?
>
> MUMMY: Crime and guilt bind us together. We have broken our bonds and gone apart innumerable times, but we are always drawn together again.

Every attempt to break out, to tell the truth, is met by a revelation of the truth-teller's complicity. The Student, finally, learns that there is no liberation but death. He sits with the Young Lady under the starlike flowers, but knows that marriage and fulfilment are impossible, in this house of guilt and decay. The girl dies, and again all that can be said is the welcome to death:

> The liberator is coming. Welcome, thou pale and gentle one. Sleep, lovely, unhappy, innocent, creature, whose sufferings are undeserved ... Sleep without dreaming. ... You poor little child, you child of this world of illusion, guilt, suffering and death, this world of eternal change, disappointment and pain. May the Lord of Heaven have mercy on you in your journey.

And the mercy, finally, is in the journey through death. The Lord is the Lord of Heaven, not the Lord of Earth. All created things have been separated from his mercy; only in the lapse back into death can the possibility of mercy reappear. Humanism has quite disappeared, as tragedy has entered the bloodstream. For such a vision of God is the late-mediaeval view that humanism had challenged: of a God separate from His creatures, who while they live are beyond his reach, and who in the act of living create hurt and evil, their energy turning to fever and the flow of desire turning to self-destruction, until death comes to release them.

It would be difficult to overemphasise the persistence of this pattern in twentieth-century literature. It is a characteristic half-world from which God is absent, or is present only in absence, but in which evil and guilt are close and common, not only in particular relationships but as a kind of life-force: an element that is finally recognised below and beyond individual aspirations and beliefs. While this pattern holds, every actually destructive relationship can be brought, as experience, to its support, and we often fail to notice how interpretation and selection are being consciously and unconsciously guided by the conviction of a general truth. Superficially, this literature is empirical, and it is significantly often autobiographical or founded on reported cases. But the kind of warrant this gives has to be set against the presence in such works of the characteristic absolutes, which are held to be empirical or even scientific in character, and which support a determining general pattern. This is normal in any structure of feeling which is powerfully supported by a particular culture. What is called dogma is the dead tissue, of used and separated beliefs. But the real dogma is in the assimilated pressures, the habitual ways of perceiving and acting, which create an experience and then offer reflection as truth.

The line from Strindberg can be traced in a number of ways. In the drama, the significant line is American, through Eugene O'Neill to Tennessee Williams. In England, the clearest example is the work of John Osborne, though here it is joined or entangled with a particular kind of social feeling, which can be superficially related to the liberal tradition.

O'Neill's relation to Strindberg was explicit.

> It was reading his plays ... that, above all else, first gave me the vision of what modern drama could be. .... If there is anything of lasting worth in my work, it is due to that original impulse from him. ...

Working in the Provincetown Playhouse, O'Neill called Strindberg the greatest interpreter in the theatre of the characteristic spiritual conflicts which constitute the drama—the blood!—of our lives today.

He singled out, for quotation, Strindberg's sentence about the 'tense and cruel struggles'.

O'Neill brought to his early plays a vernacular vigour which was certainly new in the modern theatre, but increasingly he used this to communicate an assumed pattern, especially in *Desire under the Elms* and *Strange Interlude*. Indeed the pattern became so conscious that it determined his experiments with form. His drama was governed by the need to set an absolute pattern inside the lively vernacular transcription.

At the same time, there can be no doubt that O'Neill's driving experience was tragic in a more direct sense. He wrote in 1917:

> The tragedy of Man is perhaps the only significant thing about him. What I am after is to get an audience leaving the theatre with an exultant feeling from seeing somebody on the stage facing life, fighting against the eternal odds, not conquering, but perhaps inevitably being conquered. The individual life is made significant just by the struggle.

This might be read as the ordinary version of post-Renaissance tragedy, but O'Neill continues:

> The struggle of man to dominate life, to assert and insist that life has no meaning outside himself where he comes in conflict with life, which he does at every turn; and his attempt to adapt life to his own needs, in which he doesn't succeed, is what I mean when I say that Man is the hero.

This, decisively, is the tragedy of the isolated being, for whom 'life has no meaning outside himself'. That the struggle is described as 'to dominate life' is a further turn of the screw. The isolated persons clash and destroy each other, not simply because their particular relationships are wrong, but because life as such is inevitably against them. This struggle of life against life is an exultation, but beyond it, again, is the wish for death.

More clearly than Strindberg, O'Neill identified the family

as a destructive entity, especially in *Mourning Becomes Electra* and *Long Day's Journey into Night*. A speech in *The Great God Brown* is characteristic, when a son mourns his father:

> What aliens we were to each other! When he lay dead, his face looked so familiar that I wondered where I had met that man before. Only at the second of my conception. After that, we grew hostile with concealed shame.

The emphasis, here, is not only on the inherent hostility and guilt, but also on the fact of recognition in death, when, paradoxically, some kind of living contact can at last be made. The primary relationships are in experience a profound alienation, and the self that emerges from them is a ghost who will struggle to touch life at some point, but who in the pain of this knows unreality as the greater reality. These are the 'fog people' of *Long Day's Journey into Night*. Edmund, describing being out in the fog, says:

> Everything looked and sounded unreal. That's what I wanted—to be alone with myself in another world where truth is untrue and life can hide from itself. . . . The fog and the sea seemed part of each other. It was like walking on the bottom of the sea. As if I had drowned long ago. As if I was a ghost belonging to the fog, and the fog was the ghost of the sea. It felt damned peaceful to be nothing more than a ghost within a ghost.

And later:

> It was a great mistake, my being born a man, I would have been much more successful as a sea-gull or a fish. As it is, I will always be a stranger who never feels at home, who does not really want and is not really wanted, who can never belong, who must always be a little in love with death.

Long Day's Journey into Night is O'Neill's version of himself and his own family, and it is easy to hear the intensity of this feeling. The pattern of particular relationships, and of the individuals composing them, can be seen as leading, perhaps even inevitably, to this kind of consciousness. Yet what we overlook, in such arguments for authenticity, is that the pattern itself is a creation of this consciousness, and a kind of justification for it. This is the point about a self-reflecting empiricism, made earlier. It is not, in the end, that the relationships create the consciousness. Dramatically, it is the consciousness that creates the relationships. What looks like a family drama is an isolate drama.

The point comes out most clearly in *Mourning Becomes Electra*. O'Neill said that he was trying here

> to get modern psychological approximation of the Greek sense of fate into such a play, which an intelligent audience of today, possessed of no beliefs in gods or supernatural retribution, could accept and be moved by.

The statement has a representative importance, including the reference to modern psychology. What is being offered is not primarily a set of destructive relationships, but a pattern of fate which is not dependent on any beliefs outside man. Life itself is fate, in this fundamental pattern, which is again the inherently self-destructive family. The critical difficulty, always, is that the fatal pattern is then given particularity; it is even possible to consider and confirm it along quite different lines: New England puritanism, the effects of civil war, and so on. But this, both critically and dramatically, is a false particularity. What matters, clearly, is the imposed pattern, which has the effect of conferring a sense of inevitability on what, as experience, was and could otherwise be seen as a series of living choices. The pattern comes from the consciousness of the isolate, rationalised by reference to modern psychology and to the Greeks. In this relatively constant progress from possibility to inevitability, and from the authentically particular to the willed general, it is important to distinguish a play like *Mourning Becomes Electra*, with its external elements of generalisation in the Greek analogy, from a play like *Long Day's Journey into Night*, where the generalisation is more truly internal, and to that extent more moving.

In his reworking of the *Oresteia*, O'Neill substituted psychology for the Greek action. What is less often noticed is that this psychology is curiously static: underlying and determinist, rather than active and living. In the end it is not so much that the relationships are destructive as that they are illusory:

> MANNON: ... Me as your husband being killed, that seemed queer and wrong—like something dying that had never lived.

From this basic unreality of relationship, the patterns of adultery and incest follow as it were mechanically. The pain and misdirection are bred in the original nullity. The only active feeling is the struggle of these ghosts to come alive, of these dead to awaken. Nothing is possible within this house and this family; the dream of the happy islands is of a totally alternative condition. Yet for all the careful grafting of the Freudian pattern, this is not psychology, but metaphysics: the characteristic metaphysics of the isolate, for whom life in any form but the suffering of frustration and loss is impossible. The characteristic resolution is neither Greek nor Freudian, but simply the achievement of death, which because there is no God has to be self-inflicted, by suicide or total withdrawal:

> LAVINIA: I'm the last Mannon. I've got to punish myself. Living alone here with the dead is a worse act of justice than death or prison. I'll never go out or see anyone. I'll have the shutters nailed close so no sunlight can ever get in. I'll live alone with the dead, and keep their secrets and let them hound me, until the curse is paid out and the last Mannon is let die. [*With a strange cruel smile of gloating over the years of self-torture*] I know they will see to it I live for a long time! It takes the Mannons to punish themselves for being born.

The analogy of Mannon seems finally not to Agamemnon but to Man.

The point has been reached, in our own generation, when the 'tense and cruel struggles' can be assumed as a whole truth, an orthodoxy, without anxious generalisation and argument. What we get then is not the dramatic philosopher, which O'Neill tried to be, but the dramatist of the case-book, who can afford simply to demonstrate. The plays of Tennessee Williams are the clearest examples of this: his characters are isolated beings who desire and eat and fight alone, who struggle feverishly with the primary and related energies of love and death. At their most satisfying they are animals; the rest is a covering of humanity, and is destructive. It is in their consciousness, their ideals, their dreams, their illusions that they lose themselves and become pathetic sleepwalkers. The human condition is tragic because of the entry of mind on the fierce, and in itself tragic, animal struggle of sex and death.

The purpose of the drama is then to cut through these mental illusions to the actual primary rhythms. This is, in a literal sense, drama on a hot tin roof. The rhythms are intense, yet they move, inevitably, through time, which

> rushes towards us with its hospital tray of infinitely varied narcotics, even while it is preparing us for its inevitably fatal operation.

In the brief dramatic intensity, the rhythms are isolated and heard. Then

> our hearts are wrung by recognition and pity, so that the dusky shell of the auditorium where we are gathered anonymously together is flooded with an almost liquid warmth of unchecked human sympathies, relieved from self-consciousness, allowed to function. . . .

Or to put it another way, in this world of *Baby Doll, Streetcar Named Desire, Cat on a Hot Tin Roof*, the sense of reality of the isolated human beings, the fierce *impersonal* rhythms, can be so urgently and directly transmitted that the only kind of connection known to him, 'relieved of self-consciousness', can flow like a physical act, a dissolving liquidity in the undifferentiated sea:

> a release in this work which I wanted you to feel with me.

The tragedy of individual persons, which began in the struggles of the aspiring mind, ends as the fierce animal struggle and relapse: in the single act of sex, where there is a communication in which mind has tragically failed; an act of life and death, in the same rhythms, the tense and cruel struggle consummated at last in relapse. The end of the sex, the fierce humping life-struggle, is death.

3

SOCIAL AND PERSONAL TRAGEDY

TOLSTOY AND LAWRENCE

The deepest crisis in modern literature is the division of experience into social and personal categories. It is now much more than a matter of emphasis. It is a rooted division, into which the flow of experience is directed, and from which, with their own kinds of vigour, the separated kinds of life grow. Intellectually, the division is fought out with the complete and confident apparatus of ideology: the individualist version confronts the collectivist version; sides are taken and armed. It is almost a mark of irresponsibility, the way things are going, not to take sides; not to insist on the unanswerable finality of this or that: the individual reality; the social reality. For the man who has not grasped *that* choice, the most withering contempt is reserved; he is not in touch with modern experience at all.

Tragedy, inevitably, has been shaped by this division. There is social tragedy: men destroyed by power and famine; a civilization destroyed or destroying itself. And then there is personal tragedy: men and women suffering and destroyed in their closest relationships; the individual knowing his destiny, in a cold universe, in which death and an ultimate spiritual isolation are alternative forms of the same suffering and heroism. One version of tragedy or the other, and it seems we must choose between them. In the facts of the ordinary day, there may be connections, but when we shape our imaginative world we are pressed to begin with the controlling reality. If the reality is ultimately personal, then the crises of civilization are analogues of a psychic or spiritual maladjustment or disaster. If the reality is ultimately social, then the thwarted relationships, the destructive loneliness, the loss of reasons for living, are symptoms or reflections of a disintegrating or decadent society. The ideologies, at either point, move smoothly into action. The explanations of others are merely false consciousness or rationalisation; the substantial reality is here, or here.

When the division is deep enough, there are only alternatives, only the taking of sides, until a new break comes. But the division itself has been a long process, and there are stages in it, of the greatest importance, which enable us to look for a moment beyond the finished states, at the process itself. Of all literary works which offer this opportunity, the most important are Tolstoy's *Anna Karenina* and Lawrence's *Women in Love*. In each of these major novels, an important relationship ends in tragedy, in a death given significance by the whole action. The personal reality, in these relationships, is as substantial as fiction can offer. Yet, clearly, in each of the novels, the form of the tragic relationship is defined by the form of other relationships, which appear to work out quite differently. What makes for life and what makes for death is closely explored in individual lives. Yet already, by the coexistence of these other relationships, the tragic relationship has been given a context. In this limited but important sense, a society has been formed, around the tragic experience.

But again, in each novel, it is more than this. It is impossible to read either novel without feeling the pressure of other experiences and other questions: sharply contrasted ways of living; questions of the nature of work and of its relation to how a man lives; questions, finally, about the inward nature of a given civilisation, which the form of each novel seems designed to dramatise.

It is true that in either case we can suppress or more subtly adjust those elements in the novel which we judge to be, from our taken position, secondary. Tolstoy strayed into autobiography and preaching; Lawrence into preaching and autobiography. Or neither man realised the true perspectives of his inquiry: he was forced back, by the limitations of his position, from a whole view of society into a primarily internal action; he was a critical realist, unable to touch the last lock. Then the division begins again, as it must, since we are part of it. Yet is it really too difficult, even with novels like these, to consider the issues as if division were not the predestined end; to consider their substance as throwing light on the division itself? Can we not touch, even momentarily, a kind of experience in which the personal and the social are more than alternatives, are seen growing as actions from the same life?

Read *Anna Karenina*—no matter, read it again, and if you dare to fall out with it, I'll swear aloud.

The sentence comes from a very early letter of Lawrence
(1909), and there is a good deal of evidence of his lasting
interest in the book. He called it once 'the greatest of novels',
but later he more than dared to fall out with it; he attacked it
bitterly, and accused Tolstoy of 'wetting on the flame'. There
is an important history here: not simply at the level of
influence, or of change of critical opinion, but in the working-
out of Lawrence's deepest and most challenging experience.

It is a question, ultimately, of the nature of tragedy.
Lawrence saw in Tolstoy and Hardy, as in Shakespeare and
Sophocles,

> this setting behind the small action of (the) protagonists the terrific
> action of unfathomed nature; setting a smaller system of morality,
> the one grasped and formulated by the human consciousness within
> the vast, uncomprehended and incomprehensible morality of nature
> or of life itself, surpassing human consciousness. The difference is,
> that whereas in Shakespeare or Sophocles the greater, uncompre-
> hended morality, or fate, is actively transgressed and gives active
> punishment, in Hardy and Tolstoy the lesser human morality, the
> mechanical system is actively transgressed, and holds, and punishes
> the protagonist, whilst the greater morality is only passively, negat-
> ively transgressed, it is represented merely as being present in back-
> ground, in scenery, not taking any active part, having no direct
> connexion with the protagonist.

Lawrence saw this difference as

> the weakness of modern tragedy, where transgression against the
> social code is made to bring destruction, as though the social code
> worked our irrevocable fate.

Of Anna, as of Hardy's tragic heroines, he asks:

> what was there in their position that was necessarily tragic? Necess-
> arily painful it was, but they were not at war with God, only with
> Society. Yet they were cowed by the mere judgment of man upon
> them, and all the while by their own souls they were right. And the
> judgment of men killed them, not the judgment of their own souls
> or the judgment of Eternal God.

Consequently,

> their real tragedy is that they are unfaithful to the greater unwritten
> morality, which would have bidden Anna Karenina be patient and

wait until she, by virtue of greater right, could take what she needed from society; would have bidden Vronsky detach himself from the system, become an individual, creating a new colony of morality with Anna.

Lawrence's interesting argument darts both ways at this point. He is saying in his last sentence that the tragedy can be avoided, if the people concerned will become individuals, create a 'new colony'. Whereas Oedipus, Hamlet and Macbeth, who are too full of 'real, potent life' to compromise with the social system,

> set themselves up against, or find themselves set up against, the unfathomed moral forces of nature, and out of this unfathomed force comes their death.

They fight right through, and so they are killed. But this, of course, is profoundly ambiguous. How does it happen that these heroes, who will not surrender their real potent life, are destroyed, not by society, but by nature?[1] The question is dodged in the slide from 'morality of nature' to 'morality of nature or of life itself'. Behind the rhetoric of 'vast' and 'incomprehensible', Lawrence misses the decisive question: how can it be that real, potent life is necessarily destroyed by the 'morality . . . of life itself'? The point will be very important, at a later stage in our argument. Meanwhile, we can notice the prepared escape route, in which the full claims of individual life are asserted, without the necessity of tragedy.

An escape route, of course, from the logic of his own proposition; not necessarily an escape route from life itself. The terms in which he describes how Anna and Vronsky ought to have acted are virtually a description of *Lady Chatterley's Lover*, and this novel can be seen as a conscious answer to *Anna Karenina*. A woman leaves a husband who has gone dead to himself and to her. In leaving, she finds life in herself and in another, and society is defied, by the principles of this new morality of experience. The new colony, as the book ends, seems likely to be established.

It is an interesting case, but what we must now notice is

---

[1] Lawrence almost certainly, of course, took this formulation from Nietzsche. It lies uneasily beside his beliefs in change and regeneration, which had been formed in a different tradition.

that in making his alternative action, Lawrence in fact
absorbed the essential morality of *Anna Karenina* itself. This
fact throws into relief his continued misreading of Tolstoy's
work: a significant misreading, because it is based on the false
ideas of 'the individual' and 'society' which Lawrence shared
with twentieth-century orthodoxy. We have already seen his
description of Anna as destroyed by 'the social code', 'the
judgment of men'. Elsewhere he describes the destruction of
Vronsky as 'a perverse pleasure' in Tolstoy, because he 'so
meanly envied the healthy passionate male'. Further,

> as a perverse moralist with a sense of some subtle deficiency in him-
> self, Tolstoi tries to insult and to damp out the vividness of life.
> Imagine any great artist making the vulgar social condemnation of
> Anna and Vronsky figure as divine punishment! Where now is the
> society that turned its back on Vronsky and Anna? Where is it?
> And what is its condemnation worth today?

Always the same pattern: it was the society that destroyed
them. But in fact Lawrence only read *Anna Karenina* like
that, against the evidence, in order to avoid seeing something
which would have destroyed his own moralising. It is
important to add that he only made this misreading as a critic
and a moralist. When it came to his novels, he remembered
what Tolstoy had written, and saw the issue quite differently.

What is the real action of *Anna Karenina*? Two common
errors obscure this from us. First, there is the isolation of
individual characters from the action as a whole, as if the
tragedy of Anna could be considered apart from the actual
relationships with Karenin and Vronsky, and without reference to the *varied* society in which these are lived out.
Secondly, there is the isolation of the Anna-Karenin-Vronsky
story from the novel as a whole, in which it occupies less than
half the actual narrative. The exclusion of Levin, and of the
Levin-Kitty and Stiva-Dolly marriages, is deeply distorting.
It is sometimes rationalised by the argument that Anna-
Vronsky is the real story, and that the story of Levin (though
of course occupying a great deal of space) is simply the result
of Tolstoy's incurable autobiographical itch; he had to record
his discursive observations on work and faith, even though the
real story was about the lovers. This is, of course, the fashion-

able 'personal relationships' dogma, in which certain kinds of relationship are abstracted from the other human relationships of society, work and belief, in obedience to strong and obscure pressures from our own kind of society. It is worth repeating a fact surely obvious in reading *Anna Karenina*: that it is a whole structure in which all the elements are closely related, and that the complexity of this structure (rather than Lawrence's version of one of its elements) is Tolstoy's actual morality. Critics who isolate the Anna-Vronsky story should consider, as just one example of this structure, the sequence of chapters in Part Five, where the marriage of Levin and Kitty is followed by the Italian honeymoon of Anna and Vronsky, and then by Levin and Kitty setting up house and living through the first difficulties of their marriage, to the crucial death of Nikolay and the discovery that Kitty is pregnant. This is not the interweaving of plot and sub-plot, or of two separate stories, but the enactment of a single complex design.

The strong point in Lawrence's case is, of course, the quickening of life in Anna, after her meeting with Vronsky. Equally, that Tolstoy wrote it so is sufficient answer to the accusation that he is merely embodying a conventional morality; this is the one experience there was ordinarily a conspiracy to suppress. But Tolstoy, unlike Lawrence (at least as a moralist) recognised the fact of life, to be quickened or destroyed, in all individuals, not merely in selected ones who can be called individuals while the rest are dismissed as 'society'. Thus the rejection of Karenin is certainly part of Anna's new instinct for life, but this is much too crudely taken if Karenin is seen as simply 'dead'. (The crudeness of the physical deadening of Clifford Chatterley is significantly relevant here). Tolstoy created, in Karenin, a memorable figure of the avoidance of love, but he was concerned with a whole experience, not with a figure in an isolated moral action. All his adult life, Karenin has been afraid of open emotion, of any kind, because of a characteristic fear that in exposing himself he will be hurt. Once, and once only, this fear is overcome, in the stress of the apparent imminence of Anna's death after bearing Vronsky's child, and of her powerful appeal to Karenin, accompanied by a rejection of Vronsky:

There is another woman in me, I'm afraid of her: she loved that man, and I tried to hate you, and could not forget about her that used to be. I'm not that woman. Now I'm my real self, all my self.

Here Anna, in pain and fear, living through the consequence of her love, renounces it (not from any outside pressure). Karenin responds, accepting her and the child, but then she recovers and goes back to her previous position. The pattern of Karenin's character has thus been confirmed: he has 'given way' to emotion, and he has been coldly hurt. His subsequent deterioration is then hardly surprising. The point here is, not that Anna's instinct for life has been disproved, but that Tolstoy, as a great novelist, refuses to deal with cardboard figures of the 'quick' and the 'dead'. He turns instead to the actual processes of relationship in which love and hate are confirmed or denied. By letting us see this situation from each point of view in turn, rather than predicating the 'quick' and the 'dead'—the 'quick' to be forgiven their weaknesses, the 'dead' to be ritually damned—Tolstoy shows an extra-ordinary creative and moral energy. The flow and stopping of life is seen as much more complicated than in the Lawrence version.

Yet the really decisive element is the character of Vronsky. It is important to see that he awakens Anna, but still it is one thing to wake somebody, another to live through the day. When Lawrence speaks of Tolstoy's perverse pleasure in what happens to Vronsky, we have to ask whether he is not himself surrendering to his own rhetoric of maleness. The question is, quite simply, whether Vronsky is capable, as a human being, of meeting the demands of the love he has started in Anna. When we first see him, in the relationship with Kitty, it is clear that he is not prepared for a relationship of any permanence. Anna's comment, just before her death, seems in retrospect an accurate account of a relationship with such a man:

We walked to meet each other up to the time of our love, and then we have been irresistibly drifting in different directions. And there's no altering that. He tells me I'm insanely jealous, and I have told myself that I'm insanely jealous, but it's not ture. I'm not jealous, but I'm unsatisfied.

Vronsky's qualities are obvious, but it becomes clear, as the relationship with Anna develops, that he lives in a single and limited dimension, in which there is no room for enduring passion. We can be misled here, as Lawrence was often misled, by too simple an idea of 'masculinity'. Tolstoy raises the question in the novel, significantly in Vronsky's own reflections on the foreign prince: is being a man something more than being a piece of healthy beef? More fully, it is present, throughout the novel, in the sustained comparison of Vronsky and Levin, which is one of Tolstoy's major themes, and from which Levin emerges as undoubtedly the stronger man. Levin (and Tolstoy) had lived much like Vronsky once, but he learns to grow beyond it.

It is of course quite easy, in a highly civilised society, to be carried away by phrases like 'animal vigour', but this, as Lawrence sometimes told it, is frankly a cock-and-bull story. It is not only that a man's strength has to include the tenderness of protection and the warmth of continuing care, which are biologically necessary in the human condition. Most men can give a woman a child, but less can really be fathers. It is also, in the same pattern, that passion is more easily aroused than satisfied, and that merely slaking a passion can destroy not only the woman who is used but also the man who is merely using himself: the energy, unreturned, falls back on itself and goes dead. Without relationship, vigour can be simply destructive, and this is an essential part of the story of Vronsky and Anna. When she is socially isolated, in the country and in Moscow, he repeatedly leaves her alone, to play at politics or to watch Yashvin's gambling. The cold regularity of his reply to her desperate appeals, on the day of her death, is more than a moment of carelessness: it is characteristic of the limited and powerful determination which, ironically, had first enabled him to break through Anna's frigidity. It is very illuminating that Lawrence, reworking this situation in *Lady Chatterley's Lover*, created in Mellors not a Vronsky, but a Levin. Mellors is strong and alive, but he has also a deep tenderness, and, interestingly, has that quality which Tolstoy saw as the condition of health in Levin, an intimate and deeply respecting connection with the world of natural growth. Lawrence the critic was, after all, put right on this by Lawrence the novelist.

Yet, in spite of everything, did Tolstoy kill Anna as a kind of renunciation of sexual love? It is certainly true that Tolstoy insisted, much more than Lawrence, on the social consequences of primary relationships; but then, unlike Lawrence, he set all his fiction in real societies, and could hardly avoid what they were showing him: a network of actual and continuing relationships which could not be dismissed by the easy formulas of Puritanism and the grey North. The social convention invoked against Anna is indeed shallow and hypocritical, but take a society in which there is no difficulty in divorce, in which an Anna would not be pointed at and avoided, and the human difficulty in substance remains. The child of the body is there, in any society. Frustration and hatred are there, under any laws, if the relationships are wrong. The tragedy of Anna is exacerbated by her society, but the roots of the tragedy lie much deeper, in a specific relationship (just as, in contemporary societies in which the old sexual laws and conventions have been practically abandoned, men and women still kill themselves in despair of love).

The immediate action of Anna's tragedy is that she leaves one inadequate man for another; but the inadequacy of Karenin lay with an unawakened woman, the inadequacy of Vronsky with a woman grown to passion and demanding it as the continuing centre of her life. The significance of Anna, at the highest point of her growth, is that she must live her feelings right through. Living by a limited commitment had been possible once, but it was from this that she broke away. Of course, not as a mature woman. The maturity had seemed to be there, when the pressure was no more than the limited commitment to Karenin, but it is not there, once her whole energy is released. One of the few things we do not know enough about, in the novel, is her original attitude to the marriage to Karenin (this suppression is common in romantic and anti-romantic stories alike). But it is at least clear that she has become a wife and mother without ever having been a girl in love. What breaks out from the wife and mother is this girl in love, but now in a situation where much more is needed. The rush of feeling is awakened by and attached to Vronsky, but this is not the whole story. There is also evidence, in her attitude to Vronsky, of that adolescent condition in which overwhelming feeling as it were collides with an object rather

E

than grows towards it. This can be disastrous, even for a girl, if the object is inadequate or irrelevant to the real force of the feeling. But Anna is not a girl; she is still also the guilty wife and mother, and the combination is terrifying. The ordinary married woman's affair, as with her friends in St Petersburg, is a characteristically limited commitment; it can be had on the side because it is on the side. We see this again in her brother Stiva, in many ways so like her, but unhurt because always essentially uncommitted. Anna shames the half-life of this society, but half-life is often a protection for the weak and the immature. Stiva slips away from difficulty, with his 'almond-oil smile'. Anna, in her delayed rush of feeling, must give herself wholly, without regard for safety, and whether she then survives depends on the quality of the man she is giving herself to. Nothing less is thinkable; her demand is quite absolute. Even her death is a revengeful move to make Vronsky love her more, and this tragic error (common enough in certain kinds of suicide) fuses the wholeness and the immaturity which, falling on weak hands, combine to destroy her.

It is here, in Tolstoy, that the account of a relationship extends into a pattern of relationships, and beyond them into a society. For the contrast is not only with the hypocritical half-life of conventional society, and its primary relationships. It is also with the demands of a working society, and the process of growth towards whole relationships. The story of Levin is of fulfilment, of a man who gives himself and commits himself completely. Significantly, this is a slow growth, learned as much from the death of his brother as from the love of Kitty, learned also in work and in the effort towards right working relations with other men. The density of this life of Levin's makes an obvious contrast with the single dimension in which, in their different ways, Vronsky and Karenin and Stiva live. In each of these men the attitude to work, and thence to other persons, is related to their differing yet alike inadequate attitudes to love. For Vronsky, love is like the life of an officer: vigorous, assertive, attuned in the end to the willingness to kill. For Karenin, the official, love is an aspect of an institution, a marriage conceived solely in social terms. For Stiva, the taker of business opportunities, love is the personal equivalent of conscious negotiation and the confidence trick. Levin, by contrast, learns to reject their kinds of society and their kinds of love in a single process. When he is translating a hundred-rouble note, lightly spent in Moscow, into the work of men in the fields, he is involved with values in a sense equally opposed to the conventions of fashionable society and the mere flouting of them. In learning this kind of connection with all that lives, he is learning something deeper than either respectability or personal honour. His learning to love Kitty as a wife, and then to love their child, grows within this whole attachment, which is more mature than anything Anna is allowed to live. Vronsky, in the end, wants marriage and a stake in the country, but in his terms the offer is both too much and too little for Anna: she does not want marriage and Vronsky's children, but she needs passion, which in Vronsky has gone. A meaningful society, and therefore a meaningful relationship in it, is for different reasons beyond both of them.

What we have really learned from the whole action, in its pattern of contrasts and in its breaking and making of connections, is Tolstoy's sense of the wholeness of life. In such an experience, the ordinary abstractions of 'personal' and 'social' relationships break down and are returned to reality. Here the quality of personal lives is known as related to the quality of the whole way of life, which is not a single thing called 'society' but the complex activity of many persons, making and wasting, recognising and betraying, lying and telling the truth. What is thought of as society does not determine the relationships; men can learn to grow beyond the institutionalised failures. Yet social exploitation, neglect, indulgence and cynicism are paid for not only in social and political coin; they teach ways of feeling, and in turn are taught by them, which find their way into the most personal experience. To grow anywhere is to begin to grow everywhere, but also every rejection, every weakness, finds its way into the flow of life. And then it is not only growth in this man, withering in that. It is also, as in Anna, growth and withering, strength and weakness, acceptance and rejection, in a single body. At this point, which is neither fulfilment nor resignation, there is tragedy. This is the moving field of all Tolstoy's greatest writing, and there are few writers who can live with him in it. The irony is that Lawrence addressed himself to just this field, though with less strength and in any case with less time (he died in the year of life in which *Anna Karenina* was begun). It is an instructive irony that this defence of Tolstoy should have to be made against, of all people, Lawrence.

I have said that Lawrence the critic was put right, in one important instance, by Lawrence the novelist. We must now look at the equally significant instance of a continuing image, which Lawrence understood in Tolstoy and used in *Women in Love*. The most effective embodiment of the character of Vronsky is the critically placed scene (between Anna's first giving herself to Vronsky and her confession to Karenin) in which, at the races, Vronsky kills the mare he is riding. This has a marvellous intensity and rightness because it at once embodies the vitality and excitement of the man, and the 'moment of carelessness' in which, intent on his own purpose of winning, he destroys the life that is responding to him. I believe this image played an important part in Lawrence's creative life, making new images in, for example, Ursula's meeting with the horses near the end of *The Rainbow*, and, very powerfully, in *St Mawr*. But his most direct use of it is in *Women in Love*, where the feeling and the judgement are very close to Tolstoy's. Gerald, watched by Ursula and Gudrun, holds the mare he is riding close to the level-crossing as a train passes (perhaps another unconscious image from the creative world of *Anna Karenina*). The mare is terrified, but the man takes a pride in mastering her. It is at once a cold and an exciting domination of life by the will. The future of Gerald and Gudrun is revealed in it, as surely as was the future of Vronsky and Anna, in Tolstoy's scene.

The particular connection reminds us of some of the similarities between *Anna Karenina* and *Women in Love*. There is the intended contrast between a relationship ending in coldness and death, and a relationship apparently growing towards life and continuity. There is the comparable seeing of essential connections between particular relationships and the whole way of living. Gerald's will and mastery are explicitly related to his social position as a colliery owner, with the industrialist's philosophy of the mastery and use of natural and human resources.[1] His death, when it comes, is seen as

[1] There is, I think, a glance at Tolstoy in Lawrence's portrayal of Gerald's father, Thomas Crich, who believed that 'in Christ he was one with his

more than personal; it is the death in coldness of a whole way of life.

The similarities are important, but the differences are even more instructive, when we remember our original question, about the process in which the 'social' and the 'personal' became separated. Lawrence's insistence, to the end of his life, on the essential connections, the whole flow of living, is strong and important. Thus we can see in him, more clearly than in writers by whom the separation is assumed, the pressures under which a major consciousness broke down.

The process of breakdown is indeed explicitly stated at the centre of the novel, when Birkin reflects:

> Thousands of years ago, that which was imminent in himself must have taken place in these Africans: the goodness, the holiness, the desire for creation and productive happiness must have lapsed, leaving the single impulse for knowledge in one sort, mindless progressive knowledge through the senses, knowledge arrested and ending in the senses, mystic knowledge in disintegration and dissolution. . . . We fall from the connexion with life and hope, we lapse from pure integral being, from creation and liberty, and we fall into the long, long African process of purely sensual understanding, knowledge in the mystery of dissolution. . . . It would be done differently by the white races. The white races, having the Arctic north behind them, the vast abstraction of ice and snow, would fulfil a mystery of ice-destructive knowledge, snow-abstract annihilation.

This is clearly the tragic movement of the book, to the death of Gerald. But there is a profound ambiguity in it, when we examine the whole action. The words used to describe the state from which this is a tragic fall might have been used by Tolstoy:

> the goodness, the holiness, the desire for creation and productive happiness.

But whereas in Tolstoy this is the counter-movement in his novel, in the love of Kitty and Levin and in the discovery of

---

workmen. Nay, he had felt inferior to them, as if they, through poverty and labour, were nearer to God than he'. Lawrence's implication of the failure and breakdown of this feeling is significant. He was right, in general, if not in particular, that it had to fail.

the meaning of natural work and its relations with other men and with the land, in Lawrence it is only present as a phrase and a memory (it had in fact been significantly present in the early chapters of *The Rainbow*). The counter-movement in Lawrence is different:

> There was another way, the way of freedom. There was the paradisal entry into pure single being, the individual soul taking precedence over love and desire for union, stronger than any pangs of emotion, a lovely state of free proud singleness, which accepted the obligation of the permanent connexion with others, and with the other, submits to the yoke and leash of love, but never forfeits its own proud singleness, even while it loves and yields.

The way of 'knowledge arrested and ending in the senses, mystic knowledge in disintegration and dissolution' is taken by Gerald and Gudrun, and reaches its farthest point in Loerke. The way taken by Ursula and Birkin is offered as a contrast with this: Ursula arguing against Loerke and Gudrun about art, insisting on the connections between art and life and rejecting the reduction of art to autonomous sensation; Ursula and Birkin, in their own relationship, learning

> the pure duality of polarization, each one free from any contamination of the other. In each, the individual is primal, sex is subordinate, but perfectly polarised. Each has a single, separate being, with its own laws. The man has his pure freedom, the woman hers. Each acknowledges the perfection of the polarised sex-circuit. Each admits the different nature in the other.

But as we repeat these words we know that something crucial has happened, in the contrast between death and life. It is a long way from 'the goodness, the holiness, the desire for creation and productive happiness' to 'the perfection of the polarised sex-circuit'. The mechanical image is significant enough, and it has to be said that the known relationship between Ursula and Birkin is not so different in kind from the relationship between Gudrun and Gerald as to be an effective counterpoise to what Gudrun calls that 'barren tragedy'. There is more care, more respect, between Ursula and Birkin, but they share with Gudrun and Gerald the separation of their personal relationship from 'the desire for creation and productive happiness'. This is not only a separation from society, though it is certainly that, in the action of resignation and flight. Such a separation might be widely endorsed, feeding into the orthodox division between personal life and a dead, useless environment. Gudrun and Gerald also reject society in this sense; it is irrelevant to what they have to do with each other. On that general movement, the whole novel agrees.

But what we have to notice is that behind the formula about rejecting a dead society a far more significant movement is taking place: a rejection of whole dimensions of directly personal relationship, and with this, finally, a rejection of humanity itself. When Ursula rejects the idea of a home, the usual criticism of shut-in domesticity is offered as ratifying, as if the rejection were primarily social: this is not a way to live. But the rejection is actually in terms of a 'proud single-ness', and what is then being rejected, in fact, is that whole body of personal life which is more than a relationship in a single generation. Lawrence, in all his later work, reduced the definition of personal life to a single generation, over and over again, and he has been widely followed. Parents are distant and meaningless, Ursula and Gudrun agree. The tone comes easily to any single generation, but it remains shocking in *Women in Love*, since we have known these parents as persons, this home as a home, in *The Rainbow*, and their reduction in status is arbitrary. The change in the methods of fiction, which Lawrence was actually bringing about, involved and underwrote this kind of loss. In the insistence on the proud singleness of persons, the reality of other persons had to be scaled down. But then it is not only the 'old home' that is rejected; it is any home. And this is part of an effective rejection of children, for whom there is evi-dently no place in 'the perfection of the polarised sex-circuit'. The polarised sex-circuit is single and static, in this sense; the child of two bodies would break it. Anything that can be described as creation would break it, for there would be a new living fact which is more than 'proud singleness'. A child would be a human being who is also the embodiment of a human relationship and who could not be arbitrarily reduced to a domesticity, a social fact, from which one simply breaks away.

What Lawrence achieves then, as a contrast to the 'single

impulse for knowledge in one sort' of Gerald and Gudrun, is an impulse no less single, though it is asserted as more human. The saving clause of his definition, 'the obligation of the permanent connexion with others', cannot be realised or lived at all. Human continuity, in personal generations or in a society, is rejected by Ursula and Birkin as effectively, if less sensationally, as by Gerald and Gudrun and Loerke. Birkin's difference is that he continues to insist that a personal relationship with Ursula is 'not enough'; he wants more, but the novel is a demonstration of his inability to find it.

When we realise this, the whole form of the tragedy is changed. The difference from *Anna Karenina* is fundamental, whatever the initial resemblances. This is not a tragedy resting on contrasts, though it may appear to be so. It is a tragedy of a single action, in varying forms. Gerald dies, in a 'snow-abstract annihilation', but Gudrun and Loerke ('why not be bestial?') not only survive, but are seen as capable of surviving. It is Gudrun who says:

The only thing to do with the world is to see it through.

And it is Ursula and Birkin, who want to grow beyond this reduction, this disintegration and dissolution, who reach the most tragic position. They want to get beyond what is 'so merely *human*'. The tragedy is what Lawrence originally defined, in his comments on Tolstoy and Hardy: 'the non-human mystery'. Birkin, on Gerald's death, accepts that

the mystery could dispense with man, should he too fail creatively to change and develop.

This echoes a constant theme in the book: that man is a mistake, as he is, and that the world would be better without him.[1] Nature is not, as in Tolstoy, a world where man works and learns. It is an alternative to man. This separation-out, also, is complete. It is a wood you retreat to, as a solace from human experience. It is a place of play and recreation. Its

[1] Lawrence was, after all, a child of the same world as Wells and Shaw, in which despair about actual living could be rationalised and mystified into an idea of 'evolution beyond men'. The progressive and regressive formulas, which follow from this idea, need to be connected as well as contrasted. The fight between them, though it tries to monopolise our attention, is quite secondary, and at times sham.

forms of creation are in buds, not children. All that is human, beyond the singleness of pure being, is an 'old shadow-world'. The only relationship, finally, is between the single being and the non-human mystery.

Such a tragedy is real enough. It is a death in ice, or a death in sun, as much as the death of Gerald. It is the death of a race and a world, and it has been, undoubtedly, a major imaginative experience in our century. And it is best, in writing of *Women in Love*, to acknowledge its logic, to recognise its movement towards a general death. To use it as a standard of life and health is inevitably to deceive ourselves. It is not so much a judgement of a civilisation as a judgement of life. The 'new, deep life trust', with which Birkin ends, has been learned from death. It is a very old tragic pattern.

We return to our original question, when we noticed in Lawrence's account of tragedy an important ambiguity. He argued against what he saw as Tolstoy's conception of tragic necessity. People could live, if they rejected the terms of the 'social being' and became new individuals. Yet, if they were full of 'real, potent life' they in fact moved to death, not under a social judgement, but by the 'morality . . . of life itself'. I do not think this is an intellectual confusion in Lawrence. It is, rather, a radical uncertainty, at the deepest point in his experience. The difference between *Women in Love* and *Lady Chatterley's Lover* is relevant here. Lawrence's feeling that industrial civilization is dead is perhaps even stronger in the later book, and the process of growing beyond 'social being' into responsible individuality is in fact clearer in Mellors and Connie than in Birkin and Ursula, though still incomplete. But whereas Mellors, at the end, is thinking of the flame of life that can be kindled in a loving relationship, and of the hard business of keeping this flame alive in a dead society (in which he must find work to live and look after Connie and their child) Birkin, on the other hand, sees the flame of life as having to go beyond man, and can only go on breaking away, from people and from society. It is important that Mellors is the later conclusion, but Lawrence, evidently, never really made up his mind about this final issue; he was pulled both ways, and he kept trying to get it clear and right. But in *Women in Love* the flame of life is almost out, in the end. The point of tragic breakdown is reached, even though at the last

E*

moment Lawrence kept trying to make reservations. The break in consciousness had happened, and was only ever partly healed.

I call it break, and not discovery. I think it is important to do so, now, when there are so many signs that we are trying to rest in a divided consciousness. It is a break from society, but not only in the simple sense of rejecting and going away from a bad society. It is also a break in the deeper sense that Lawrence will not even oppose what he opposes, will not enter that dimension at all, in any active way, though he has known it as torment and written it as general and inescapable.

It is possible to say this, if one believes in meaningful social action, and of course to await that summary dismissal as politician or sociologist, a simple pedlar of the old social dream. Yet it is necessary to say, at the edge of the meanings we can grasp, that this deeper break is as much personal as it is social. The turning away from the social dimension is also, and inevitably, a turning away from persons. It is an attempt to create the individual person without *any* relationships. All those elements of the personality which live in relationship— not only the formal relationships of the family, but between any persons and especially between a man and a woman—are ultimately suppressed in the name of personal fulfilment. At this farthest point of his crisis, Lawrence not only refuses to oppose what he opposes, but also refuses to affirm what he affirms. Under these tensions, only death is possible: para-doxically a death in the aspiration to life. Lawrence had the courage to live this through, but the only relevant respect is a recognition of what is actually arrived at. Others have taken over the categories of this tragic disintegration, and sought to erect them as normality. As such, they are no more than a tired orthodoxy. The contrary distinction of Lawrence is that he shows us the disintegration in progress, with an intensity only rarely breaking into hysteria.

Yet when we arrive at that final division, between society and individual, we must know that an assertion of belief in either is irrelevant. What has actually happened is a loss of belief in both, and this is our way of saying a loss of belief in the whole experience of life, as men and women can live it. This is certainly the deepest and most characteristic form of tragedy in our century.

4

TRAGIC DEADLOCK AND STALEMATE

CHEKHOV, PIRANDELLO, IONESCO, BECKETT

Anton Chekhov inherited and worked in the main tradition of nineteenth-century realism. Yet from his work we can trace an important twentieth-century tradition, in which realism is almost wholly rejected. To understand this paradox, we must look carefully at the nature of this realism, and at its critical relation to actual developments in its society.

The condition of realism in the nineteenth century was in fact an assumption of a total world. In the great realists, there was no separation in kind between public and private facts, or between public and private experiences. This was not, as it may easily appear in retrospect, a wilful joining of disparate things. Rather, it was a way of seeing the world in which it was possible to experience the quality of a whole way of life through the qualities of individual men and women. Thus, a personal breakdown was a genuinely social fact, and a social breakdown was lived and known in direct personal experience. But then to take breakdown as an illustration of this continuity is itself a mark of a very deep kind of change. Chekhov is the realist of breakdown, on a significantly total scale.

Such a way of seeing the world is not willed but given. When it has broken down, as an ordinary way of seeing, it of course appears as naïve. To retain its methods, in artistic creation, is then almost always paradoxical. What was once a habit of realism becomes a habit described in quite opposite terms. This happens, notably, between Chekhov and Pirandello.

The key to this difficult analysis is the continuing emphasis on a total condition. Elsewhere, the breakdown has led to quite different kinds of literature. Where it led to the isolation of the individual, it moved, inevitably, towards the methods of expressionism: the dramatic conflicts of an individual mind. In the novel, it moved through the stream of consciousness to the fiction of special pleading. What had formerly been

seen as a way of life, a society, became now neutral or hostile:
an indifferent flux, or a background, or a rat-race, or a jungle.
The element of neutrality extended to other persons, who
became in this sense merely objects in an environment (the
word which characteristically has replaced society). The
element of hostility, increasingly present as this structure of
feeling developed, is different in kind from the earlier active
hostility, between an individual and his society, which was so
widely recorded in liberal tragedy. In the new structure, the
hostility is neither engaged and active, nor at all specific. It is
not against a condition of society that the individual reacts,
but against the fact of society as such. From this, inevitably,
no action but withdrawal can follow.

Meanwhile, attempts to restore a sense of society, largely
on doctrinaire grounds, on positions taken rather than given,
bear witness only to the same facts of breakdown. For now the
society is isolated, and its specific kinds of fact are given a new
literary status. The general conditions of social life—kinds of
work, kinds of housing—are converted into absolutes, by a
process similar to the isolation of the individual. Society, that
is to say, is converted again into an environment, though on
apparently quite different assumptions about life. The
materialism inherent in the dominant movements of socialism
has been the ratifying theory for this kind of literature. A
shadow battle has indeed been fought (by habit is still being
fought) between this kind of materialist literature and what is
described as the idealist literature based on the isolation of the
individual. But what the contending parties have failed to
notice is that both, by different methods certainly, and with
very different literary results, have converted the realism of
man in society to the quite different mode of man in an
environment. What is significantly absent from both is any
sense of a total condition, in which public and private facts are
not in kind to be distinguished. Each party is prepared to
diminish the other kind of fact: the whole way of life is an
illusion or indeed an ideology; the individual is significant
only as his life acquires social (that is, environmental) connections. But as the priorities are disputed and taken, the
humanist sense of totality, which had given realism its
strength, is in any case lost.

The complexity of this development becomes further

apparent when we return to the main tradition and are forced
to see that it, also, has been qualitatively changed. The sense
of total condition, so clear in Chekhov even when what is
being seen is breakdown, has indeed continued, but has been
transformed in its characteristic substance. In the best
literature of the nineteenth century, the whole way of life and
the individual human beings were not only simultaneous and
contemporary, but were both real. The ironic condition of
such a total vision, in the middle of the twentieth century, is
that while still simultaneous, contemporary, and inseparable,
the way of life and the individual beings are alike illusory. A
general consciousness of illusion has taken over from the
reality of both.

The farthest developments of expressionism, and the
fiction of special pleading, had converted all but one individual
to illusion, but then his reality was correspondingly emphasised. The distinguishing characteristic of the new total vision
is that even this individual has gone. Indeed the work of art
itself, maintained in those other forms by an emphatically
personal consciousness, takes on more and more the quality of
illusion, in its own mode. Illusion has often been used as an
element of dramatic action, and the nature of art has always
been a willing and shared illusion, which is made real. But
what we have now reached, in some notable work, is a wholly
illusory action, or an action attempting to be so. The illusion
is not a means to reality, but an expression of illusion itself.
Then the work itself protests, the artist protests, against those
conditions of its expression by which it threatens to become
real. Traditional procedures can be rejected on this ground
alone. The credibility of successful illusion is itself menacing.
Art must not aspire, even in its own mode, to any false reality
which might disturb or shatter the experience of total illusion.
The ordinary tension of expression is seen as damnable. Art
must be anti-art, the novel must be anti-novel, the theatre
must be anti-theatre, for this compelling reason. The most
dangerous thing about any utterance, in this movement, is
that it creates the possibility of communication, which is
already known to be an illusion. The total condition of life,
when seen in this way, leaves no theoretical basis for art,
except its existence, which yet, ironically, has at some point
to be willed. Then the very will to art has itself to be converted

to bad faith. The creative process has to be separated from will and, at its extremes, from design. A condition of total illusion is thus precariously achieved by a method which must continually turn back on itself and dissolve what it has created. For without this continuous dissolution, the experience itself will be made unreal, by becoming falsely real.

We must now follow, in detail, the process of this transformation, in drama itself. Its beginning is evident in Chekhov's *Ivanov*. Here we see the conscious individual, the liberal hero and victim, already turning his opposition to a condition of society back on to himself.

> It seems to me that I've strained myself, too. The high school, then the university, then farming, schools for peasant children, all sorts of projects. I had different ideas from all the other people, I married differently, I took risks, I threw my money about right and left, I got too excited, as you know. I've been happier and I've suffered more than anyone in the district. Those have been my sacks, Pasha. I hoisted a load on my back, but my back gave way. At twenty we're all heroes, we undertake anything, we can do anything, but at thirty we're tired already and good for nothing. Tell me, how do you explain the way one gets so tired?

Here we are still within the liberal consciousness. Ivanov sees what has to be done, and tries to do it. He is left to struggle alone, is misunderstood and is broken. He also breaks others, in his own fall. But this kind of deadlock, familiar to us from Ibsen, is already being transformed by Chekhov into a new condition: that of stalemate. In a deadlock, there is still effort and struggle, but no possibility of winning: the wrestler with life dies as he gives his last strength. In a stalemate, there is no possibility of movement or even the effort at movement; every willed action is self-cancelling. A different structure of feeling is then initiated:

> My whining inspires you with a sort of reverent awe . . . but in my opinion this neurotic state of mine and all the symptoms that go with it are just something to laugh at, and nothing else. People ought to laugh till their sides split at all my affectations, but you—what a wonderful fuss you make!

This is the victim turning on himself. Its end is a suicide which the others cannot interpret or comprehend. For the victim, who has once struggled, is still seen in contrast with his social group.

In *The Seagull* the structure begins to extend. Trigorin, who has tried to make something new, takes the weight of the guilt of his group, and is broken:

> You have found your right path, you know which way you're going —but I'm still floating about in a chaotic world of dreams and images, without knowing what use it all is. I have no faith, and I don't know what my vocation is.

The end again is a suicide, which the others cannot comprehend, and from which, in its starkness, they must even be temporarily protected.

With *Uncle Vanya* the structure is further extended, until it becomes a sense of a total condition:

> Here we have a picture of decay due to an insupportable struggle for existence. It is decay caused by inertia, by ignorance, by utter irresponsibility.

Individuals vary in their attitudes and responsibilities, but the sense of a general failure has decisively entered. The structure and method of Chekhov's drama begins to change to its true originality, in which a whole group, a whole society, can be seen as victims. It is not a question now of the dramatic resolution of the fate of a single individual, but of an orchestration of responses to a common fate. *The Three Sisters* and *The Cherry Orchard* are the mature examples of this essentially new form.

> T: Migrant birds, cranes for example, fly and fly, and whatever thoughts, high or low, enter their heads, they will still fly and not know why or where. They fly and will continue to fly, whatever philosophers come to life among them. They may philosophise as much as they like, only they will fly.
>
> M: Still, is there a meaning?
>
> T: A meaning? Now the snow is falling. What meaning?
>
> M: It seems to me that a man must have a faith, or must search for a faith, or his life will be empty, empty. To live and not to know why the cranes fly, why babies are born, why there are stars in the sky. Either you must know why you live, or everything is trivial, not worth a straw.

v: Still, I am sorry that my youth has gone.

m: Gogol says: life in this world is a dull matter, my masters.

t: And I say it's difficult to argue with you, my masters. Hang it all.

c: Balzac was married at Berdichev. That's worth making a note of. Balzac was married at Berdichev.

The breakdown of meaning is now so complete that even the aspiration to meaning seems comic. The hold on reality is so tenuous that any 'fact', however incidental (like the information on Balzac) supplies the illusion of temporary control.

Still, in a tragic tension, the failing memory that there has been significance comes through as heartbreaking, for even a failing memory of a past that has meant something (for the three sisters, Moscow) implies a condition other than the present, and this can turn into a breaking hope for the future:

> They will forget our faces, voices, and even how many there were of us, but our sufferings will turn into joy for those who will live after us, happiness and peace will reign on earth, and people will remember with kindly words, and bless those who are living now. . . . If only we could know, if only we could know.

The way to the future is seen, consistently, in work:

> We must only work and work, and happiness is only for our distant prosperity.

Or in *The Cherry Orchard*:

> Everything that is unattainable for us now will one day be near and clear; but we must work; we must help with all our force those who seek for truth.

> Do not human spirits look out at you from every tree in the orchard, from every leaf and every stem? Do you not hear human voices? Oh, it is terrible. Your orchard frightens me. When I walk through it in the evening or at night, the rugged bark on the trees glows with a dim light, and the cherry-trees seem to see all that happened a hundred and two hundred years ago in painful and oppressive dreams. Well, we have fallen at least two hundred years behind the times. We have achieved nothing at all as yet; we have not made up our minds how we stand with the past; we only philosophise, complain of boredom, or drink vodka. It is so plain that, before we can live in the present, we must first redeem the past, and have done with it; and

it is only by suffering that we can redeem it, only by strenuous, unremitting toil.

This element is crucial in Chekhov's whole structure of feeling. But it is easy to misinterpret it. We have seen, in our own period, what we can call English Chekhov and Soviet Chekhov. In English Chekhov the dominant tone is pathetic charm. The call to work is ironically displaced, by the undoubted fact that it is made by those who do not work, and apparently will never work (as Trofimov, the 'eternal student', in the speeches just quoted). Thus the aspiration is converted into just another idiosyncrasy. In Soviet Chekhov, on the other hand, the call to work is sometimes positively displaced, towards the voice simply prophetic of the future. These interpretations are interesting, for they show how difficult the whole structure is to grasp.

The aspiration is genuine. To deflect it ironically is to cheapen and sentimentalise the whole feeling. But, equally, to abstract it from the whole process of disintegration is to miss the point. For the energy to work is consumed, in this context, by the very effort to conceive it. This is a common form of tragedy in a stagnant society. Or, to put it another way, for Chekhov a social breakdown *is* a personal breakdown. Even when you can see beyond a pressing situation, still the actual pressure is disintegrating. And a disintegrating society extends its process into individual lives. It is not something external, towards which an attitude would suffice, but is directly lived, in the fibres of body and mind. In a disintegrating society, individuals carry the disintegrating process in themselves. Even aspiration is a form of defeat.

In a note published after his death, Chekhov wrote:

They cry out there are no ideals and so on, but all this was already going on twenty or thirty years ago; these are worn-out forms which have already served their time, and whoever repeats them now, he too is no longer young and is himself worn out. With last year's foliage there decay, too, those who live in it.

It is as hard as that, in the world of his plays. The judgement cannot be mitigated, towards either prophetic hope or pathetic charm. When the rot enters, it produces the *nedotepa*, the unfinished and useless who are still human beings and suffering. What redeems is not the aspiration to the future, but the future itself, and from this they are cut off:

> There is boiling up around us a life which we neither know nor notice. . . . Before the dawn of a new life has broken, we shall turn into sinister old men and women, and we shall be the first who, in our hatred of that dawn, will calumniate it.

This is the harder, and more actually prophetic, voice. But also it turns back on itself, as it must. For even to show the disintegration as it is becomes disintegrating:

> To scare society as we are doing now, and as we shall continue to do, means to deprive it of courage.

Yet the total condition has still to be shown, by a method which continually turns back on itself: creating a tragic situation, and inviting us to laugh at it; creating a ridiculous situation, and making it end in tragic breakdown.

All Chekhov's work is rooted in a sense of society, and in the inescapable connection of what a less honest but more complacent period calls 'public' and 'private' facts. It is not that human beings are simple, or simply determined. It is that society is, inevitably, the sum of their relationships, and when these are badly wrong, or when people cease to understand them, there is a complicated structure of guilt and illusion which is lived through in every corner of experience, as well as at the most obvious meeting-points. Yet there is a stage beyond this, when the condition is so complete that it is taken for granted, and the particular structure becomes general and is taken for life itself. This seems to me to happen, decisively, in Pirandello.

Here the dramatic world is one of guilt and illusion: the guilt interlocking and complicated, in a series of false personal relationships; the illusion elaborate and persistent, as a way of avoiding or living with the guilt. Yet this is not only a particular world; it is deliberately generalised. Straight and truthful relationships have become impossible, and the only defence against suffering, the only source of innocence, is fantasy.

The simplest case is *Right You Are (if you think so)*. Here Mrs Frola asserts that her daughter is Ponza's wife, while Ponza asserts that this daughter died and his wife is another woman. The wife declares that she is each of these contradictory alternatives, but in herself is nothing.

The point is developed from a common uncertainty:

> What can we really know about other people? Who they are? What sort of people they are? What they do? Why they do it?

But the uncertainty goes much wider, into the self and the world:

> Thinking back on those illusions which you no longer have, on all those things that no longer *seem* to be what they *were* once upon a time, don't you feel that—I won't say these boards—no—that the very earth itself is slipping away from under your feet, when you reflect that in the same way this *you* that you now feel yourself to be— all your reality as it is today—is destined to seem an illusion to-morrow?

Thus reality is at best temporary. As 'Henry the Fourth' puts it, in his simultaneous masquerade of sanity and insanity:

> To think that the men of the twentieth century are torturing them-selves, in an absolute agony of anxiety, to know how things will work out. Painstakingly they rush around, frantic about fate and fortune, and about what they have in store for them. Whereas you are already in history with me. And sad as my lot is, hideous as are the events of my life, with all the bitterness and all the struggle, with all the sorrow and all the strife, nonetheless it's all history. Nothing can change. Do you understand? Nothing can possibly change. Everything is fixed for ever. And you can peacefully gaze on in admiration as effect follows obediently upon cause, with the most perfect logic, and as every event happens precisely and coherently, right down to the smallest detail. Yes, the pleasures of history, the pleasures of history. . . .

Only when life is over, and has become history, can a common meaning, a common sense of reality, be found. But this state of mind is only available, to the living, in a masquerade. To the living, a common reality is an illusion:

> They have created, she for him and he for her, a world of fantasy that has all the substance of reality itself, a world in which they now live in perfect peace and harmony. And it cannot be destroyed, this reality of theirs, by any of your documents, because they live and breathe in it. They can see it, feel it, touch it. At most a document

might comfort *you* a little, might satisfy your stupid curiosity. But such a document is just not to be found, and so you're condemned to the wonderful torment of having before your very eyes, suddenly very close to you, on the one hand, this world of fantasy and on the other, *reality* . . . and of not being able to distinguish one from the other.

Then, even to the observer, reality is this illusion:

Reality for me lies in the minds of those two, and I can only hope to penetrate to that reality through what they tell me about themselves.

When others probe for 'the real facts of the case', they merely threaten this precarious balance. The probing is inevitably destructive, for the truth cannot be discovered, but only an illusion of the truth:

It doesn't matter *what* truth it is, provided only that it's good, solid, categorical stuff.

Truth is unattainable, and in any case incommunicable, because of the nature of our selves and our language:

Each one of us has a whole world of things inside him, and each one of us has his own particular world. How can we understand each other if into the words which I speak I put the sense and the value of things as I understand them within myself, while at the same time whoever is listening to them assumes them to have the sense and value that they have in the world that he has within him? We think we understand one another, but we never really do understand.

We have then to resign ourselves to a tragic distance from each other:

There's a little basket that we send up and down in the courtyard. It always carries a note from me and a word or two from her. Just giving the day's news. I'm quite content with that. And now, well I'm quite used to it now. Resigned, if you like. I don't suffer any more.

Or, trying to force a meaning, we become involved in deception:

You know it's just words, which he says simply for the sake of talking. . . . You *give* them a meaning, yourself; you put a meaning into them, whatever meaning best suits you. But you pretend *he's* put a meaning into them. He'll be delighted to find his own words actually making sense. In that way you can gradually make him into

exactly what you want him to be, and he'll be under the impression
that that's what *he* wants to be. . . .

Yet the end of this is tragedy:

To crush a man like that, with the weight of a single word.

Whether in good or bad faith, the whole making of
relationships is a process of illusion and tragedy:

Each one of us is many persons. Many persons, according to all the
possibilities of being that there are within us. With some people we
are one person, with others we are somebody quite different. And
all the time we are under the illusion of always being one and the
same person for everybody. We believe that we are always this one
person in whatever it is we may be doing. But it's not true. It's not
true. And we see this very clearly when by some tragic chance we
are, as it were, caught up in the middle of doing something and find
ourselves suspended in mid-air. And then we perceive that all of us
was not in what we were doing, and that it would, therefore, be an
atrocious injustice to us to judge us by that action alone. To keep us
suspended like that, to keep us in a pillory throughout all existence,
as if our whole life were completely summed up in that one deed.

This is the tragic father in *Six Characters in Search of an
Author*, where the nature of the action is just this being caught
up in a suspended life. Yet the tragedy is in the relationships
thus revealed. The truth about the relationships is not, it is
argued, the whole truth about the persons involved in them,
yet the relationships must take their tragic course. When there
is this radical uncertainty about the self, the whole business of
becoming involved with others is a tragic farce:

Do you see what these lunatics are up to? Without taking the slightest
notice of their own phantom, the phantom that is implicit within
them, they go haring about, frantic with curiosity, chasing after
other people's phantoms. And they believe they're doing something
quite different.

To accept the state of illusion, the 'phantom' existence, can
seem the only realistic conclusion. As Henry puts it, near the
end of his masquerade:

Ladies and gentlemen, I am cured. Because I know perfectly well
that I'm playing the madman here. And I do so very quietly. You

are the ones to be pitied, for you live out *your* madness in a state of
constant agitation, without seeing it, without knowing it.

There is an interesting structural parallel here. With the
breakdown of a general morality, we have been offered the
consciously dishonest man as a type of virtue. Similarly, with
the breakdown of a general reality, we are offered the man
conscious of his unreality as real. The types operate at
different levels of experience, but in so widespread a breakdown as we have seen in this century, the formal resemblance
is important.

Pirandello recognises and urgently conveys the suffering
which leads to self-deception and fantasy. Thus illusion, in
his world, is not to be mocked; he is starting with common
experience. But he extends this process to a general stalemate.
The tragedy is not, essentially, in what this or that person
does, but in a total condition. We can construct an illusion for
ourselves, and may temporarily interlock it with the illusion
of another. But while life continues, the interlocking is
threatened, and both the pressure of the other, playing out his
own illusion, and yet his distance, the impossibility of genuinely reaching him, are tragically felt:

> It's a terrible thing if you don't hold on tight to what seems true to
> you today, to what will seem true to you tomorrow, even if it's the
> complete opposite of what seemed true to you yesterday. I would
> never wish you to think, as I have had to do, of that horrible thing
> which really drives you out of your mind. You're there, very close to
> someone, looking into his eyes, just as, one day, I looked into some-
> one's eyes, and you see yourself mirrored there. But it's not really
> yourself. No, you see yourself as a beggar, standing before a door
> through which you will never pass. The man who goes through that
> door will not be you, you with that secret life, the world you have
> within you, the familiar world of sight and touch. It will be someone
> quite unknown to you who will pass in at that door. The man *he*
> sees you as. The one he, in his own personal, impenetrable world, sees
> and touches.

Thus the tragedy is in the fact of the 'personal, impenetrable
world'. This must be defended, and yet the act of defence
destroys others, by destroying their reality. This is what is
meant by stalemate, since no valid move is possible. It is

perhaps the final crisis of individualism, beyond the heroic
deadlock of liberal tragedy, where the individual could pit
himself against a total condition outside him, even at the risk
of his life. Here the very thing that must be defended, the
'personal, impenetrable world', is, by the fact of its existence
in others, the thing that turns back and destroys oneself. By
a paradoxical procedure, the other individuals, defending
their personal, impenetrable worlds and their consequent
ways of seeing and living, become a hostile society, which
threatens to destroy one's own personal way:

> Those people always demand that the rest of us should behave exactly
> as they wish. That every moment of every day should be lived out
> as they dictate. But of course there's nothing arrogant about that.
> Oh no, no. Of course not. It's merely *their* way of thinking, *their*
> way of seeing, *their* way of feeling. Everybody's got his own way
> of. . . . You've got yours, too, haven't you? Of course you have. But
> what *is* your way? Your way is that of the common herd. You're a
> flock of sheep, wretched, uncertain, feeble, and *they* take advantage
> of it. They make you submit to their will. They make you accept
> their way of life. So that you feel and see as they do. At least, that's
> the illusion to which they blissfully cling. For, after all, what is it
> that they've succeeded in imposing upon you? Words. Words that
> each one of us understands and gives out again in his own particular
> way. And that, that is how so-called public opinion is formed.

This sounds like a call to personal revolt. The aspiration,
and the familiar description of the 'common herd', are
characteristic.

> Oh yes, it's a joke here all right. But suppose we leave here and go
> out into the world of the living. Dawn is breaking. All time is before
> us. Dawn—and the dawn of—and the day that lies before us. You
> say to yourselves this day is ours to make of it what we will. And do
> you? *Do* you? To hell with tradition. To hell with the old con-
> ventions. Go on, talk away. You'll do nothing but repeat the same old
> words, over and over again, like countless generations before you.
> Do you really believe you're living? All that you're doing is chewing
> the cud of the life of the dead.

This is a tragic despair, about other people. The false society
is seen, for a moment, as a fact in itself. But there is no way
out, within Pirandello's world, for the pressure is constant:
the pressure of the reality of others, with their own impene-

trable ways of thinking and feeling, their own inevitable conversion of your meanings into their meanings, and such a
world is only negotiable by interlocking illusion. The day
before us is never really ours but theirs, and so the personal
stalemate becomes a general stalemate, an impenetrable
general condition.

It is important, finally, to see how widely this version of
life has been extended. In the years since 1945, it has become
the theme of a whole school of dramatists. Ionesco is the
clearest example:

> The fact of existence, the very use of language—these are what seem
> to me to be inconceivable.

The world in which we live

> appears illusory and fictitious . . . human behaviour reveals its
> absurdity, and all history its absolute uselessness; all reality, all
> language seems to become disjointed, to fall apart, to empty itself of
> meaning, so that, since all is devoid of importance, what else can one
> do but laugh at it?

Here is the same ultimate perception, and the same tone, as in
Pirandello. The comic possibilities of such a world, evident in
Pirandello, have been more fully realised, often brilliantly as
in *La Cantatrice*, by Ionesco. Yet at the same time, within the
deliberately crazy structure, the fact of tragedy has become
more arbitrary and more brutal. The individual is isolated, in
a permanently meaningless world, so that even the connections within the personality break down. Yet to know people
and the world as unreal is not enough to dispose of them.
Indeed, to recognise the platitudes which sustain a conformable world is to be released beyond them into a state of silence
and terror, which is still densely inhabited by the material
pressure of others. The tragic then manifests itself in two
forms: the habitual brutality which holds a meaningless
world together; and that 'state of paroxysm . . . where the
sources of tragedy lie'. By definition, there can be no clear
connection between the apparent action and the sudden
violence. The ritual murders in *The Lesson*, the killer in *Le
Tueur sans gages*, the monstrous corpse in *Amédée*, seem to
emerge by their own momentum from the world of unreality
and platitude. The one fact that is not questioned, in the
general doubt of reality, is death, and this, significantly often,

is violent and arbitrary. In the total condition of human illusion, these facts alone seem certain: death and anguish. Behind the ridiculous facade, a separate violence, acting by its own laws, is waiting. To know this is both anguish and liberation. Indeed, the only authentic society that can be created, as Ionesco sees it, must be based on a general discovery of the total condition of illusion, and consequently on 'our common anguish'.

This coexistence of illusion and violence is found again in Pinter (*The Dumb Waiter*, *The Birthday Party*). The more general pattern of unreality, failure to communicate, and meaninglessness is indeed now so widespread that it is virtually, in itself, a dramatic convention. For many writers, including at times Pinter, it is often no more than convention: a particular kind of theatrical opportunity. The convention of total illusion, and of man's inability to communicate, seems then merely the most recent and most bourgeois of platitudes. But when this is so, we are in danger of missing those few works which go beyond the formulas and create the experience in depth.

The most remarkable example, in this kind, is Beckett's *Waiting for Godot*. It is clear that in certain respects it belongs to the tradition we are tracing. It presents a total condition of man, and this belongs within the familiar structure of feeling:

> . . . One day we were born, one day we'll die, the same day, the same second, is that not enough for you? They give birth astride of a grave, the light gleams an instant, then it's night once more.

> Astride of a grave and a difficult birth. Down in the hole, lingeringly, the grave-digger puts on the forceps. We have time to grow old. The air is full of our cries.

Yet the dramatic method is in fact unlike that of Chekhov and Pirandello, where the movement is normally a single action showing how the characters fit in with each other, sharing comparable illusions. The method of *Waiting for Godot* is older. The play is built around an unusually explicit set of contrasts: between the tramps, Vladimir and Estragon, and the travellers, Pozzo and Lucky; and the further contrasts within each pair.

This polar opposition of characters was used in early expressionism to present the conflicts of a single mind. But now the method has been developed to present the conflicts within a total human condition. It is an almost wholly static world, with very narrow limits set to any significant human action. Yet the struggles for significance, of each of the pairs, are sharply contrasted. The movement of the play is the action of waiting. In each of the two acts, the tramps come together to wait, meet the travellers, who pass on, and then the tramps are left waiting for an appointment that is not kept. But while in the travellers there is change between the acts, in the tramps there is no change. This follows from the different responses they have made. The simplest illustration can be taken from the two speeches quoted above: the first by Pozzo, the second by Vladimir. The sense of life in each is identical, but Pozzo's next word is 'On!', the command to movement, while Vladimir's next words are 'But habit is a great deadener', the patience and the suffering of waiting. Pozzo and Lucky belong to the world of effort and action; Vladimir and Estragon to the world of resignation and waiting. Neither response is more significant than the other, in any ultimate way: the travellers fall and the tramps wait on in disappointment.

Neither the way of progress nor the way of salvation leads out of this human condition. But the way chosen affects the human beings who choose it. The way of the travellers is marked by power and exploitation, which in the end consume themselves. Pozzo, the comfortable accommodated man, leads Lucky as a slave with a halter on his neck, but in the second act the same rope is that of the blind being led by the dumb. It is a way of domination and dependence: relationships which can only be reversed. The way of the tramps, on the other hand, is one of compassion in degradation. Irritation drives them apart, and the power of sympathy is always likely to fail. Hysterical cruelty waits at the edge for these breakdowns. Yet, under pressure, the relationship holds, and within the tradition we have been tracing this is the main originality of the play. The compassion which was always present in Chekhov had virtually disappeared by the time of Pirandello and his successors. Their exposure of illusion (as indeed in Beckett's own other work) carried a mocking harshness which could not go beyond itself. The world and life had been 'seen through', and that was that. In the Pozzo-Lucky sequences, Beckett continues this tone, but he combines it with what had seemed to be lost: the possibility of human recognition, and of love, within a total condition still meaningless. Strangely, this answering life, at a point beyond the recognition of stalemate, is convincing and moving:

ESTRAGON: Do you remember the day I threw myself into the Rhone?

VLADIMIR: We were grape-harvesting.

ESTRAGON: You fished me out.

VLADIMIR: That's all dead and buried.

ESTRAGON: My clothes dried in the sun.

VLADIMIR: There's no good harking back on that. Come on.
[*He draws him after him. As before.*]

ESTRAGON: Wait.

VLADIMIR: I'm cold.

ESTRAGON: Wait. [*He moves away from* VLADIMIR.] I wonder if we wouldn't have been better off alone, each one for himself. [*He crosses the stage and sits down on the mound.*] We weren't made for the same road.

VLADIMIR [*without anger*]: It's not certain.

ESTRAGON: No, nothing is certain.

[VLADIMIR *slowly crosses the stage and sits down beside* ESTRAGON.]

VLADIMIR: We can still part, if you think it would be better.

ESTRAGON: It's too late now.

[*Silence.*]

VLADIMIR: Yes, it's too late now.

[*Silence.*]

ESTRAGON: Well, shall we go?

VLADIMIR: Yes, let's go.

[*They do not move.*]

The condition is absolute, and the response confirms it. But as they stay together, with nothing to go for and nothing but disappointment to wait for, yet staying together, an old and deep tragic rhythm is recovered.

5

TRAGIC RESIGNATION AND SACRIFICE

ELIOT AND PASTERNAK

The rhythm of tragedy, it is said, is a rhythm of sacrifice. A man is disintegrated by suffering, and is led to his death, but the action is more than personal, and others are made whole as he is broken.

As a matter of fact we need particular contexts, if we are to discuss sacrifice at all. It has been said that tragedy took its origin, in Greek culture, from an active ritual of sacrifice. But this is at best an hypothesis, and has been vigorously disputed. In its most popular forms, it is based on a romantic anthropology, which characteristically took patterns of ritual from this culture and from that. Integration was at the level of the abstracted patterns, which appeared available in literary evidence, rather than at the level of actual relationship between a particular ritual pattern and the body of the society in which it was practised. Significance, then, was a general arrangement of patterns, irrespective of actual societies and irrespective of history.

Sacrifice, even if it is a single kind of action, can have many meanings in particular contexts. Yet behind the powerful word, is it not possible to see, in fact, different kinds of action? In our own culture, the idea of sacrifice is profoundly ambiguous. The simplest form of sacrifice, in which a man is killed so that the body of men may live or live more fully, we have almost wholly abandoned. We know the idea, from other cultures and periods, but it retains emotional significance in one case only: at the centre of Christian belief. There, the manner of its retention proves the distance we have moved away from the idea as such, since the man Jesus is also, for believers, the Son of God, and the action, if it is to be significant, must be seen as part of a divine rather than a merely human history. Other apparently comparable cases, deprived of this sanction, are seen as essentially primitive—the scattering of the body for fertility, the sharing of the blood of the man who died. If it is not a divine action, it is a primitive magical action, and flat comparison of one with the other is even offensive. Here the decisive importance of context is most ironically proved.

In a continuing religious tradition, the martyr can be seen in the rhythm of sacrifice. He dies in order that the faith may live, or the result of his death is a general renewal of faith. This interpretation has been extended, beyond the context of religion: notably, in the history of political movements and parties. Even to mention the variation is to be reminded of the decisive significance of context: martyrdom will be denied, another name will be found for it, if the faith is not shared. An evident instance of this continual variation is the case of the soldier who dies in war. He is ordinarily seen, by the men of his own country, as having made what is still called the supreme sacrifice, and any questioning of this can be profoundly offensive. Yet the death of an enemy soldier (and the condition of war is that all are enemies) is, while the action lasts, seen in quite different ways: he is destroyed, liquidated, wiped out, even mopped up. Thus identity of cause, whether religious, political, or national, is the keystone of martyrdom.

Sacrifice is judged, in fact, by its cause and its effects. The significance of the word is often refused by others. But martyrdom, in our own time, has taken on a particular emotional content, which further distinguishes it from simple sacrifice. Martyrdom now is defensive; it is a death under pressure. Just as all wars are now seen or justified as defensive, by all sides, so this sacrifice of a life is negatively seen. It is not a consummation, the climax of a general history. It is often a willing event, but to preserve, not to renew. The sense of loss is ordinarily keener than the sense of revival. The martyr is formally described as a hero, but he is more often mourned as a victim.

We have lost, then, the rhythm of sacrifice, in its simple original form. Our heroes often move us most closely when they are in fact victims, and are seen as victims. Our emotional commitment, in a majority of cases, is to the man who dies, rather than to the action in which he dies. At this point a new rhythm of tragedy enters, and the ceremony of sacrifice is drowned, not in blood but in pity. There are important exceptions, as we shall see.

But the ambiguity returns, while the older rhythm is

remembered. We ask, when men sacrifice their lives, whether this is a chosen or a forced destiny. And we include questions of character in the discussion of forcing, often undermining the fact of the public choice. He did not die, as he said, for a cause, but for private reasons elevated or rationalised to a cause. As we see the character differently, so, inevitably, we choose our viewpoint on the action. Thus our other word for sacrifice is scapegoat; logically so. Public reasons also can be elevated or rationalised to a cause. When a man is driven to die, we scrutinise the need, and say scapegoat more often than sacrifice. Further, we see the action of finding the scapegoat as tragedy, just as the death of the scapegoat is for us tragic: new rhythms again. After such an action, there is not a renewal of our general life, but often a positive renewal of our general guilt, which can move us more deeply than the consummation of any order of life. Indeed, in our world, resignation to a general guilt has become an order of life, or its shadow.

In any literary work, the true context (of a divine order or of history or of a particular society) has to be present in the work's substance, or it falls short of significance. This presence can be explicit, in the forms of the action, or implicit, in its conventions. Its significant presence is also in the language of the action, which in the deepest sense is inseparable from the action itself. While the significance holds, within the work, it appears to be possible (and this is all that now matters) to be moved by rhythms that we do not ordinarily share. Our response is a discovery or else a remaking, so that the action can seem, at least temporarily, autonomous. This kind of autonomy is a condition of art, and is what distinguishes it (though there can be overlapping) from ritual. Thus we can be moved by the rhythms of sacrifice, even when we have formally detached ourselves from them. And it is clear that this often happens, in tragedy. It most notably fails to happen when the rhythms are carried, not by the work, but by a forgotten ritual, a disintegrating pattern. In our own time the question is complicated, for in a way the whole context is known, and we cannot easily separate it from the work where the rhythms are active. It is at such a point that the timeless rhythm of sacrifice is most ratifying and most tempting. That connection is simpler than the connections the context forces. And the context, finally, is ourselves.

What happens, in fact, when we hear, not from the past but from the present, what seems the rhythm of sacrifice? What happens as we watch the actions leading to the deaths of Becket and Celia Coplestone and Yury Zhivago? I take these examples as the clearest known to me, in modern work, to which the idea of sacrifice seems relevant. I have been moved, though in different ways, by *Murder in the Cathedral*, by *The Cocktail Party*, and by *Doctor Zhivago*. I find my thoughts about each leading back to the rhythm of sacrifice, but equally to the varieties of this rhythm, and to its present ambivalence. We have to know, in these actions, the subtle ways in which the rhythm of sacrifice is always dependent on context, and what kind of context this can be, in a literary work which is also of our own time. We have to know the movements in which hero becomes victim, and in which either can be seen as the other. We have to know the processes of a chosen or a forced destiny, not only at the level of statement, but at the level of the whole action. We have to know elevation and rationalisation, of public and private causes. We have finally to know, as the most searching question, the process of transformation, in making and responding, by which an order becomes a conspiracy, and a conspiracy an order; by which renewal and guilt change places or become identified or confused; by which a death is offered and received —more truly is *seen*—as a defeat or a victory, as a consummation or a simple breakdown.

The three works mentioned are characterised by an endorsement as necessary of a destiny ending in willed death. The central characters, though in different ways, are not seen in the end as victims, as in most modern tragedy. Willy Loman, in *Death of a Salesman*, ends by deliberately sacrificing his life, but the sacrifice, like the whole life, comes through as an indictment. What has been shown to be necessary, within the terms of the action, is still not endorsed; another and qualifying context is present. In *Murder in the Cathedral*, in *The Cocktail Party*, and (I admit the controversy) in *Doctor Zhivago*, the context offered, in the whole action, is not alternative but ratifying. We have to see how this can be so.

The action of *Murder in the Cathedral* is based on an

historical martyrdom, but in all essentials is taken out of its particular context and made part of an 'eternal design':

> *Even now, in sordid particulars*
> *The eternal design may appear.*

Thus, for the martyr,

> *It is not in time that my death shall be known;*
> *It is out of time that my decision is taken*
> *If you call that decision*
> *To which my whole being gives entire consent.*
> *I give my life*
> *To the Law of God above the Law of Man.*

The centre of the play is the consciousness of the martyr, but the action is the making over of this consciousness into an element of the eternal design:

> *an eternal action, an eternal patience*
> *To which all must consent that it may be willed*
> *And which all must suffer that they may will it,*
> *That the pattern may subsist. . . .*

Thus Becket's life is sacrificed, his independent will to life conquered, by the demands of an absolute and timeless law which the particular ritual enacts:

> *His blood given to buy my life*
> *My blood given to pay for His death*
> *My death for His death.*

Not only the ordinary desires of life, but also the willed heroism of being a martyr, must be set aside:

> The true martyr is he who has become the instrument of God, who has lost his will in the will of God, and who no longer desires anything for himself, not even the glory of being a martyr.

Thus the action moves towards acceptance of the ritual of blood, and even to thanksgiving for it:

> *We thank Thee for Thy mercies of blood, for Thy redemption by blood.*
> *For the blood of Thy martyrs and saints*
> *Shall enrich the earth, shall create the holy places.*

This pattern is stronger, in the play, than the alternative

pattern through which the historical event, and indeed the general fact of martyrdom, have often been seen. The idea of a church persecuted by a powerful state, and of a believer dying rather than renounce his faith, is deliberately weakened so that the structure of ritual sacrifice may be more clearly seen. It is not to the heroic will of the martyr that our response is directed, but to his subjection of himself to his part in the pattern, and then to the fertilising effects of his blood. The third priest gives the alternative pattern:

> the Church is stronger for this action
> Triumphant in adversity. It is fortified
> By persecution: supreme, so long as men will die for it.

But the general movement is not of this kind. The dominant imagery is of the land and the seasons, the lives of men and beasts, the redemption through blood. Redemption is a consciousness of this natural order, and of the place of sacrifice in it, for this is a consciousness of God. The natural order, without the sacrifice, is merely bestial. It is the act of blood, and the receiving of the blood, which creates consciousness, and separates man from the beasts. Through the chorus, the drive of the play is towards general acceptance of the blood of the sacrifice. In the beginning,

> For us, the poor, there is no action,
> But only to wait and to witness.

Fear of the act of blood drives the people to appeal against the pattern:

> Do you realise what you ask, do you realise what it means,
> To the small folk drawn into the pattern of fate, the small folk who
> live among small things,
> The strain on the brain of the small folk who stand to the doom of the
> house, the doom of their lord, the doom of the world?

Yet, whatever their fear, they go on to acknowledge that

> the world must be cleaned in the winter, or we shall have only
> A sour spring, a parched summer, an empty harvest.

F

So the cry becomes:

> *Clear the air! clean the sky! wash the wind! take the stone from the stone, take the skin from the arm, take the muscle from the bone, and wash them. Wash the stone, wash the bone, wash the brain, wash the soul, wash them, wash them!*

It is not only the acceptance of consciousness, of 'the strain on the brain of the small folk'. It is also the perception of the filth of the beast who is man without God. The blood of the martyr not only fertilises the world, but also cleanses the world of its ordinary filth, and marks the heads of the believers, as a permanent reminder of the sin of their normal condition:

> *The sin of the world is upon our heads . . . the blood of the martyrs and the agony of the saints*
> *Is upon our heads.*

It is in this movement that we notice the special character of this rhythm of sacrifice, in the Christian tradition. It is not the act of the body of men, convinced of the need of sacrificial blood for the renewal of their common life. On the contrary, this need has to be brought to the people, by the exceptional man. The need for blood has to be shown by the man who is offering his life. The sacrifice is not only redemption, but conversion. It is in this particular rhythm that the sacrificial victim becomes the redeemer or the martyr.

Eliot's pattern of sacrifice, his insistence on this kind of willed death, is determined by a context which is clearly offered as a ratification. It is a response to a state of unconsciousness, which becomes either smallness or bestiality, among the general body of men. It rests on a division of humanity into the many unconscious and the few conscious, in terms similar to the division between unauthentic and authentic man. Yet the pattern is such that it is the role of the conscious not to save themselves but to save the world. Tragedy rests not in the individual destiny, of the man who must live this sacrifice, but in the general condition, of a people reducing or destroying itself because it is not conscious of its true condition. The tragedy is not in the death, but in the life.

Though the pattern is clear, in *Murder in the Cathedral*, it can slip away in the mind, and often in the theatre, by the emphasis of the martyr, at the centre of the play. There is a clear difference from Robert Bolt's *A Man for All Seasons*, in which another martyr, Thomas More, is ratified by a superficially similar context: the minor contrast between the honesty of More and the corruption of others in power; the major contrast between More's nobility and the craven time-serving of the 'Common Man', who appears under this name as accomplice and executioner, though meaning no harm. Bolt's play is not sacrificial but, as far as it goes, ethical: this good man against the rest. Though Eliot's play is quite different, it can be easily confused with the same pattern, as the structure of the play pushes Becket towards an heroic position which is in fact irrelevant. It is, moreover, an historical death, and thus in a sense indifferent.

The essential pattern comes through more clearly, though with a marked lessening of dramatic force, in *The Cocktail Party*. Here the martyr, the life sacrificed, is not at the centre of the play. Celia Coplestone is one of several characters at the same apparent level. The true centre of the play, now, is the common condition, seen not so much in the alternative of bestiality as in the more negotiable alternative of the trivial round which gives the play its title.

At this weakened level, the sacrificial pattern is again enacted. Celia becomes conscious (in ways reminiscent of Chekhov and even more of Pirandello) of the illusion covering the common condition, and her insight is offered to mark the true condition:

> *That I've always been alone. That one always is alone.*
> *Not simply the ending of one relationship,*
> *Not even simply finding that it never existed—*
> *But a revelation about my relationship*
> *With everybody.*

The possibility that this is simply a personal breakdown is dramatically argued:

> *I should really like to think there's something wrong with me—*
> *Because, if there isn't, then there's something wrong,*
> *Or at least, very different from what it seemed to be,*
> *With the world itself—and that's much more frightening!*
> *That would be terrible.*

But the action of the play makes it perfectly clear that this 'much more frightening' condition is in fact the case. Celia's breakdown is not an illusion, but an epitome of the breakdown of illusion—our ordinary understanding of our condition—which the play as a whole is designed to show. The action is a search for love, and this search is shown as a necessary failure, except when it is the apparent rejection of human love which leads Celia to her death. The way she takes

> leads towards possession
> Of what you have sought for in the wrong place.

The search for human love, in relationships, is illusory:

> Can we only love
> Something created by our own imagination?
> Are we all in fact unloving and unlovable?
> Then one is alone, and if one is alone
> Then lover and beloved are equally unreal.

This, in fact, is the play's context. It is offered to ratify a death which would otherwise seem wasteful and horrifying. Once again, the real tragedy is not in the death but in the life.

The heroic status which hovers over Becket, but against the pattern of the play, is paralleled by the social status which, in the tone of action and dialogue, enfolds Celia and the others, again blurring the decisive pattern. The play shows, convincingly, an empty round of life, but particularises this in a place and among people somewhat removed from the common condition. It is a social world of temporary relationships, transience, and bright emptiness, but it is as easy to relate the essential triviality of this life to the particular place and the people as to a common human condition. Eliot, of course, will have none of this, but it is what the play does that matters, and it is difficult in the end to believe that he has done more than *assert* a condition. Moreover, the analogy between the particular and the general is weakened by the play's evident delight in its chosen particulars. The pattern dissents, but the tone accepts.

These facts have an important effect on the play's final meaning. Celia, rejecting the human illusion, chooses the way that leads to crucifixion. The guardians who direct her approve this, as a happy death, though

> *she paid the highest price*
> *In suffering. That is part of the design.*

But this is only one of two ways, each an alternative to the 'final desolation of solitude':

> *Neither way is better.*
> *Both ways are necessary. It is also necessary*
> *To make a choice between them.*

The second way is that of the Chamberlaynes, and

> *the consequence of the Chamberlaynes' choice*
> *Is a cocktail party.*

This is crucial. The effects of Celia's sacrifice are mentioned:

> *Who knows . . .*
> *The difference that made to the natives who were dying*
> *Or the state of mind in which they died?*

And at home, in London:

> *If this was right—if this was right for Celia—*
> *There must be something else that is terribly wrong,*
> *And the rest of us are somehow involved in the wrong.*

'Who knows?'; 'somehow': these tentative phrases are dramatically on a level with the ambiguous guardians, who are at once the mystifying agents of grace and yet whole-hearted and full-blooded (those are not, on reflection, quite the adjectives) participants in the world of the cocktail party. The Chamberlaynes resign themselves to this world:

> *Two people who know they do not understand each other,*
> *Breeding children whom they do not understand*
> *And who will never understand them.*

This is a resignation to unconsciousness, or at best to a consciousness of being unconscious. It is also a resignation to sub-humanity—what might still be called bestialism—as the characteristic word 'breeding' shows. It is a resignation to making a bad job of life, because

> *The best of a bad job is all any of us make of it—*
> *Except of course, the saints.*

And as this position is reached, it is necessary to look again very critically at the idea of sacrifice. For sacrifice now does not redeem the world, or bring new life to the waste land. Rather, in an obscure way, it ratifies the world as it is. Eliot's Christian action is not tragic redemption, but tragic resignation. 'Something' may be terribly wrong, and we are 'somehow' involved in this wrong, but at this level of consciousness we begin again, with the cocktail party. It is difficult to resist the conclusion that this is a social pearl of some price: a theoretical justification for continuing this kind of half-living, but with a consciousness of disorder as a saving clause. As the guests arrive, and the drinks are poured, life will go on much as usual (we are resigned to that), but of course we will not forget Celia, who died so terribly. Sacrifice, really, is what saints are for, but we, we go on with the cocktail party. Thus an ironic footnote is written to the original division of humanity between the conscious elite or elect and the unconscious majority. Theirs is the tragedy, ours the comfortable farce. Neither way is better, but we must choose between them. We choose.

Indeed Eliot, in *The Cocktail Party*, abandons the Christian tradition of sacrifice and redemption. He removes its action elsewhere, and to a minority. He replaces it, as the controlling structure of feeling, with a socially modulated resignation. Yet perhaps he does not altogether abandon sacrifice, in one of its senses. It looks to me very much as if Celia had to die, for the needs of this group. Elsewhere, naturally. Terribly, of course. But in such a way that the blood does not stain or shame, or at least not for long. In such a way that redemption, in any whole sense, is fine but is for others. In such a way that a gesture can be made to her blood, but what will be drunk at the party is the same old cocktail. The darker wine, of an involving crucifixion, is richer and stronger, but we are not in its class. We'll put up with the cocktails, making the best of a bad job.

We need not pursue Eliot further. After *The Cocktail Party* there is a radical loss of substance. As a dramatist he chose the sociable way, but he was never, in any case, very sociable. Those of us who were moved by his tragic challenge, even against the claims of the actual fulfilments of life, cannot be moved in his final half-world, where there is no longer challenge, and where there was never living fulfilment.

To move from the world of Eliot's cocktail party, where the sound of human beings was heard as the rubbing of insects' legs, to the world of Zhivago, where a whole society is in known torment, is to be reminded sharply of the true status of literature. Here, with remarkable intensity and seriousness, life and death reappear as experiences, rather than as literary attitudes. The preoccupation with tone, which has for so long imprisoned us, is challenged and swept aside by the whole content of literary art. The importance of Pasternak's work, in this sense, is beyond question.

Dr Zhivago has been given two contrary interpretations: that it is the story of a sensitive individual crushed by a soulless collective action; and that it is the story of a man unable to change as his world changes, and so breaking and dying. But each of these readings is partial. The theme of the second, while undoubtedly present, is unacceptable as a whole reading because of the significance given to the individual history, which is clearly much more than a demonstration of incompatibility. One incompatible is highly valued, and we must see why. At this point the first reading asserts itself, in a context prepared by politics. The novel is what happens to 'the individual' in a socialist revolution. We are with Zhivago and Lara, in their fidelity to personal experience, against the brutality and meaninglessness of the collective scheme of things. But this sort of thing is so easily said—the half-truths and evasions involved in it so taken for granted—that we ought in any case to be wary of it. I believe that in accepting this pattern, for which again there is partial justification, we are missing something quite crucial, and much more important. We are missing the conception of life as sacrifice, which in the end gives meaning to both the individual and the social histories, and around which, essentially, the novel is built.

It is worth rejecting the ordinary ethical reading at once. If the positive value in the novel is fidelity to personal experience, it has to be said that Pasternak has quite disastrously failed to embody it. At the level of personal experience, the pattern is consistently one of betrayal, or apparent betrayal. Zhivago, as an ethical hero, is monstrous. It is not merely the revolution, the collective formula, that he abandons, but every person with whom he is in any way involved. Three times in the book, with a patterned consistency, he abandons the woman he loves or to whom he has given children. As a doctor he abandons the practice of his life-caring skills, and the persons by whom they are needed. His whole development, indeed, is as consistently away from individual human beings as from the collective action itself.

Of course this can, after a fashion, be seen as personally authentic. A fidelity to personal experience can (fifty years of Western literature have been proving it) practically exclude other persons. But the novel is not written in this way. The separation of Zhivago, as a character, is a product of criticism rather than of the actual narrative. The error is comparable to that of the editors of *Novy Mir*, who produced an ethical case against the central character and thought they had produced a critical case against the book. What both readings miss is the shape of the narrative as a whole. Neither, for example, can include in its reading the important penultimate scene, in which the daughter of Yury and Lara, deserted and suffering, is given great emphasis of feeling. Is this lost girl merely a hurried postcript to a humane love? Or is the emphasis on her compatible with the ethical underwriting of Zhivago which the Soviet critics saw as the purpose of the novel?

We must begin in another way, with a recognition that the novel is about men and women in history:

> Now what is history? Its beginning is that of the centuries of systematic work devoted to the solution of the enigma of death, so that death itself may eventually be overcome.

That is Nikolai, in an early conversation. It can be paralleled, later, from Yury:

> He realised, more vividly than ever before, that art has two constant, two unending preoccupations: it is always meditating upon death and it is always thereby creating life.

To make art is then to participate in the release of spirit which is the movement of history. Nikolai describes this release as

> firstly, the love of one's neighbour—the supreme form of living energy. Once it fills the heart of man it has to overflow and spend itself. And secondly, the two concepts which are the main part of the make-up of modern man—without them he is inconceivable—the ideas of free personality and of life regarded as sacrifice.

The design of the narrative springs from these ideas. I mean design in the formal sense, in the pattern of thought and action. This pattern is controlled, at the structural level, by the network of meetings and repetitions which have been described as coincidences (and sometimes blamed as clumsy). In fact, quite clearly, this design is beyond the wills of any of the characters, and is meant to be seen as such. 'The way God brings us together', Lara says at Yury's death, and this is more than a conventional phrase. As Nikolai says,

> it is possible to be an atheist, it is possible not to know if God exists or why He should, and yet to believe that man does not live in a state of nature but in history.

This is the world the novel creates. 'History began with Christ', Nikolai says, and the sense here is of the response to death, and the living resurrection. It is not so much that Yury is a Christ-figure as that the whole novel is this action.

The Russian Revolution is not, in this design, an external collective action; it is, as it was, an historical process. Of the child Lara, Strelnikov says:

> You could indict the century in her name.

Lenin is seen by Strelnikov as this indictment and retribution:

> And side by side with him there arose before the eyes of the world the immeasurably vast figure of Russia, bursting into flames like a light of redemption for all the sorrows and misfortunes of mankind.

This is not merely the view of 'the opposition' in the novel. The making of Pasha Antipov into Strelnikov is one of the many instances of the reality of the general process. The revolution is fire and redemption, but it is also fire and hardening, fire and destruction. The personal and the general are connected in the beginning, as Yury says:

> The revolution broke out willy-nilly, like a breath that's been held too long. Everyone was revived, reborn, changed, transformed. You might say that everyone has been through two revolutions—his own personal revolution as well as the general one. It seems to me that socialism is the sea, and all these separate streams, these private individual revolutions, are flowing into it—the sea of life, of life in its own right.

F*

But

> this new thing, this marvel of history, this revelation is exploded right into the very thick of daily life without the slightest consideration for its course

Similarly,

> mourning for Lara, he also mourned that distant summer in Melyuzeyevo when the revolution had been a god come down to earth from heaven . . . when everyone's life existed in its own right and not as an illustration to a thesis in support of higher policy.

But

> revolutions are made by fanatical men of action with one-track minds, men who are narrow-minded to the point of genius. They overturn the old order in a few hours or days; the whole upheaval takes a few weeks or at most years, but for decades thereafter, for centuries, the spirit of narrowness which led to the upheaval is worshipped as holy.

This is what happens to the 'revolution for life in its own right', but it is not only degeneration; it is also dialectical in its movement:

> However much we look at (the forest), we see it as motionless. And such also is the immobility, to our eyes, of the eternally growing, ceaselessly changing life of society, of history moving as invisibly in its incessant transformations as the forest in spring.

The antithesis to the revolution for 'life in its own right' is the destruction of

> everything established, settled, everything to do with home and order and the common round.

This, significantly, is said by Lara, mistress and adulteress. She and Yury are at once the witnesses and the victims of this process, as is their daughter, abandoned by them:

> all that's left is the bare, shivering human soul, stripped to the last shred, the naked force of the human psyche for which nothing has changed because it was always cold and shivering and reaching out to its nearest neighbour, as cold and lonely as itself.

The human crisis of the revolution is that

> man is born to live, not to prepare for life.

The tragedy of Yury and Lara, as of Tanya and of Strelnikov, is a progressive loss of personality, as the destructive force of the revolution extends. Here indeed is the key to the novel: not the assertion of personality, against the collective action, but the loss of personality which is at once the result of the revolution and the greatest danger to it. At the end, Tanya and the revolutionary society are virtually identified: the daughter of the love of Yury and Lara, and the daughter of the revolution. Her exposure is the result of the whole action, in which we cannot significantly set one part against the rest. It is only in comprehending this total design that Yury's life is given its pattern.

The Revolution, that is to say, is seen as a sacrifice of life for life: not simply the killing, to make way for a new order, but the loss of the reality of life while a new life is being made. It is on this death that the novel meditates, and from it that it creates life. Here are its ideas of free personality and of life regarded as sacrifice. Yury is the embodiment of these ideas, in a single action, and his poems, which end the book, are its essential definition:

> *Surely it is my calling*
> *To see that the distances should not lose heart*
> *And that beyond the limits of the town*
> *The earth should not feel lonely?*
> *That is why in early spring*
> *My friends and I gather together*
> *And our evenings are farewells*
> *And our parties are testaments,*
> *So that the secret stream of suffering*
> *May warm the cold of life.*

The calling is a particular kind of redemption through suffering, as the revolution itself had originally been. It is a loss of personality, so that the stream may flow again, and bring human warmth to the earth, where there is now a general loneliness. He lives through his loneliness, towards a general redemption, a movement towards others that is a loss of himself:

And life itself is only an instant,
Only the dissolving
Of ourselves in all others
As though in gift to them.

Or again:

I feel for each of them
As if I were in their skin,
I melt with the melting snow,
I frown with the morning.
In me are people without names,
Children, stay-at-homes, trees.
I am conquered by them all
And this is my only victory.

In this kind of action, there is no hero and no victim. Yury cannot be separated out for ethical approval or disapproval. His action is the general action: the seemingly paradoxical design of a sacrifice or a revolution. This is only finally clear in the epilogue: first in the reflections on the war:

> The war has its special character as a link in the chain of revolutionary decades. It marks the end of the direct action of the causes inherent in the nature of the upheaval itself. By now, secondary causes are at work: we are seeing the fruit of its fruit, the result of its results—characters tempered by misfortune, unspoilt, heroic, ready for great, desperate, unheard-of deeds. These fabulous, astounding qualities are the moral flowering of this generation.

The dialectic has worked itself through, and the paradox of a man saving his life through losing it, of a people renewing its life through destroying it, has been understood. 'The fruit of its fruit, the result of its results.' 'I am conquered by them all, and this is my only victory.' It is not a pious hope, but the completion of Pasternak's pattern, when in Moscow, after the war,

> this freedom of the spirit was there . . . on that very evening the future had become almost tangible in the streets below . . . they had themselves entered that future and would, from now on, be part of it.

It is an emphasis of this pattern, again, when it is through Yuri's poems that this future is known—the art that has meditated on death has created life—and when the salvation is seen not as personal but as general:

> Moscow below them and reaching into the distance . . . now appeared to them, not as the place where all these things had happened, but as the heroine of a long tale of which that evening, book in hand, they were reaching the end.

It is not surprising that both in the West and in the Soviet Union this structure of feeling should have been misunderstood. It is a very original fusion (though with some precedents in Russian literature) of the Christian idea of redemption and the Marxist idea of history. It is thus open to attack from both sides. Much western Christianity has separated redemption from social change, even if it accepts both. And orthodox Marxism has separated history from the personal reality which is its inescapable process, substituting an historical impersonality through which men and women are finally seen and judged. Pasternak, seeing the action of sacrifice as the action of growth and change, has moved, doctrinally, into no-man's land, and can expect rejection and dilution. Yet literature, as he affirmed, carries its own kinds of energy. The action of sacrifice, a giving of life to renew the general life, is limited, in Eliot, to dogma, or reduced to a marginal significance within a general resignation. In either case, the answering vitality is small. The extraordinary vitality of Pasternak's novel makes the essential contrast. Here, against all the odds, the idea of sacrifice creates and controls a much deeper and richer life than one would have believed possible. It is nature and history, man and society, in a single pattern. It is a story of absolute suffering and sacrifice, yet, through its controlling idea, it is also an account of

> joy in the whole universe, its form, its beauty, the feeling of their own belonging to it, being part of it.

It is in this sense that we can agree with Zhivago's own note:

> every work of art, including tragedy, witnesses to the joy of existence. . . . It is always meditating upon death, and it is always thereby creating life.

6

TRAGIC DESPAIR AND REVOLT

CAMUS, SARTRE

Albert Camus said in 1945:

> The public is tired of the Atridae, of adaptations from antiquity, of
> that modern tragic sense which, alas, is all too rarely present in ancient
> myths however generously they may be stuffed with anachronisms.
> A great modern form of the tragic must and will be born. Certainly I
> shall not achieve this; perhaps none of our contemporaries will. But
> this does not lessen our duty to assist in the work of clearance which
> is now necessary so as to prepare the ground for it. We must use our
> limited means to hasten its arrival.

This is not simply an aspiration towards a new dramatic form.
The desire for a new form is a recognition that our modern
sense of tragedy is of a new kind, needing radically different
expression. This should hardly need arguing, but we have in
fact been oppressed by a traditional persistence, in the
definition of tragedy, which has often succeeded in persuading
us that it has a kind of copyright both in the experience and
in the form. The humanism of the twentieth century, we have
been told, is so shallow in its optimism, so beguiled by
rationality, so helpless when faced by resolute evil, that
tragedy is necessarily beyond its powers.

Nothing will be gained, no clarity will be achieved, if what
is attacked as humanism, by these familiar critics, is simply
the ordinary parody. If the argument is to become honest,
Camus, inevitably, will be a central figure. It is not only that
in his best work he can be accurately described as a tragic
humanist. It is also that humanism itself, in the violence of
this century, is of a new kind, which cannot be rendered back,
for convenience, to its nineteenth-century forms. The important and still active transition from a liberal to a socialist
humanism is only one of these permanent changes.

'Today tragedy is collective', Camus wrote, in the course
of that political journalism which was one form of his
deliberate exposure to the tragic experience of his time. (The

French intellectual tradition, which made this kind of participation normal, is in this respect notably more humane and more alive than the prim specialisation which still tries to prevail in England.) The recognition of this new scale of events is decisive. Yet Camus brought to this recognition, without which nothing is possible, his own deeply rooted attitudes to life, which were also, in themselves, tragic. The words which summarise these attitudes are despair and revolt, and we must look into them more closely, in his developing work.

The condition of despair, as Camus describes it, occurs at the point of recognition of what is called 'the absurd'. This 'absurdity', in Camus, is less a doctrine than an experience. It is a recognition of incompatibilities: between the intensity of physical life and the certainty of death; between man's insistent reasoning and the non-rational world he inhabits. These permanent contradictions can be intensified by particular circumstances: the decline of spontaneous life into mechanical routines; the awareness of isolation from others and even from ourselves. By whatever channel the recognition may come, the result can be an intense despair: a loss of meaning and value in one's world, one's society, one's own immediate life. In *The Myth of Sisyphus* Camus describes and communicates this despair rooted in a sense of fundamental absurdity, and faces what appears to be its logical outcome: the act of suicide.

This much is generally known, and has been willingly received. In its power and authenticity, it has been taken up into that post-war orthodoxy which I have described as the tragic stalemate. What is less known, and even less acknowledged, though the facts are clear, is that Camus did not find this a position in which he could rest (though he may later, ambiguously, have returned to it). Indeed it was precisely here, where the denial of humanism ordinarily begins, that Camus most notably affirmed his humanism. He rejected suicide, both as a physical act, and in the more common form of retreat into an irrational philosophy. He rejected it because the problem, after such a recognition, is still how to live. It is no solution to collapse the tension between life and death, by merely choosing death, or between our insistent reasoning and our non-rational world, by choosing irrationalism. The essential problem is to live in full recognition of the contradictions and within the tensions they produce, yet the weight is then such that we are always seeking, by open or covert means, to collapse or reduce them. Despair itself, which has been presented as an inevitable conclusion, is in fact merely one of our means of evasion.

As Camus put it:

> A certain kind of optimism, of course, is not my strong point. With the rest of my generation I grew up to the drumbeats of the First World War, and our history since then has continued the tale of murder, injustice or violence. But real pessimism, as we meet it today, consists in trading on all this cruelty and infamy. For my part, I have fought unceasingly against this degradation; I hate only those who are cruel. In the darkest depths of our nihilism, I have sought only for the means to transcend nihilism.

This is the essential challenge to that tragic resignation which we have seen, for example, in Eliot. Camus, as writer and humanist, put all his strength into going beyond that point at which humanism is supposed to break down into despair. As he wrote:

> Real despair means death, the grave or the abyss. If despair prompts speech or reasoning, and above all if it results in writing, fraternity is established, natural objects are justified, love is born. A literature of despair is a contradiction in terms.

It is at this point that his tragic humanism begins.

The achievement would be less interesting if Camus had not known, or had been unable to create, the sense of tragic absurdity and despair which he wished to transcend. *The Outsider* cannot be read as autobiography; it is essentially an objective presentation. Yet its extraordinary power makes it seem much more than the taking of a case. The loss of connection and relationship in Meursault, combined with his intense awareness of himself in all other respects, is a genuinely tragic situation of a new kind. That it leads to murder is convincing. The loss of connection with others, which is also a loss of connection with reality, is in that sense fatal. Meursault kills feeling that he is being attacked, but he has lost connection, at this point, not only with what the other is actually doing, but with what he himself is doing. When the reaction comes, from a society that must punish murder, it can still not reach him. In this sense it is accurate to say that he is being condemned to death because he did not weep at his mother's funeral. The continuity of feeling and action, and of their negatives in Meursault, is real. But equally, the society is to punish killing by killing. Its own loss of connection is dramatically demonstrated, at the central point of its legal and moral assurance. Certainly the crime is absurd, but so is the punishment absurd, its assumption of authority over life and death absurd. The novel ends in a tension which is in fact an awakening in Meursault: an intense awareness of his own life and situation, as he is condemned to death. The legal, moral and religious authorities have no such awareness, of either life or death. Merely an alienated world claims one of its own, and in the sudden act of consciousness is despised for its blindness. This is not despair, but a tragic affirmation. As Camus wrote: 'the opposite of the suicide is, precisely, the man who is condemned to death'. Or again, in the definition of Sisyphus, which reminds us of the final position of Meursault:

> The lucidity that was to constitute his torture at the same time crowns his victory. There is no fate that cannot be surmounted by scorn.

Or so Camus hopes, at least. This is a position open to the individual consciousness, in one kind of revolt against the absurd condition. It is the position of Caligula, who, when asked what is his secret solace, replies again 'Scorn'. Yet in Caligula the revolt against despair is not a lucid indifference but an assertion of freedom, in an active way:

> This world has no importance; once a man realises that, he wins his freedom. And that is why I hate you, you and your kind; because you are not free.

It is on this that Cherea opposes him:

> All I wish is to regain some peace of mind in a world that has regained a meaning. What spurs me on is not ambition but fear, my very reasonable fear of that inhuman vision in which my life means no more than a speck of dust.

Caligula, in power, follows his own logic:

> There's no understanding Fate; therefore I choose to play the part
> of Fate. I wear the foolish unintelligible face of a professional god.
> . . . Any man can play lead in the divine comedy and become a god.
> All he need do is to harden his heart.

The indifferent and arbitrary cruelty of the world is then
positively enacted, but Caligula is not merely a tyrant; he
extends the indifference to himself:

> It's a fact that I don't respect (human life) more than I respect my
> own life. And if I find killing easy, it's because dying isn't hard for
> me.

So Caligula becomes, in his own terms, free; free to create the
world in his own image: arbitrary, indifferent, cruel.

> When I don't kill, I feel alone. The living don't suffice to people my
> world and dispel my boredom. I have an impression of an enormous
> void when you and the others are here, and my eyes see nothing but
> empty air. No, I'm at ease only in the company of my dead.

The logic of the absurd, and of its consequent despair, seems
complete, but the play, finally, is

> an account of the most human and most tragic of mistakes. Caligula
> is faithless towards humanity in order to keep faith with himself.

This is the redefinition of humanism, on the other side of
despair. Caligula knows in the end that

> I have chosen a wrong path, a path that leads to nothing. My freedom
> isn't the right one.

As Camus put it, later:

> The moral lesson which I think emerges from the play . . . is that one
> cannot be free by being against other people.

This, in its way, is another ending of liberal humanism, and its
replacement by a tragic humanism. Tragic because the error
of Caligula is common and understandable; only the ruthless
logic of its execution is exceptional. The facts of absurdity and
despair are seen as a common condition, most notably perhaps
in *Cross Purpose* (*Le Malentendu*). In a sense this is the most
tragic, or at least the most desperate, of Camus' works. For

he is not here dramatising an individual consciousness, set in relief against an unknowing world, but a total condition. At this point, most clearly, Camus interlocks with the worlds of Pirandello and Eliot.

A man returns, after a long absence, to the inn kept by his mother and sister. He does not reveal his identity, for he wants the pleasure of recognition. But the sister, actively, to regain her freedom of movement, and the mother, indifferently, kill any guest who is alone and has money. On the edge of recognition, but still unknowing, they kill the man who is brother and son. And in this, again, they are not exceptional. Failure of recognition is general; the relationships are not seen, or are not seen in time. 'Life', the sister claims, 'is more cruel than we are'. And again:

> Neither for him nor for us, neither in life nor in death, is there any peace or homeland.

Nor is there any pity from outside; the gods are stonily deaf, like the manservant who ends the play, speaking to the widow:

MARIA: Hear me and raise me from the dust, oh Heavenly Father. Have pity on those who love each other and are parted.

MANSERVANT: What's all this noise? Did you call me?

MARIA: Oh! I don't know. But help me, help me, for I need help. Be kind and say that you will help me.

MANSERVANT: No.

The mother and sister, having realised their guilt, take their own lives.

A problem arises here, of the most profound importance. The voice speaks of pity and kindness, but the action speaks of fate, an indifferent, arbitrary and tragic fate. And we have to ask (Camus would have insisted on asking) what are the sources of this perceived condition, especially when it is asserted as common. There is an ambiguity, an honest ambiguity, at the centre of Camus' work, for he recognises the sources of this condition in particular circumstances, and yet also asserts that it is absolute. The point is particularly interesting in relation to *Le Malentendu*, which is said to be based on the report of an actual murder in Czechoslovakia.

The play is in fact remarkably similar to Lillo's *Fatal Curiosity* (1736), which is said to be based on an actual murder in Cornwall. There a father and mother kill a stranger who is in fact their son, for a casket of jewels which he has brought from India and deposited with them. When the son's identity is discovered, the father kills his wife and then himself.

What interests me most is not the similarity of plot, but the similarity in structure of feeling. Lillo's play was a very early example of bourgeois tragedy, and can be seen as a response to the actual disruption of relationships, and particularly of the family, by the abstract emphasis on money as the only living currency. Yet, if it is such a response, it is also disguised. At the centre of this perception, in most early bourgeois tragedy, something abruptly called Fate is made into the active agent. How fatal, how terrible, that it was a son! Yet the destructive agent is in fact money: not simply greed (that ethical diversion, creating a separate class of the guilty) but the need for money, in a society governed by it. The parents in Lillo's play are poor. In Camus' play, the sister's need is to get away to the sun, where she can reach the fullness of her own life. The frustration of life by money is known as tragedy, but its detailed workings are called Fate. Certainly in Lillo, and as certainly, I think, in Camus, a false consciousness has intervened, making the recognition ambiguous. It is not an evasion of the permanent contradictions of life to recognise and name a more particular and temporary contradiction. Rather, the naming of the latter as Fate is itself evasion.

This is a continuing problem, in Camus. For one looks back to *Caligula*, and remembers that part of the arbitrariness of the man is the essential arbitrariness of the Caesar. The tyrannical power, masking itself as divine, is the necessary agent of execution on such a scale. The mask of Fate is then again a process of evasion. Even in *The Outsider*, the condition of Meursault is in part the condition of Algeria. Camus, convincingly, in the novel and in such essays as *Summer in Algier* and *Return to Tipasa*, puts great emphasis on the physical conditions of the country: especially the blinding sun, and the sense that after youth there is in any case nothing to live for: a wholly physical culture finds the period after youth meaningless. And the man Meursault kills is, after all, an Arab.

We have to ask, of so honest a writer, the most difficult question. For any man, his own particular condition is absolute. To argue otherwise is to reject actual men. Yet the assertion of an absolute condition as *common* is something else again. We have to ask how much rhetoric, how much lying rhetoric, is involved in that almost unnoticeable transition, under the power of art, from absolute to common. The point is unusually subtle in relation to Camus, for indeed the assertion of a common condition was an especially valuable part of his own humanist revolt.

Perhaps the key lies in the movement from despair to revolt, which is also the movement from being an exile to being a rebel. Camus has brilliantly described this:

> In absurdist experience, suffering is individual. But from the moment that a movement of rebellion begins, suffering is seen as a collective experience—as the experience of everyone. Therefore the first step for a mind overwhelmed by the strangeness of things is to realise that this feeling of strangeness is shared with all men and that the entire human race suffers from the division between itself and the rest of the world.

Or again:

> If men cannot refer to common values, which they all separately recognise, then man is incomprehensible to man. The rebel demands that these values should be clearly recognized as part of himself because he knows or suspects that, without them, crime and disorder would reign in the world. An act of rebellion seems to him like a demand for clarity and unity. The most elementary rebellion, paradoxically, expresses an aspiration to order.

Included in rebellion, by the facts of consciousness and of speech, is the artist. The general condition is:

> I *rebel*, therefore we *exist*.

And it is so, now, for the artist:

> The artist, whether he likes it or not, can no longer be a solitary, except in the melancholy triumph which he owes to all his fellow-artists. Rebellious art also ends by revealing the 'We are', and with it the way to a burning humility.

Everything depends, here, on the definition of revolt, which we shall have to examine. But the movement from individual to collective suffering is crucial in Camus. In *Le Malentendu* the movement is still rhetorical; in *The Plague*, convincingly, it is actual. Or, to put it another way, in *Le Malentendu* there is an aggregation of individual absurdist suffering, whereas in *The Plague* there is a common process of collective suffering. To distinguish these conditions is our central problem.

The humanity of Oran, before the plague, is a humanity of habit. People work, love and die

> with the same feverish yet casual air. The truth is that everyone is bored, and devotes himself to cultivating habits.

The facts of the epidemic are at first accommodated within these habits, after the initial refusal to accept the facts at all. But, inevitably, the plague at its full extent disrupts the ordinary social consciousness. In the presence of a collectively arbitrary death, the people of Oran take on a

> family likeness. . . . These men and women had come to wear the aspect of the part they had been playing for so long: the part of emigrants whose faces first, and now their clothes, told of long banishment from a distant homeland.

It is within this condition of common exile that Rieux expresses his characteristic revolt:

> Whenever tempted to add his personal note to the myriad voices of the plague-stricken, he was deterred by the thought that not one of his sufferings but was common to all the others and that in a world where sorrow is so often lonely this was an advantage. Thus decidedly it was up to him to speak for all.

He learns during the plague

> that there are more things to admire in men than to despise.

Yet, while the suffering and the sense of exile are common, the essential revolt is not. After the exhilaration, the sense of equality and brotherhood, which the end of the plague brings, people will in fact forget and resume their habits.

> The tale he had to tell could not be one of a final victory. It could only be the record of what had had to be done, and what assuredly would have to be done again in the never-ending fight against terror

and its relentless onslaughts, despite their personal afflictions, by all who, while unable to be saints but refusing to bow down to pestilences, strive their utmost to be healers.

The true dimension of the tragic humanism of Camus is now evident. The humanism is insistent: a refusal to despair; a commitment to heal. But the tragedy lies in the common condition, against which the revolt is made. There, among most people, both despair and commitment are shut off by habits, which may be interrupted but will always be resumed.

Thus while the suffering is genuinely collective, the revolt is inevitably individual. The last rhythm of liberal tragedy is again heard. The capacity of history to change the common condition, in any essential way, is implicitly denied. Thus revolt is sharply distinguished from revolution.

This important distinction is made again in *The Just*. But now it is a harder case, because while the suffering of the plague could be seen as unhistorical and external to men, at most as the product of indifference and neglect, the suffering against which Kaliaev and his group rebel is undeniably historical; the Tsarist tyranny. However, as Camus interprets their rebellion and terrorism, this is again revolt, and not revolution. The value of their action is in their own negation of it:

> Their only apparent victory is to triumph, at least over solitude and negation. In the midst of a world which they deny and which rejects them, they try, one after another, like all courageous men, to reconstruct a brotherhood of man. The love they bear for one another which brings them happiness even in the desert of a prison, which extends to the great mass of their enslaved and silent fellow-men, gives the measure of their distress and their hopes. To realize this love, they must first kill; to inaugurate the reign of innocence, they must accept a certain degree of culpability. This contradiction will only be resolved for them at the very last moment.

Thus the value of their terrorism is not in any historical inauguration, in the common sense. Simply, they live the whole contradiction: that violence is at once inevitable and unjustifiable. To appeal to history, like revolutionaries, would be an evasion of this actual tension, in their own lives. So, they conceived the idea of offering themselves as a justification and of replying by personal sacrifice to the question they asked themselves. For them, as for all rebels before them, murder was identified with suicide. A life is paid for by another life, and from these two sacrifices springs the promise of a value.

In feeling, Camus is here very close to Pasternak, except that there is a direct commitment to activity, rather than the acceptance of sacrifice within an apparent resignation. Stepan, in *The Just*, marks the next and, to Camus, disastrous stage. Stepan is prepared to kill, as a revolutionary, without offering his own life. He will risk his life, but not sacrifice it. Thus he accepts what is, to Camus, an intolerable guilt, masked only by the evasion of the appeal to history.

Camus touches, at this point, what is undoubtedly our central tragic preoccupation. Certainly his exposure of the ordinary lying of the appeal to history is convincing. He is right to say that it is putting an abstraction above actual life. Yet there is an ambiguity here, nevertheless. Camus seems, again and again, to take an historical action, and to draw much of his feeling from it, only to put it, in the end, outside history. This sense of a history outside history is continually disturbing. For the reality we have to face in the end is that while history is an abstraction it is still an abstraction from the actual lives of ourselves and others. There is a point at which the refusal of history, the limitation of significance to the personally known and affirmed, becomes in effect the refusal of others, and this also can be evasion and even complicity.

It is here that the famous quarrel with Sartre takes on a central importance in the experience of our century. Sartre accused Camus of 'a bitter wisdom which seeks to deny time', and argued that while Camus was ostensibly in revolt against historical suffering, he was less concerned to end this than to find a personally satisfying position: a metaphysical revolt against an eternal injustice. There is obviously some truth in this, though it omits the essential qualification of 'personally satisfying'; 'I rebel, therefore we exist.' The authentic personal voice is a voice speaking for, and not simply of, a common condition.

The essential argument is confused, for two reasons: first, that Sartre, as his early work shows, shares with Camus those perceptions of the absurd which are the starting-point of the metaphysical rebel; secondly, that when Sartre speaks of history, he in fact takes the Marxist version of history as its substance, and so, ironically, for the purposes of argument, does Camus. Thus their argument, which at times has the appearance of a confrontation between absolute positions, is in fact a series of variations on two relative positions and their consequences.

Already, in *The Flies*, Sartre is creating his own version of the metaphysical rebel. The action of Orestes is a rejection of guilt and despair, and of any order beyond man:

> Your whole universe is not enough to prove me wrong. You are the king of gods, king of stones and stars, king of the waves of the sea. But you are not the king of man.

Orestes becomes free by assuming the personal consequences of his defiance. At the same time, by this personal action, he liberates his city from the cloud of flies and blood. By the form of the Greek story, he is the man destined to the decisive action; thus the metaphysical rebel can be seen also as the liberating hero. Diego, in Camus' *The State of Siege*, has the same double role.

The more difficult question returns in *Crime Passionel*, where the confrontation is not with pestilence but with history. It is probable that the play is confused, certainly by Sartre's own afterthoughts about it. It is possible to read it as in part the familiar Freudian gloss on historical actions: Hugo could not kill Hoederer for public reasons, but he can kill him in personal jealousy. The public reasons are themselves made ambiguous by the shift in the party line which makes Hoederer first a traitor and then a hero. Of such ironic reversals and ambiguities of motive, history, the play seems to assert, is in fact composed. Authenticity is then a matter of personal intention, of the meaning given to the act by the man who commits it. Other kinds of meaning are inevitably secondary and confused. This is then still the morality of revolt, and not of revolution. A personal meaning can be asserted, and confirmed by dying for it, but there are no effective meanings beyond this.

Sartre's attempts to move from this position are important. Already in *Men without Shadows* the essential argument has

begun. The values of the Resistance are not in question, but
the particular operation in which the group have been
captured may have been wrongly conceived. Henri's motives
in killing the boy who might have talked are questionable, or
at least are questioned. In the extremes of exile and despair,
after capture, the decision has to be taken between a self-
justifying death and the limited actions by which they can
still be useful to the cause. They make the decision to be
useful, by a common morality, but are killed anyway, by a
cruel lie which has all the effect of the wholly arbitrary.

This movement towards the morality of usefulness is continued in *Le Diable et le Bon Dieu*. Here Goetz comes to see
that in a world without God, and in a time of violent social
conflict, the important commitment is not to goodness, which
is impossible, but to the cause of liberation. This is the
position reached by Kaliaev and his group in *The Just*, but
the difference of resolution is crucial. Goetz assumes the
weight of the same contradictions, but will resolve them by
action rather than by offering his own life:

> I shall fill them with horror since I have no other means of loving
> them, I shall give them orders since I have no other way of obeying.
> I shall remain alone with this empty sky above me since I have no
> other way of being with everybody. There is this war to be waged and
> I shall wage it.

This is the final point of development, from revolt to
revolution.

The quarrel between Sartre and Camus occurred, precisely, at this point of transition. For Sartre, revolution must
be accepted, if any final personal authenticity is to be attained.
And if revolution, then political realism and if necessary
violence. Camus, however, continued to insist on the distinction between revolt and revolution, and saw revolution as
a collapse of authentic tension.

> Revolt demands unity, historical revolution demands totality. The
> first starts from a 'no' based on a 'yes', the second starts from absolute
> negation and condemns itself to every kind of slavery in order to
> create an affirmation transferred to the end of time. The one is
> creative, the other nihilistic.

The argument is important, but the point comes when one

can see it as taking place on altogether too narrow grounds. It is not only that Camus identifies revolution with only one kind of revolution, in which slavery and draining the present of value are inevitable. It is also that Sartre, defending revolution, puts his whole stress on its violence, which indeed seems at times to be not merely necessary but actively purifying. For or against, both writers identify historical revolution with a kind of willed violence, and of course they have much of the experience of our century on their side.

At the same time it is worth noticing that this particular colouring is continuous with the view of man which both writers, as a matter of creative practice, seem to hold. If we compare Sartre's early *Huis Clos* with his most recent *Altona*, we discover that in the later play a political dimension has been added to the identical (Pirandellian) version of human beings as inevitably mutually destructive and frustrating. It is true that in *Altona* the destructive and frustrating elements are related to capitalism and to imperialist war, but whether this is a primary or a secondary relation we cannot say. If people are as they are in *Huis Clos*—and nearly all Sartre's work confirms that this is his view—it is indeed difficult to believe that revolution could be anything more than nihilism. Even if, at a political level, this corruption is reserved to the old civilizations, and innocence is transferred to the new peoples now entering history, it is difficult to feel that this is more than a tactic, within the long conviction that man as such is evil. The mysticism which follows from any such simple projection is inevitably destructive. If Camus suspected this, he was right to suspect it, and to insist on some kind of immediate affirmation.

To say that there is a conviction that man as such is evil may well be going too far. The truth is that it cannot be a matter of precise demonstration and argument. We can only attend to the kinds of life Sartre in fact adduces, and these, we have to recognize, are of an overwhelmingly negative kind. That he has the courage to believe in freedom, and to support revolution, in spite of such evidence, is important but again secondary. Camus, in this respect, is not his most critical opponent. Certainly, Camus makes closer if very limited affirmations, and has, in his rejections of cruelty and in his delight in physical existence (so different from anything in

Sartre) the voice and tones of an active humanist. But he also begins, and usually ends, in an assumption about the human condition to which this humanism can never be more than a counterpoint.[1] This is the common ground in their versions of tragedy. That one is a tragic humanist, the other a tragic revolutionary, is a divergence at a very much later stage of the experience.

The irony is that the interpretation of experience which bases itself on the absence of pre-existing values, and on the consequent human dereliction, seems itself both metaphysical and a product of a particular historical stage. The contradictions assumed seem neutral, but they are in fact partial. Life is not only negated by death, but is also renewed by birth. The reasoning mind is only *contradicted* by the universe when the supposed irrationality is not merely indifferent but hostile—an assumption about nature (in fact, a late bourgeois version of evolution) that is very near the creative roots of all this writing. The life-death contradiction is limited, in fact, to the kind of individual consciousness especially characteristic of bourgeois philosophy. 'I exist—I shall die' seems absolute, within this experience, but Camus sometimes recognized, at the limits of his strength, that 'we exist' is a permanent alternative proposition, and if this is so, then 'we exist—we shall not die' is in fact a resolution, and one which many men have in practice attained. Just as the experience of life and death is limited, by the unnoticed assumption, to individual and even isolate experience, so, by a related assumption, nature is converted to a kind of theatre; indeed, it had often previously been thus converted, but now the producer has vanished. The universe that is taken as given is in fact the shadow of a supernatural universe. Absence of purpose has weight because of the memory and denial of purpose. Atheism, as so often, is merely a heresy, and not an authentic belief. The hostility that is so often added, as an

---

[1] It is not really surprising that Camus could write *The Fall*, after his works of tragic humanism. His abstraction of a permanent human condition, dressed as the twentieth century, stands alone there, counterpointed only by a falsely mature and evasive irony. The first-person narrative allows a true or false passage from individual to common guilt; a rhetoric, and a possible reservation, behind a literary gesture. As a calculated but guarded retreat from humanism, the book has much in common with Miller's *After the Fall*.

emotional tone, is partly related to this, and partly to an episode in that long history of exploitation which is translated as 'the conquest of nature'. Whether in the bourgeois and bourgeois-marxist versions of nature as matter to be dominated, or in the existentialist version of nature as indifferent or resistant, there is no sense of common process or common life, and this, itself an analogue of individualism, leads inevitably to despair. In these ways, I see the work of Camus and Sartre as the latest and most notable struggle within the deadlock which has, historically, taken over our consciousness. The conclusions they draw, whether of revolt or revolution, are convincing only to the extent that one's own mind remains within the deadlock itself.

It has often been said that tragedy is impossible, in the twentieth century, because our philosophical assumptions are non-tragic. What is then often adduced, as evidence, is the humanism of the Enlightenment or perhaps the Renaissance. I have already argued that this is useless; the humanism that matters is not now of those kinds. What is more important to notice is that the three characteristically new systems of thinking, in our own time—Marxism, Freudianism, Existentialism—are all, in their most common forms, tragic. Man can achieve his full life only after violent conflict; man is essentially frustrated, and divided against himself, while he lives in society; man is torn by intolerable contradictions, in a condition of essential absurdity. From these ordinary propositions, and from their combination in so many minds, it is not surprising that so much tragedy has in fact emerged. The tragic humanism of Camus, the tragic commitment of Sartre, are as far as any of us have reached, and each experience, evidently, is of our own time; these men are at least not Atridae. But the question remains, inevitably, whether this is really as far as we can go, whether under the weight of a common suffering this is our own last word.

7

A REJECTION OF TRAGEDY

BRECHT

The rejection of tragedy has many motives and takes many forms. In the case of Bertolt Brecht, we find at least two kinds of rejection, in different periods of his work, and we find also a series of experiments towards new dramatic forms. In this complicated development, the response to suffering is crucial. Brecht wrote in his poem, *An Die Nachgeborenen*:

Indeed I live in the dark ages!
A guileless word is an absurdity. A smooth forehead betokens
A hard heart. He who laughs
Has not yet heard
The terrible tidings . . .

I came to the cities in a time of disorder
When hunger ruled.
I came among men in a time of uprising
And I revolted with them.
So the time passed away
Which on earth was given me.

I ate my food between massacres.
The shadow of murder lay upon my sleep.
And when I loved, I loved with indifference.
I looked upon nature with impatience.
So the time passed away
Which on earth was given me.

In my time streets led to the quicksand.
Speech betrayed me to the slaughterer.
There was little I could do. But without me
The rulers would have been more secure. This was my hope.

Here, clearly enough, is a consciousness of the weight of suffering, in the modern tragedy of Europe, which is not hyperbole but is precise and literal.

The variety of response to this weight, which we have all, though not equally, borne, is a key to our literature. Brecht lived at least two of its modes: here the identification of a

political system as a main cause of suffering, and the finding
of hope in the fight against it. But it was not always so. In his
early work, Brecht expressed, with characteristic power, one
of the main alternative reactions: a cynical disillusion about
the coexistence of public virtue and public murder, public
morality and public poverty. In his work of the 1920s we find
the characteristic sickness of a mind calloused by so established a coexistence. It is not the callousing of acquiescence,
as it has been with a majority of men. It is rather the deliberate
hardening against open sympathy, the sealing and covering
of a too naked tenderness. If the substance of suffering enters,
with its natural weight, the spectator will be broken, for he
will become a participant. Yet as a participant, he can only
condemn or comprehend the suffering by some active
principle, and this he cannot find. Principle, it seems, is part
of the world he rejects. An evil system is protected by a false
morality. This balance is always delicate, and it can seem
easier and clearer to turn, not against the system, but against
the morality. Then the fact that the morality is part of the
callousing leads to a bitter irony:

> You see, my business is trying to arouse human pity. There are a few
> things that'll move people to pity, a few, but the trouble is, when
> they've been used several times, they no longer work. Human beings
> have the horrid capacity of being able to make themselves heartless
> at will. So it happens, for instance, that a man who sees another man
> on the street corner with only a stump for an arm will be so shocked
> the first time that he'll give him sixpence. But the second time it'll
> be only a threepenny bit. And if he sees him a third time, he'll hand
> him over cold-bloodedly to the police. It's the same with these
> spiritual weapons.
> [*A large board is let down from the flies and on it is written*: '*It is more
> blessed to give than to receive*'.]
> What's the use of the finest and most stirring sayings painted on the
> most enticing boards if they get used up so quickly? There are four or
> five sayings in the Bible that really touch the heart. But when they're
> used up, one's daily bread's just gone.

The operative irony, here, is that this is Peachum, in *The
Threepenny Opera*, using pity as a trade, in his establishment
for beggars. But the structural irony is deeper, and more easily
overlooked. The assumption that human beings can and do

192 MODERN TRAGIC LITERATURE

'make themselves heartless at will' is not only the complaint of the speculator who is exploiting pity. It is also the outraged but controlling assumption of the dramatist, and so the spring of his characteristic tone. Pity and suffering can deceive anyone, if men are like this. And if sympathy can exploit us, it is the last thing we must admit.

The perversion of values, by a false system, can go so deep that only a new and bitter hardness seems relevant. Instead of sympathy, there must be direct shock. In Brecht's plays of the 1920s there is a raw chaotic resentment, a hurt so deep that it requires new hurting, a sense of outrage which demands that people be outraged. So deep is this that it is often expressed in the crudest physical imagery: a revulsion from spit and excrement which demands the exposure and the handling of both; a revulsion from false loving which leads straight to the whore. Many writers have used this simple exposure of dirt, this conscious turning to whores and criminals, as a way of expressing the tragic collapse of virtue. In Joyce, Mayakowsky and Brecht the same patterns of attraction and disgust are clear. In much *avant-garde* writing between the wars, and especially in the 1920s, the naming of filth and the open gesture of anti-morality were felt as creative. Brecht is more open than most, both in his gestures and in his marginal capacity for a different kind of response. *The Threepenny Opera*, for example, is offered or rationalised as a portrait of respectable bourgeois society. If all property is theft, and the institutions of property cold and false, then thieves and whores are the true if shocking portraits of a society trying to pass itself off as respectable. The shock of seeing this will penetrate the established false consciousness.

It does nothing of the kind, of course, and it is not difficult to see why. Nothing is more predictable, in a falsely respectable society, than the conscious enjoyment of a controlled and distanced low life. All such work reveals itself, finally, as a protection of conventional moral attitudes. The thieves and whores are the licensed types, on to whom a repressed immorality can very easily be projected, and through whom a repressed conscience can be safely controlled. There is no real shock, when respectable playgoers confront them, because they are seen, precisely, as a special class, a district. So we get, again and again, the consciously outrageous which

nobody even pretends to be outraged by, but simply settles
back to enjoy.

Brecht, in *The Threepenny Opera*, was caught in his own
paradox. The more people sat back and enjoyed this kind of
action, the safer their ordinary view of life was. When the play
was published, he wrote:

> It is a sort of summary of what the spectator wishes to see of life.
> Since, however, he sees at the same time certain things that he does
> not wish to see and thus sees his wishes not only fulfilled but criticised
> . . . he is, in theory, able to give the theatre a new function[1]. . . .
> Complex seeing must be practised. . . . Thinking *above* the flow of the
> play is more important than thinking from *within* the flow of the play.

'In theory' is right. Brecht had found his theory, in the idea
of complex seeing, but its practice was not there, in the actual
play. He had considered that his 'epic style' would enforce
'thinking *above*', whereas the 'narrative style' of 'Aristotelian
drama' (these terms make no historical or critical sense, but
they are the manifesto terms of Brecht's own creative development) enforced 'thinking from *within*'. He had used distancing effects to push the spectator into 'the attitude of one who
smokes at ease and watches'. But he was himself still confused,
himself not distanced, and there was more ease than either
watching or thinking. The play in fact fitted easily into 'what
the spectator wishes to see': crime and coldness not structural
in the society, but lived out in a romantic and theatrical
district. Of course many speculators, accepted in their generation as writers and artists, have agencies in this district:
making crime and vice theatrical, colourful, and in a simple
way distanced, so that a false society can avoid having to look
at itself. Brecht, I suppose, was never one of them, but he
settled, for a time, in a neighbouring district, in which suffering also is masked. He settled for a conventionally dissident
pattern of feeling, in which he still has company: the bitter-

[1] Brecht, like nearly all important dramatists in the past hundred years,
knew that a 'new function' for the theatre was *resisted* most strongly by 'the
theatre itself': 'today we see the theatre being given absolute priority over the
actual plays. The theatre apparatus's priority is a priority of means of pro-
duction. This apparatus resists all conversion to other purposes, by taking any
play which it encounters and immediately changing it so that it no longer
represents a foreign body within the apparatus. The theatre can stage anything; it theatres it all down'.

G

sweet professional who faced with an immoral society can display immorality as a kind of truth. People buy and sell each other, in *The Threepenny Opera* and on screens and pages beyond counting, with cold hearts and only occasionally covering sentiments, but always with colour, with wit, with the big musical number. And yes, of course, that's life; for who, while the number lasts, finds the nerve to say 'that shouldn't be life', 'that needn't be life'? When he does find the words, he's naive anyway, and a moraliser. But the actual moral is that we can all pretend to be livelier and brighter than we are, dispensing the cold-hearted muck about the warm-hearted whores and engaging crooks who at least are *honest*, who have seen through hypocrisy, who have lived past the earnestness of the old quotations.

In ways like this, the writer who 'shocks', by his rejection of 'conventional morality', becomes rich and admired, and this is no paradox: he has done the State some service, even when he is disposed to deny it. Human wrong has been sealed off. Human suffering is a sick old joke. There is even a kind of moral stability, now that outrage itself is lapsed to a convention. Except that the callousing can become so general that a more openly vicious society can go on with its business of enforcing stability, of violent protection against change, unchallenged, since the moral reserve is deliberately played out.

Fascism, the ultimate protection of propertied society against radical change, fed on much of this bittersweet toughness. What had been imagined and conventionalised could now be done. But not, in the end, by Brecht. He was able to grow quite differently. He thought he had seen through the conventional establishment: that kind of seeing-through which is a parody of opposition and revolt. The society was false and the moralising hypocritical; so. But he came to realise that at this point you have really seen nothing, seen through nothing. For what you have seen is what the society wants you to see: 'eats first, morals after'. Brecht thought he was detaching himself from this by calling it bourgeois morality, but in *The Threepenny Opera* this is so external, so really casual, that it is in effect an indulgence. The displacement of feelings about modern capitalism on to a group of pseudo-eighteenth century thieves and whores is no more than an escape clause. The real detachment, the real distancing, required a new principle and a new start.

In the idea of 'complex seeing' Brecht had his new start, but under the pressure of danger he moved, for a time, in a different direction. He set himself to oppose false society by the idea of a true society, and in his first conscious acceptance of this principled opposition he simplified both his feelings and his plays. The linking work is *Saint Joan of the Stockyards*, where the charity of Joan Dark in the labour struggles of Chicago is not only shown as a false morality, covering crime and exploitation, but as a feeling to be consciously rejected and replaced by a new hardness:

> *The ones that tell them they may be raised in spirit*
> *And still be stuck in the mud, they should have their heads*
> *Knocked on the pavement. No!*
> *Only force helps where force rules. . . .*

For saying this, Joan is of course first suppressed and then canonised, in her former charitable innocence. Something of the later complexity is briefly present. But the new positive line soon takes over. In *Die Massnahme* Brecht offers what he takes to be a revolutionary morality: that the party worker who shows too much human sympathy (being moved by the presence of suffering to an attempt at alleviation and partial reform) endangers the revolutionary effort and must be killed. But this is not any dialectical transformation of goodness into its opposite. It is a willing rejection of goodness as it is immediately known. We must say of this play what Orwell said of Auden's line in *Spain*:

> *The conscious acceptance of guilt in the necessary murder. . . .* It could only be written by a person to whom murder is at most a *word.*[1]

[1] There are other things to say about Auden's line and Orwell's description of it. Murder is usually either a personal act or part of a specifically criminal pattern. There are, of course, political murders, but these are only one aspect of the general fact of political violence. Auden is simplifying, perhaps deliberately, to the norms of his own world, but so, in another way, is Orwell. It is interesting to imagine the line rewritten as 'the conscious acceptance of guilt in the necessary killing' and then ask how many people, in reality, dissent from this. Most people I know, and most humane liberals I have heard of, accept killing in this sense again and again: from Dresden to Hiroshima, and from Stanleyville to Da Nang. If Auden got his commitment too easily and cheaply, Orwell and others have got their humane dissent on much the same terms.

The complicated issues of revolutionary violence cannot be settled by a simple formula, either way. The weight of the choice of killing is, in experience, tragic. But its reduction to a hard formalised gesture is merely wilful. Indeed, the most important thing to be said about such a gesture is not political, but cultural. This brittle literary voice, which can set a tone towards killing that appears anti-romantic, is simply the perverted romanticism of the earlier uncommitted decadence. As a literary line, it follows directly from the bittersweet amoralism, sharing with it a persuasive capacity to keep real experience at a distance. The literary revolutionary, with his tough talk of necessary killing, turns out in fact to be our former acquaintance: the honest criminal or the generous whore. This connection between the decadence and what was supposed to be a positive response to it has been widely and dangerously overlooked.

The extraordinary thing about Brecht is that he was able to grow through this position. Relapse from it is easy, as the later Auden has shown. The emphasis of love can look like growth, but is often a simple withdrawal from the human action in which love is being affirmed and fought for. Love is then defined and capitalised in separation from humanity. Brecht, however, learned to look beyond either formula, into the genuine complexity: the connections and contradictions between individual goodness and social action. It was this dimension of experience and perception which required his method of complex seeing. His first achievement, in this new kind, was *Mother Courage and her Children*, but it will be convenient, in describing the method, to look first at *The Good Woman of Sezuan*.

In this play Brecht invites us to look at what happens to a good person in a bad society: not by assertion, but by a dramatic demonstration. Shen Te is linked to some of his earlier figures in that she first appears as the conventional kind-hearted prostitute (in an alienated society the most alienated person is good). But this is almost incidental to the main action. Brecht seeks to show, through Shen Te, how goodness is exploited, by gods and men. Where goodness cannot extend, but is merely used and abused, there is a split in consciousness. The only consistent way out is through sacrifice: an acceptance of sacrifice which can become redeeming, as in Christ. Brecht rejected any such acceptance, as he similarly rejected the idea that suffering can ennoble us. Christ, after all, was the son of God as well as the son of Man, and the significance of his action depends ultimately on a superhuman design. Rejecting the superhuman design, Brecht had the courage to reject sacrifice as a dramatic emotion. For even sacrifice is used, in the continuing human game (it had been used, he might have seen, in *Die Massnahme*). The ratifying fact about the martyr is that he is dead. Life can pass him by with a timeserving bob to his nobility. And just as it is a bad society that needs heroes, so it is a bad life that needs sacrifices. By a change of dramatic viewpoint, we have to look not only at the isolated experience of the martyr, but at the social process of his martyrdom. For this is where we live, we who are not martyrs. And at this point we reach the profoundly ambiguous question: is it not a sin against life to allow oneself to be destroyed by cruelty and indifference and greed?

Brecht's mature drama works continually around this question. In *The Good Woman of Sezuan* goodness, under pressure, turns into its opposite, and then back again, and then both coexist. For the individual person, the dilemma is beyond solution. And this is conveyed with simplicity and power in Shen Te's transformation of herself into her tough male cousin, Shui Ta, who is first a disguise but then in effect takes on an independent existence. Thus the experience is generalised within an individual. It is not the good person against the bad, but goodness and badness as alternative expressions of a single being. This is complex seeing, and it is deeply integrated with the dramatic form: the character who lives this way and then that, enacting choice and requiring decision. No resolution is imposed. The tension is there to the end, and we are formally invited to consider it. The ordinary responses which we might use to cover the tension are clearly expressed by the other characters, so that we can discover their inadequacy while the tension is still there to see. The methods of expressionist drama, which had normally been used to manifest this breaking tension within a single consciousness, are here extended to examination, where they normally stop short at exposure. Brecht has in fact transformed that method of special pleading which insists on the spectator seeing the world through the actions and tensions of a single mind. He achieves this transformation by deliberate generalisation and by the appeal to impersonal judgement. He grows through the ordinary decadence of the form (which had been rationalised in a theory of art as exposure, all other intentions being defined as impure), and grows through also the crude reply of didacticism. The play becomes, in its essential movement, a moral action.

Yet *The Good Woman of Sezuan* remains a minor play, because the substance of this moral action is not so much created as given. It is in *Mother Courage and her Children* that he finds a new kind of dramatic action which creates a substance comparable in intensity with the moral inquiry. To call this action Shakespearean is not to put the praise too high. History and people come alive on the stage, leaping past the isolated and virtually static action that we have got used to in most modern theatre. The drama simultaneously occurs and is seen. It is not 'take the case of this woman' but 'see and consider what happens to these people'.

Criticism of the play has usually got off on the wrong track by starting with the question whether Mother Courage, as a person, is meant to be admired or despised. But the point is not what we feel about her hard lively opportunism; it is what we see, in the action, of its results. By enacting a genuine consequence, Brecht raises his central question to a new level, both dramatically and intellectually (though in the play there is no such separation). The question drives through the continuing action: what else can we do, here, where blind power is loose, but submit, chisel, try to play safe? And then by doing these things—either submitting and pretending to virtue, or submitting and cheating round the back—a family, see, is destroyed. The question is then no longer 'are they good people?' (the decision taken before or after the play). Nor is it, really, 'what should they have done?' It is, brilliantly, both 'what are they doing?' and 'what is this doing to them?'

All Brecht's dramatic skill is deployed to lead us to these essential questions. The contradictions in the characters— that they are sometimes hard, sometimes generous, and so on —are real, but they exist not only as personal qualities; they exist also in the play as a whole. The action is continually open, through the fact of these contradictions. It is not the inevitability of tragedy, as in the traditional tragic acceptance or the modern tragic resignation. The choices are made in a dimension that is always potential, and so the action is continually played and replayed. It could genuinely go either way, at any time. The action of consequence is intrinsically human, and in no way external:

> So we shall all be torn in two if we let ourselves get too deep in this war.

But not torn once, torn again and again. Much of the speech is then the play speaking, drawing strength from its characters but also moving beyond them.

> CHAPLAIN: Mother Courage, I see how you got your name.
> MOTHER COURAGE: The poor need courage. They're lost, that's why. That they even get up in the morning is something, in *their* plight. Or that they plough a field, in wartime. Even their bringing children into the world shows they have courage, for they have no prospects. They have to hang each other one by one and slaughter each other in the lump, so if they want to look each other in the face once in a while, well, it takes courage.

At the level of direct comment, this is, in summary, the dramatic action. But at the same time the naming of courage, and of Mother Courage, extends its scope. We need this woman if we are to look ourselves, and her, in the face. The drama, with this character at its centre, is a way of looking at a continual action.

Mother Courage and her Children is a dramatisation of conflicting instincts, conflicting illusions, and commanding insights that are not, but might be, lived through. Its crisis is properly reached in the frantic drumming of the dumb girl: a desperate articulation of the blood, to protect the city. The final paradox is genuinely tragic: the dumb girl, speaking for life, and being killed; the living going on with a living that kills; the final song of the soldiers

> *And though you may not long survive*
> *Get out of bed and look alive.*

It is action illuminated by a tragic consciousness, in contrast with *The Life of Galileo*, where the consciousness is the action. Galileo is fully conscious, and to that extent free, in ways that the pressed and the driven are not. In abstraction, the choice presented to him looks the same: accept our terms or be destroyed. But in detail the choice is quite different. Because he is conscious, he can not only foresee consequence and calculate it. He stands also for more than himself. In his own person, he is reason and liberation.

Once again, the question is not: 'should we admire or despise Galileo?'. Brecht is not asking this. He is asking what happens to consciousness when it is caught in the deadlock between individual and social morality. Galileo's submission can be rationalised and justified, at the individual level, as a way of gaining time to go on with his work. But the point this misses is what the work is for. If the purpose of science is that all men can learn to understand their world, Galileo's betrayal is fundamental. To detach the work from its human purpose is, Brecht sees, to betray others and so betray life. It is not, in the end, what we think of Galileo as a man, but what we think of this result.

The play brings this issue to consciousness, not as a problem, but as a living action. It is sometimes said that Brecht's Marxism was a handicap or at best an irrelevance to his drama. Yet it is just in this way of looking at the world that the dramatic action resides. We are used to martyrdom, and to the individual in conflict with his society. But we are not used to this radically different way of seeing an experience that is normally negotiated by these older conventions:

> Could we deny ourselves to the crowd and still remain scientists? The movements of the stars have become clearer; but to the mass of the people the movements of their masters are still incalculable. . . . With time you may discover all that is to be discovered, and your progress will only be a progression away from mankind. The gulf between you and them can one day become so great that your cry of jubilation over some new achievement may be answered by a universal cry of horror.

It is true that, trained to a different consciousness, we struggle to reduce the play to a different meaning, or, more plausibly, argue that this explicit conclusion is only there in this one speech and is not in the play as a whole. But of course we come to the story of Galileo with our own powerful image of the liberal martyr, and have real difficulty in seeing what is being actually presented. Certainly the play itself is explicit, through all its action. It is not only Galileo but the play that speaks. Thus Galileo's first speech sets the terms of the subsequent moral action:

> The most solemn truths are being tapped on the shoulder; what was never doubted is now in doubt. And because of that a great wind has arisen, lifting even the gold-embroidered coat-tails of princes and prelates, so that the fat legs and the thin legs underneath are seen; legs like our legs. . . . I predict that in our lifetimes astronomy will be talked about in the market-places. Even the sons of fishwives will go to school.

And then this is followed in the next scene, that of the presentation of the telescope, by this speech of the Curator of the Grand Arsenal of Venice:

> Once again a page of fame in the great book of the arts is embellished with Venetian characters. A scholar of world repute here presents to you, and to you alone, a highly saleable cylinder to manufacture and put on the market in any way you please. And has it occurred to you that in wartime by means of this instrument we shall be able to distinguish the build and number of an enemy's ships a full two hours earlier than he can descry ours?

The opposition is hardly too subtle to be seen. If we miss it, it is because we are resolutely interested in something else. The final scene, in which the manuscript of the *Discorsi* crosses the border, looks like a romantic liberation, unless we see also that the boys playing round the coach are still talking of witches.

The *coexistence* of these facts is always the point: the more moved we are by the one, the more ashamed we must be of the other. Galileo, committed to a universal and humanist view of science, has been trapped by another view: the imperatives of a different loyalty, to the ruling group that maintains him, to produce for the market and for war. It is not that as an individual he is a hypocrite. It is that under real pressures he embodies both a true consciousness and a false consciousness; the fact of their coexistence is what Brecht invites us to see. The movement of the play is from the ironic acceptance of false consciousness—what you say to get by, in an imperfect world—to the point where false consciousness

G*

becomes false action and is not irony but tragedy. It is like Mother Courage, who picked up her cart but to go on to the war.

In the end it is not only complex seeing. It is a very complex kind of feeling. Tragedy in some of its older senses is certainly rejected. There is nothing inevitable or ennobling about this kind of failure. It is a matter of human choice, and the choice is not once for all; it is a matter of continuing history. The major achievement of Brecht's mature work is this recovery of history as a dimension for tragedy. The sense of history becomes active through the discovery of methods of dramatic movement, so that the action is not single in space and time and certainly not 'permanent and timeless'. Struggling always with his own fixed consciousness, Brecht could only begin this transformation. But his epic theatre is at once a recovery of very early elements in the humanist drama of the Renaissance, where this capacity for historic action seemed at its full creative power, and a remaking of these elements in a modern mind. Continually limited by his own weaknesses, by his opportunism, which often comes through as dramatic cheating, and by his vestigial jeering and coarseness (the real dregs of his time and ours) he struggled towards a transformation and in part achieved it. Instead of trying to convert his work to the complacencies of our fashionable despair, or more easily to the grossness of our defensive cynicism, we should try to see what it means to drama when in recovering a sense of history and of the future a writer recovers the means of an action that is both complex and dynamic.

In most modern drama, the best conclusion is: yes, this is how it was. Only an occasional play goes further, with the specific excitement of recognition: yes, this is how it is. Brecht, at his best, reaches out to and touches the necessary next stage: yes, this is how it is, for these reasons, but the action is continually being replayed, and it could be otherwise.

The trap, at this last moment, is the wrong kind of emphasis on the undoubted fact that it could indeed be otherwise. To make it already otherwise, by selecting the facts and by subtly reducing the pressures, is to go over to propaganda or to advertising. We are committed to an actual process, and to seeing not only this movement but also that, so that not only this but also that must be said. We have to see not only that suffering is avoidable, but that it is not avoided. And not only that suffering breaks us, but that it need not break us. Brecht's own words are the precise expression of this new sense of tragedy:

The sufferings of this man appal me, because they are unnecessary.

This feeling extends into a general position: the new tragic consciousness of all those who, appalled by the present, are *for this reason* firmly committed to a different future: to the struggle against suffering learned in suffering: a total exposure which is also a total involvement. Under the weight of failure, in tragedy that could have been avoided but was not avoided, this structure of feeling is now struggling to be formed. Against the fear of a general death, and against the loss of connection, a sense of life is affirmed, learned as closely in suffering as ever in joy, once the connections are made. The affirmation begins where Brecht ended, in his poem *An die Nachgeborenen*:

> For we knew only too well:
> Even the hatred of squalor
> Makes the brow grow stern.
> Even anger against injustice
> Makes the voice grow harsh. Alas, we
> Who wished to lay the foundations of kindness
> Could not ourselves be kind.

In a continuing action—the word to posterity—such a recognition is absolute. It is the reality, in our time, of the struggle for happiness. But as a fixed position, in the manner of the early Brecht to which it is sometimes assimilated, it quickly degenerates, yet again, into a professional hardening: not the recognition but the acceptance of contradiction.

The recognition is a matter of history, the known harshness of the revolutionary struggle. But while this is seen as a process it can be lived through, resolved, changed. Whereas if it is seen, even briefly, as a fixed position—an abstract condition of man or of revolution—it becomes a new alienation, an exposure stopped short of involvement, a tragedy halted and generalised at the shock of catastrophe. In our own day, in a known complexity, it is the fixed harshness of a revolutionary regime which has turned to arrest the revolution itself, but which finds, facing its men turned to stone, the children of the struggle who because of the struggle live in new ways and with new feelings, and who, including the revolution in their ordinary living, answer death and suffering with a human voice.

PART THREE
Koba

KOBA

ACT I

SCENE I

Time: The Present

PRINCIPAL: Very well. Next.

SECRETARY: The next, sir, is a boy called Joseph. A cobbler's son. The father is dead. We have very good reports of the boy. His vicar and his headmaster both confidently recommend him for a scholarship. The mother apparently lives by going out cleaning, and the boy is what you would expect: a bit rough, of course, but quiet and serious at his work.

PRINCIPAL: Political sympathies?

SECRETARY: None known, sir. There's just this one occasion when he was heard expressing the usual popular sentiments, in a typically adolescent way.

PRINCIPAL: My predecessor was assassinated by one of these typical adolescents. You must learn to take nothing of that kind lightly.

SECRETARY: Oh, I don't take it lightly, sir. On the contrary. But it was, as I say, only this one occasion.

PRINCIPAL: My predecessor was assassinated on only one occasion. However, bring the boy in.

[*The* SECRETARY *claps his hands.* JOSEPH *enters, carrying a book.*]

PRINCIPAL: Stand there. In the light. I want a good look at you.

JOSEPH: Yes sir. Of course.

PRINCIPAL: What book is that you're carrying?

JOSEPH: It's a book of ballads, sir.

PRINCIPAL: Ballads? You have a taste for poetry?

JOSEPH: For some poetry, sir.

PRINCIPAL: There is poetry that the Church recognises, and other poetry that it condemns. Which kind is yours?

JOSEPH: I don't know, sir. Wouldn't that be for the Church to say?

SECRETARY: Watch your tongue, boy. And stand up straight when the Principal is looking at you.

PRINCIPAL: Well, Joseph, I'm waiting for your answer.

JOSEPH: I don't know, sir. I love my country, and these poems are by our popular writers.

PRINCIPAL: Put the book on the table. You say popular writers? These? But can you take the name of writer—that calm and beautiful name—from Homer, from Vergil, and from Dante, and give it to men like these: agitators, demagogues, criminals?
[*Pause.*]

PRINCIPAL: Have you nothing to say, boy? They did not tell me you were sullen.

JOSEPH: There is nothing I can say, sir.

PRINCIPAL: At least you know your limitations. If you do, we can train you. Our training is strict, but it has to be. You have come here, Joseph, to be trained in the service of the Church. It is a hard service, but it is Christ's service. You will learn what it is our duty to teach you: the difference between true glory and false.

JOSEPH: Yes sir, I wish to learn that.

PRINCIPAL: And you will dedicate your life to it? To the hard and often lonely life of the servant of God?

JOSEPH: I am prepared for it to be hard, sir. And I am prepared to be lonely.

PRINCIPAL: And these are your reasons for coming here, that you may be a priest of the Church?

JOSEPH: My mother wishes that, sir.

PRINCIPAL: But you don't?

JOSEPH: I didn't say that, sir. I honour my mother, and I am eager to be trained as is necessary.

PRINCIPAL: Very well. We shall see. But as your Principal, I must make certain things clear from the beginning. When you enter here you will leave the world and its business behind you. You will live your days and nights here, except on special application, when the father in charge of your class may, at his discretion, give you leave of absence for periods not exceeding two hours. Any breach of this or any other regulation is punished by confinement to the cells.

JOSEPH: Yes sir. I understand.

PRINCIPAL: Your work each day will be your religious

instruction and your prayers. When you are not working you will conduct yourself soberly and decently. And remember this, Joseph: if you hear or overhear, at any time, among your fellow students, any blasphemous language, any talk of political sedition, any incitement to revolt against those set in authority over you, then it is your absolute duty not only to resist such ideas, but to report them at once to the father in charge of your class.

JOSEPH: I will remember all this, sir.

PRINCIPAL: Yes, you will remember it. We will see to it that you do. But still you have made a bad start, a very bad start, by possessing this book. There are good books and there are evil books. You, Joseph, are too young to distinguish them, but the Church distinguishes. This that you have brought is an evil book: a collection of idle romances glorifying criminals and outlaws.

JOSEPH: But the stories are exciting, sir. And they are about my own people.

PRINCIPAL: Very much that is exciting is also evil. The virtues of your people are decency and humility, not rebellion and crime. These stories incite to rebellion. They have already done so, within these walls.

JOSEPH: The students' strike, sir?

PRINCIPAL: Yes, strike is what it was called, but that is the corrupt language of the world. Young men in the service of God refusing their duties, demanding to be taught the history and the literature of their own country, stubborn and insolent. When I called in the police, and the college was closed, eighty-seven young men, eighty-seven like you, Joseph, with all their hopes and plans for the future, had to be expelled, driven out, before the others could get back to their appropriate education.

JOSEPH: I know the whole story of the strike, sir.

PRINCIPAL: I see. And you have drawn, I hope, the correct conclusions. This is a house of God, not a hothouse of politics. With them, ignorance and violence; with us, learning and service. It is for you to choose, Joseph.

JOSEPH: I wish to learn and to serve, sir.

PRINCIPAL: Well, we shall see. I may seem harsh, Joseph, but I am not unkind. You come here, you young men, with an exceptional opportunity. Others, without your chances, may grow up in darkness, but for you, if you are patient, there is the road to light. Make use of your chances, Joseph. Don't throw them away in a moment of foolishness. You are a good boy, Joseph. Your mother is hardworking and devout. She sees you already as a learned man, a priest and father in God. Will you sin against her, against Mother Church, against yourself? Will you throw down that future for this: this romance of Koba the outlaw?

JOSEPH: But Koba, sir. He was only an outlaw because the laws were cruel and bad. He called himself the avenger of his people, sir, and Koba means the man who cannot be mastered.

PRINCIPAL: He burned and he robbed and he killed, beyond reckoning. These are the facts, under the romantic cloak. Is a criminal like that to be glorified, against the blessed example of the Saviour of mankind, who called all peoples to the love and the mercy of God?

JOSEPH: Jesus was made a criminal, sir. The rulers crucified him.

SECRETARY: That was a long time ago. And it was the Jews who crucified him.

JOSEPH: The Romans crucified him: the imperialists. With the help of the ruling Jews. Because Jesus spoke for the people.

PRINCIPAL: He spoke for a kingdom which is not of this earth. When we enter his service we leave the world behind us, beyond these doors. This is what you must learn, Joseph. This is what you will be taught. Now go and wait for the bell. I wish you well, my son.

JOSEPH: Thank you, Father.

[JOSEPH *bows low and goes out.*]

SECRETARY: Well, sir. Very much what we expected.

PRINCIPAL: Not what you expected, what I expected. But he won't be especially dangerous. They can be stubborn and bitter at first, these boys from the hovels. But why are they here, why did they come to us, if they are not willing to conform? Those who stay will change themselves, because in the end they are ambitious. They know what it is to be poor, and so they are anxious to get on in the world and to do what's expected of them. That is the price, and in coming here they have decided to pay it. We must grant them their bitterness for a time. It is the only way in which they can learn to reconcile themselves.

SECRETARY: Yes sir.

PRINCIPAL: Report on him with the others, in three months. And now come, quickly, or we shall be late for assembly. [*The bell is tolling. The* PRINCIPAL *goes out, while the* SECRETARY *stands and bows low at the door.*]

SCENE II

The tolling of the bell has quickened to alarm. There is distant shouting. PETER *and* GEORGE *enter, hurrying.* PETER *sits where the* PRINCIPAL *was sitting.* GEORGE *goes back to look out at the street.* LADO *and* JOSEPH *enter, but stay in the shadows near the door.*

PETER: Are you sure this is safe? The police seem everywhere.

GEORGE: Nowhere is safe, but this will do. An old shed by the quay: one of a hundred. And the police have their hands full. The demonstration is enormous.

PETER: Yes, this is a great day. A great and wonderful day when after centuries of weakness these people at last learn their strength. I admit I've doubted it often. I've thought the Revolution was a thing we only wrote and talked about —a distant idea of man's freedom and dignity. I never thought to see it here, on the streets of our own town. The ordinary people, the despised and rejected, at last with the courage to assert their humanity.

GEORGE: Yes, feel like that if you like, Peter, but this isn't the Revolution. That's still very distant, and as it comes nearer there will be nothing wonderful about it. Today is only a strike, with shouting and stoning in the streets.

PETER: But still it's a beginning. We've scattered the seed, on ground that seemed barren and hopeless, but now, at last, the first shoots have come up.

GEORGE: Have you listened to it, Peter? This isn't a pastoral. And it isn't our harvest these men are gathering, it's their own. The difference, now, is not in us but in them. They are no longer peasants, held by the quiet villages and the seasons. They are miners, railwaymen, oil workers, engineers in the factories. The machines are the seed.

PETER: You're probably right. But still the revolution isn't for oil and railways and factories. The revolution is for man, for his freedom and his dignity. We who were born free have a duty to teach that freedom.

GEORGE: Yes, when there is no strike, we can write and talk as we please. But when the men are in the streets, when the stones are flying, don't go out and talk about dignity, don't insult their anger by turning it back to an idea. All we can do now is watch and learn.

[LADO *comes forward.*]

LADO: Not go out? Not turn this anger to an idea? But this is weak and stupid. I say go out, put the anger on paper, print it, distribute it. Get me a printing press and I'll make your revolution.

PETER: Lado, you'll say anything to get your press. I think what you really like is messing about with the type.

GEORGE: It isn't that. It's a simple question of money. When this strike ends, as it is bound to end, these men and their families will be cold and hungry. Can we dare to spend on a press what we could otherwise spend on blankets and food? Because that is the choice.

JOSEPH: Then we should choose the press.

[*Pause.*]

PETER: Who's your young friend, Lado? I don't think I've met him.

[JOSEPH *comes forward.*]

LADO: His name is Joseph. He's from the college.

PETER: He seems a very definite young man. Won't you come closer, Joseph? Here, in the light, where I can see you.

JOSEPH: Yes, sir.

PETER: Now, Joseph, you mustn't call me sir. I'm chairman of the organisation, certainly, but we're all equals here, all friends and comrades. I know it will be hard for you to break the habits of the college, but you're among very different people now, Joseph, as I'm sure you'll learn.

JOSEPH: I shall learn what is necessary.

PETER: Yes, I'm sure you will. It's ironic, isn't it, how many recruits we get from the college. Is it the desire for service, perhaps, that first led them to the Church, leading them now to us?

LADO: It isn't to serve that they go the college. It's to get an education. There's nowhere else.

JOSEPH: In the college we learn much that is false. But at least we learn discipline there. A necessary discipline.

GEORGE: If you knew more of movements like ours, Joseph, you wouldn't make us smile by talking of discipline. If we have fifty members then we have fifty ideas of the revolution, all different.

JOSEPH: Perhaps. But then why are you so pleased about it? If you have fifty different ideas then you are fifty times weaker and will get nothing done. We have to learn discipline, or we shall all be destroyed.

LADO: Yes, that's good college talk. Not that it comes to much. In my day they had to fetch the police to us. I was the first of the eighty-seven expelled. Your generation, Joseph, is much more careful.

JOSEPH: Yes. Because to expose yourself to your enemy, before you are ready for him, is a stupid heroism. We must never make a move until we know we are strong enough.

PETER: Well, Lado, we're all being rebuked, by this marvellous boy. But seriously, Joseph, what is it you want to do? Are you a writer? A speaker? What exactly?

LADO: He's published poems.

PETER: That's fine. We can't have too many poets.

JOSEPH: We have too many already. Too many in proportion. If you read their books the revolution is just round the corner, or has even begun. And while you can write about revolution there is no need to make it. Yet put the books down and look out in the streets, there is nothing.

GEORGE: You call this strike nothing?

JOSEPH: It's been badly organised. By tomorrow it will be broken and the leaders arrested.

GEORGE: It's easy to talk, Joseph. Even one day's victory is much harder work than you've ever done.

PETER: And in any case, he just told us, he's written poems himself.

JOSEPH: No, I didn't tell you. And it was three years ago, and of no importance. I grew up reading poems, and like most other boys I started copying them out, in slightly different words. I've come past that now, to the real work.

GEORGE: And what is the real work?

JOSEPH: Organisation. The people need organisers who can also teach.

GEORGE: And can you do that?

JOSEPH: I will do what the Party instructs.

GEORGE: Having told us, however, what the Party should be.

LADO: I'll take you up on it, Joseph. I've got three groups in the railway workshops. You can take them over, from tomorrow. If you make a go of it there's better work waiting. At the oilfield we can really organise, organise to fight.

JOSEPH: I shall be glad to do this.

PETER: You must realise, of course, you risk being expelled from the college.

JOSEPH: Yes, my mother will regret that. But I've had more than four years there. I've learned what I need.

GEORGE: And it will be dangerous work, Joseph, quite apart from the risk of expulsion. It's an unusual group, these days, without at least one member who's being paid by the police. And it's never easy to pick him out, except perhaps that he's keener, more convinced and more active. You'll need an underground name, as some sort of protection.

JOSEPH: Yes. You can call me Koba.

PETER: Koba the outlaw. That's very good.

JOSEPH: Not Koba the outlaw, but Koba the avenger of his people. My father was born a serf. My grandfather, my great-grandfather, every man through the generations that have given me life, was a serf and was bought and sold. These are my people, and there is much to avenge.

GEORGE: It's a dangerous emotion, though, vengeance.

PETER: I understand how he feels. And it is our duty, we who were born free, to take this bitterness and transform it to brotherhood, to a new vision of man.

JOSEPH: This is wasting time. We must get back to the streets. And by staying too long we risk being taken.

GEORGE: The streets are as dangerous.

JOSEPH: Yes, but they are fighting there.

LADO: All right. Koba.

[JOSEPH *and* LADO *go out.* PETER *and* GEORGE *hesitate, and then follow.*]

SCENE III

JORDAN *enters, followed by* MAX

MAX: Jordan.

JORDAN: Yes.

MAX: The credentials so far are checked. They're all in order.

JORDAN: Of course. Even the police have their credentials in order. Is there any more news from the capital?

MAX: What there is is good. All the strike committees are firm. The city administration only exists on paper. The troops and police are shooting, but we have held so far.

JORDAN: We must get back there quickly, as soon as this congress is over. Though it's no use going until we've made our decisions. How many more are to come?

MAX: It's difficult to say. There'll have been the usual arrests, on the way here. There's nobody yet from the South.

JORDAN: Who would it be, from the South? There's a Koba, isn't there?

MAX: Koba? I don't know. It sounds sufficiently barbarous.

JORDAN: He's done good work in the oilfields. I know no more about him.

[JOSEPH *enters.*]

JOSEPH: Excuse me. Are you Max?

MAX: Yes, I'm Max.

JOSEPH: I was told to find you and present my credentials.

MAX: Right. Where are you from?

JOSEPH: From the South. I am Koba.

MAX: Koba, did you say? How would I spell that?

JOSEPH: K-O-B-A. Is it all that difficult?

MAX: Not now. But I wasn't familiar with it. All right, give me your papers.

JOSEPH: Here. You'll find them in order. But has Jordan arrived yet? I can't wait to see him.

MAX: You can't wait, Koba? Why?

JOSEPH: Because Jordan is the leader. Because I've thought of him from a distance, in prison and exile. Because I've read all his writings, and learned them by heart. He is a great leader, and I have waited to see him.

MAX: Well yes. If you say so. That's how things are, I suppose, in the South. Anyway, if you want to see Jordan, it won't be difficult. You won't have far to go.

JOSEPH: Not far? Where is he then? Has he already appeared?

[JORDAN *steps forward.*]

JORDAN: Koba, I'm Jordan. I'm glad to meet you. I've heard good reports of your work in the South.

JOSEPH: You? Jordan? But that's impossible!

JORDAN: Impossible? Why?

JOSEPH: Because Jordan is the leader. Jordan is a very great man.

JORDAN: And I don't look like a very great man? Is that it?

JOSEPH: Well to be frank, you don't. That is, if you are Jordan. You're not a bit what I expected.

MAX: A giant fifteen feet high, I suppose, with a sheepskin cloak and an eagle's feather in his cap. You've some primitive ideas, Koba, in the South.

JOSEPH: But are you really Jordan? You're not fooling me?

JORDAN: Yes, Koba, I'm Jordan, for better or worse. And I'm sorry I can't oblige in the way of a more striking appearance. I went bald early and I've always lacked height. But still, as I am, you'll have to take me.

JOSEPH: I didn't mean to insult you. I apologise. And the appearance doesn't matter, though of course it would be an advantage. But even as you are, and great as you are, you're making a basic mistake. We work in the underground in silence and exile. We work in danger, where every effort seems hopeless. And what do you think sustains us? The idea of the people, of course, but the people themselves are not ready. To lead the people is to be the best of the people: to show, in yourself, all their future strength. Then you must not only be great, but seem great. You must get people asking: when will he come, when will Jordan be here? We are all only men, all equal in that. To be a leader needs emphasis, and emphasis must be organised. You shouldn't say 'I'm Jordan', and step from a corner. You can't be the father if you behave like the son.

JORDAN: You're still young, Koba, and you have, inevitably, these romantic ideas. Yes, I am leader, but not as myself. I am only leader so long as I am right. When I am wrong I

am nothing. It is never one man, but history, that is
leading us.

JOSEPH: History is made by ordinary men, and ordinary men
need a cause they can see. What you call history is still in
the books. We must bring it out from the books to the
streets.

MAX: You talk well, Koba, and in many ways you are right.
But here, you must understand, we are all leaders, the
vanguard of the revolution. The display you talk about
would be quite out of place.

JORDAN: This is wasting time. You say you are practical,
Koba. Then talk about practical things. You weren't sent
from the South to make speeches.

JOSEPH: I speak as I find, Jordan. Even to you.

JORDAN: Very well. But speak of the work. Are your people
strong?

JOSEPH: The people are strong, or they would not have lasted.
The people have always been strong, that is not in question.

JORDAN: Exactly, comrade. But leaving slogans aside.

JOSEPH: The people need slogans, to direct their strength.
Yes, in the South, we are fighting, and we fight better with
every encounter. We are learning unity, we are learning
discipline, we are hardening ourselves under fire.

JORDAN: There have been many disputes in the South.
Disputes in the Party.

JOSEPH: We move from building to building, avoiding the
police. We speak, we write, we organise, preparing the
people for their tasks. This is the real work, among the
people. But from outside, from the exiles, we hear dis-
cordant voices. We watch strength being dissipated in
futile arguments. This we condemn.

JORDAN: Condemn it if you like, Koba, but what are the facts?
You've been, yourself, at the centre of these arguments.
You've been fighting, haven't you, the whole leadership
of the Party in the South?

JOSEPH: It's the same issue. Can't you see this, Jordan? I fight
all those who are weakening the people. The leaders I have
fought, and in fact beaten, are just like your exiles. The
revolution for them is a speech, a pamphlet, a theoretical
point. But for me, for the people, it is a fight for power.

MAX: The people need eyes, Koba, to see how to use their

strength. This giant has been blind. The speeches and the pamphlets are to help him to see.

JOSEPH: This giant is hungry, and needs bread. This giant is bleeding, and must reach for the whip.

JORDAN: He has always reached, but he has never held. All that matters, now, is to learn how to hold, and this, inevitably, is what we must teach.

JOSEPH: Yes, this is true.

JORDAN: We have all taught, and we have all been arrested. It isn't the arrest that makes us teachers; it is only the idea.

JOSEPH: Since I was expelled from the college I have been twice arrested. The first time I escaped, within a week. But the second was harder. They moved me from prison to prison, and at last to the North. In the end I escaped and travelled South again, in a farm cart. I got frostbite on that journey, but it has healed.

MAX: We have all been to prison, Koba. We have all been sent to the North.

JOSEPH: I am not boasting. It was little enough. I had a friend, Lado, who was my first political teacher. Lado was shot, last year, by his gaolers. It is one more death to avenge.

JORDAN: Not to avenge, but to justify. We are in constant danger, and we must stay calm and disciplined. The correctness of theory is calm. An educated party is disciplined. There is no room, as we are, for any other emphasis.

MAX: Exactly. And it is time for the meeting. Come on, Sir Jordan, or shall I go and catch you your eagle's feather?

JORDAN: I'll have to make do as I am. It's a heavy agenda.

[MAX *and* JORDAN *go out.* JOSEPH *waits, watching them, and then follows slowly.*]

SCENE IV

Enter LUKE *and* WARDER. *The light is fading*

WARDER: Here you are then, Luke. Here's your happy home.

LUKE: A wooden box in a desert of snow. Do you call that a home?

WARDER: Well, it's not a palace, admitted, but it's not such a bad little place. The stove's all right, when you get it cleaned out, and you'll get fresh straw over the barn. You see, you'll soon settle down.

LUKE: That is always the word: settle down. But I am not in exile, I am in the heart of this country. Here, in prison, in this barren landscape, I am living the truth of this people. To be exposed and guarded, in this endless silence, where nothing grows and nothing moves: that, everywhere, is the life we are offered.

WARDER: I don't know about that. But there you are, if you don't like it up here, you don't have to come. It's your own choice, you know, picking quarrels with the government.

LUKE: I taught children, in an unauthorised school. That was my quarrel.

WARDER: Well, there you are. I mean, things like that, the Government has to decide.

LUKE: Yes, you believe that. And because you believe it, you are the prisoner. I am a free man, caught for a moment. You are the prisoner, a life prisoner, not even knowing your sentence.

WARDER: Well, we won't argue about that. I'll just lock you in and get off home for some supper. There'll be another chap in with you, in a bit. I saw them carting him to the office.

LUKE: I expected at least to be alone here.

WARDER: You wouldn't say that, brother, if you knew anything about prisons. Put men on their own, they get to screaming like animals, or they just slouch and die. We're only alone when we're dead. You'll find that out. Now come on, settle down.

[*The* WARDER *goes out.* LUKE *crosses to the window.*]

LUKE: The home in my mind. I can close my eyes and remember. I can see the ice break, on the silent river, and the deep snow melts, in that distant valley, where the black earth will breathe, in the April winds. I have closed my eyes, for that spring seems distant and hopeless. I have closed my eyes, for here where I live there is darkness. Yet will not the spring come, in this far country? Cannot the flower be known, here where the seed lies dormant? May not the darkness flower, in its own season?

[*The* WARDER *re-enters, with* JOSEPH *behind him.*]

WARDER: Are you there then, Luke?

LUKE: Yes. By the window.

WARDER: Here's the company I promised you. You'll be glad to see him.

JOSEPH: That's enough. Don't taunt us. Do your duty and go.

WARDER: Now look, brother, there's no call to be unfriendly. I was only trying to act decent.

JOSEPH: You will not succeed. The whip can never be decent.

WARDER: Yes, but look here, I carry the whip, but we only use it on the very worst cases, what they call the recalcitrants. Like they told you in the office, a detention centre's got no use for violence. You just be sensible, and there'll be no trouble.

JOSEPH: When you learn to be sensible, there will be trouble. But not for us. For them.

WARDER: Aye, you all talk the same. Tomorrow the Judgement. Like the priest at home used to say: the last reckoning will come, and you'll all be weighed in the balance. Just scaring the life out of decent people, that's all it amounts to. We could see for ourselves, they don't weigh corpses, they just shove them down in the earth. Nobody gets at you past that.

JOSEPH: At least you've broken with one superstition.

WARDER: Maybe I have. I've got my own life to live. Only now there's your lot, and the same old story. St Peter's gates or this great revolution: it all comes the same to us. One way or another, if we listen to you lot, we've got it coming to us, the day after tomorrow. But what I say is, let the future feed the future. We've got enough where we are, just feeding ourselves. This bloody politics kills people, I've seen it over and over. And don't try and tell me, I've heard it too often. Making out that for me or for you things could ever be different.

JOSEPH: But things will be different, and you will be part of the difference.

WARDER: All right, I don't blame you, if it keeps your spirits up. Like my old aunt, she had to sleep on her own, but she'd got something much bigger, a god or something, coming up later on. Go on. Sweet dreams. I'll just lock you in.

JOSEPH: You can never lock us in. We are everywhere.

WARDER: Aye, well tonight you're here, under lock and key, and every blessed night for the next seven years, God help you. So settle down, make the best of it.

JOSEPH: We shall make the best of it.

[*The* WARDER *goes out.* JOSEPH *puts down his things, and turns to* LUKE, *who is still by the window.*]

JOSEPH: Did I hear him say Luke?

LUKE: Yes, Luke is my name.

JOSEPH: I'm Joseph. They call me Koba. Where are you from?

LUKE: From the West.

JOSEPH: I've been to the West. To the Congress. On my way back they arrested me. How about you? Where did they pick you up?

[LUKE *turns from the window and goes to sit in the shadows.*]

LUKE: I'd rather not talk, friend, if you don't mind.

JOSEPH: Not talk? What else can we do?

LUKE: I shall try to write, if I can.

JOSEPH: Write? Well that's an idea. I used to write, a long time ago. In the way you mean, that is. I only write now in terms of the struggle. Afterwards, I dare say, it'll be different. But writing is strange. I know I only write when there's an audience waiting to be written to. Writing, for me, is just a way of talking to people. That's what I don't understand. I've known lots of writers, good writers, and all they ever think about is getting away on their own somewhere, sitting down to write. As if writing, really, was a sort of talking to themselves. Well, there it is. You're as good as your word. But don't think I shall bother you. You sit there, comrade, as long as you like. Sit with your head in your hands, and when you want to, write. For me, as I said, it would be no good. When I'm away from people I've got nothing to write about.

[JOSEPH *looks around, and then crosses to the window.*]

Only sometimes, if you like, look across as I stand by the window. Look across at me, and then look back at your writing. I am an ordinary man, but I am also the people, watching from the window and waiting. In this dark hut, in prison and exile, I stand looking out for the first sign of the light, and the chance to break free.

[LUKE *turns and watches him.*]

You're thinking I'm mad, standing talking like this. Only
prisoners and lunatics have such great ideas of themselves.
But I know I am nothing. I have no name, for I am the
people.

[*The stage darkens further.*]

They call me Koba, but my name is not Koba, my work is
Koba. Tell me what you can see, as your eyes strain in the
darkness. Can you see these men, my fathers and brothers?
Generation on generation, poor and hungry and dying.
These men are my seed, and I am their seed.

[*In the shadows near the door, men and women are moving,
slowly.*]

The child at the breast becomes the man at the plough,
gives the earth his blood and gives others his harvest. The
girl screams on the bed of straw, in new blood, in new
hands, and still the harvest is taken. War and tyranny and
fever and ignorance: generation on generation, taking and
destroying our children. Watch now if you can. Watch.
This man, this taller man, is called Lado. A teacher and a
fighter, a young man.

[LADO *crosses and kneels beside* JOSEPH. *The* WARDER *enters
and stands behind* LADO. *He draws his pistol and shoots him
in the back of the neck. Then he goes out, dragging the body.*]

He spoke and he was killed. He is many men. And I, Koba,
am many men. In myself I am nothing, but I have become
Koba.

[*The stage darkens completely, and there is a clear silence.*
JOSEPH *and* LUKE *are alone.*]

Can you not see how it is, in this darkness? Look. Watch.
The generations of killing, by act or neglect. Yet our life
goes on, and our bodies have learned from this killing. Life,
in this darkness, has found its own answer. It has taken my
body and changed it, taken my name and changed it. I
have become Koba, the man who cannot be mastered. I
have become Koba, the avenger of my people.

[*A light appears near the window.*]

Look. Watch. Do you see?

LUKE: The darkness flowers, in its own season.

The darkness flowers, passing beyond its source.

In this far instant, when the darkness flowers,

There is a new country, between earth and sun.

[*The light has been growing as he speaks, and continues to brighten. There is shouting outside, coming nearer.*]

JOSEPH: You hear the shouting. Listen now, they are shouting for peace and for bread. Listen, listen, how many are shouting.

LUKE: Yes, I see you now, you are Koba the avenger.

JOSEPH: Listen to the shouting. The giant has woken, and is reaching with his hands.

LUKE: I can see you, Koba. The darkness has flowered.

JOSEPH: We've no time to waste. We must get away tonight. We must get to the capital.

LUKE: You are the man who cannot be mastered, but they are shouting for peace and for bread.

JOSEPH: Yes, the shouting, listen to it. And look, our door has been opened. We are free, free to go. Come on, friend, I'll help you. Come on, come on, you can walk.

LUKE: I can walk but there is nowhere to go. Or nowhere for me. Your work is Koba.

JOSEPH: The name doesn't matter. Let it go back to the underground. This is the day I've been waiting for, the day of freedom. I must get to the capital.

[JOSEPH *hurries out. The shouting reaches its climax.* LUKE *stands, looking after him, and then goes out slowly, in another direction.*]

SCENE V

Enter GEORGE *and* MARK. *They close the door on the shouting.*

GEORGE: I tell you again, Mark, there's nothing to celebrate, there's everything to organise.

MARK: Yes, of course. You are an old revolutionary. The years have soured you, and you have that much excuse. But is nothing enough for you? Not even the revolution? Now, today, when the people are in the streets?

GEORGE: We can't live in the streets. It's easy enough, marching this way and that with your banners. But if we mean business, there are more important things to do.

MARK: We mean business all right, but without the excitement nothing real can be done.

GEORGE: The banners are fine, but it is time to put them away. The reality, now, is not banners, but committees, white papers, administration, supplies. These images of the Revolution are a luxury. We must make the real revolution.

MARK: The revolution, surely, is supplies *and* images.

GEORGE: Exactly. And we haven't got the supplies.

[*Enter* JOSEPH *and* RUTH.]

JOSEPH: Is this headquarters? I am Koba.

GEORGE: Joseph! You've escaped then?

JOSEPH: I escaped three days ago.

GEORGE: I'm very glad, Joseph. We weren't even sure you were alive. And is this your wife?

JOSEPH: This is Ruth, the daughter of one of our members here. She has written and sent me supplies while I've been in the North.

GEORGE: You must be glad to have him back, Ruth.

RUTH: Yes, I'm glad for his sake. He was there in the darkness for so many years. He used to ask me to send post-cards, so that he could see what living country was like.

JOSEPH: This is no longer important. We have a great deal to do. As an elected member of the committee of the Party, I take it I'm senior here.

GEORGE: Yes, Joseph, you are senior. Or say Koba is senior.

JOSEPH: The name doesn't matter. But I need to see all the reports. The city's excited, but the real situation's obscure.

GEORGE: You can see the reports, Joseph, and the situation will still be obscure. Never mind, come and look. I've got all the papers in here.

[GEORGE *and* JOSEPH *go out.*]

MARK: Well, Ruth? You must be very proud, to be so close to one of the leaders.

RUTH: Who? You?

MARK: Me? Good heavens, no. I'm just what they call a wild student. No, I meant Koba.

RUTH: Yes, he is one of the leaders.

MARK: You don't sound very impressed. Don't you like him?

RUTH: I hardly know him. When he must hide from the police, he would lodge, sometimes, with my father. But I was only a child then, before he was sent to the North.

MARK: Yet you wrote to him there?

RUTH: My father cannot write. I was glad to do what I could.

MARK: Well, Koba must have liked it, having a pretty girl writing to him.

RUTH: I am not pretty. You mustn't tease me.

MARK: Yes, you are pretty. You are even beautiful. But then today, really, everybody is beautiful. That is what it means, this excitement. Not that the others will see it, the old ones, even Koba. They've been cut off for too long, from any ordinary world. They come back now like ghosts, pale and bitter and grey.

RUTH: My father says only one thing of Koba, that he is entirely reliable.

MARK: Reliable, yes. Well, there are worse things to be. But also there are better things. Don't you feel it yourself, like your own life beginning?

RUTH: I can't tell. I don't know. I'm not sure what is happening. All my father says is that the situation is still obscure.

MARK: Your father says. Have you no feelings of your own?

RUTH: They say this is no time for feelings of your own.

MARK: Of course they say that. The grey disease. We shall all catch it in time. I can feel it already, as these ghosts bring it back with them.

[JOSEPH *enters as* MARK *is speaking.*]

JOSEPH: That's enough. Be quiet.

MARK: I'm sorry, Koba. I didn't mean to insult you. But still I speak as I find. Even to you. And don't tell me to be quiet, as if you spoke to a dog. Those are the ways we are ending, with this revolution.

JOSEPH: I see. Have you finished?

MARK: Nothing is finished. This is only the beginning.

JOSEPH: Your name is Mark, is that right?

MARK: Yes, I am Mark.

JOSEPH: Then let me make this clear, Mark, to you and to others. How you are spoken to is of no importance. You are one single person, a tiny individual among millions. Can you dare to think of yourself, when the lives of millions are in danger?

MARK: I think of myself because I think of those millions. You also, Koba, are only one among many.

JOSEPH: Yes. Certainly. As myself I am nothing. But I am here to speak for the Party, and the Party speaks for the people. We have worked and suffered to make this revolution, and nothing, now, will be allowed to defeat it.

H

Yet we shall in fact be defeated—defeat is staring from
every report—unless there is authority, discipline, order.
Like you I was a student, with my dreams of the future.
Like you I lived for the shout, the great shout, that would
transform my world. But it doesn't happen like that. My
first political teacher, a student hardly older than myself,
was shot in his cell by his gaolers. The groups I organised
were raided and broken up, dragged away to prison and
exile. I have learned, very clearly, the strength of the people
but I have learned even more clearly the strength of the
enemies of the people. As you open your mouth to cry
freedom, they will hit you, without pity, across the face, hit
you until it is not freedom but blood that jumps from your
mouth.

MARK: Blood, certainly, but also freedom. Have you never
learned that? That people can be trusted? That we can only
make freedom by knowing it in the face of our neighbour?

JOSEPH: That is the ordinary piety, while the blood runs. But
this struggle is desperate, and is beyond piety. The people
are strong, or there would be no revolution. Yet also the
people are weak, and their weakness, precisely, is the
business of the Party. Where they are weak we must
strengthen them, as part of themselves. We must be their
eyes, their hands, the blood in their veins. Our interests as
individuals, our rights as individuals, are of no importance
except in that duty. We exist only as eyes, hands, blood.
We exist as a Party, and as the duty of the Party. And
this involves from you, now, first: order, discipline,
obedience.

[PETER *has entered, while* JOSEPH *is speaking. He now claps
his hands.*]

PETER: Order, discipline, obedience. You could hardly have
said better, Joseph. You said this to us first in that hut by
the docks. You, fresh and young from the college, as the
strike gripped the city. Do you remember, Joseph?

JOSEPH: I remember many things, Peter.

PETER: But order, discipline, obedience: these three, above
everything. And of course you're quite right. This is why
I have come. I have authority to speak for the Revolutionary Government. To speak, plainly and urgently, to your
own party. The Revolution is not only in danger, but on

the edge of defeat. The army is massing against us, and we
have only our spirit and our hands to fight with. Only one
thing can save us: the unity of all parties in the Revolutionary Government. But at a time like this, in such
desperate danger, your party, Joseph, is breaking that
unity. Your whole policy is senseless. It isn't even that
you're the strongest party, though in some centres you are
strong. And since you can never hope to govern alone, you
are bound to work with the rest of us, loyally, honestly.
That is why I call you, Joseph, in the name of the Revolution, to discipline, order, obedience.

JOSEPH: We cannot be loyal both to you and to the people.

PETER: The people? But the people are divided in a hundred
ways: even brother against brother, father against son.
Nobody can speak for the people as a whole. That is just
arrogant rhetoric. Look at the facts, Joseph. We've over-
thrown the tyranny. The essential revolution has occurred.
But we are weak and divided, and the enemy is literally at
the gates. We must have government, if we are to survive
at all. Whatever our differences, we must unite on this.

JOSEPH: There can be unity for the revolution, or unity
against it.

PETER: Of course. This doesn't need saying. What I'm asking
from you is unity and loyalty in the Revolutionary
Government.

JOSEPH: On what terms, exactly?

PETER: There can be no terms. It is all too urgent for that. We
must just sink our differences, for the sake of unity in the
Revolutionary Government.

JOSEPH: You have said this before. You are merely repeating
yourself.

PETER: Yes, but I want an answer, Joseph.

JOSEPH: An answer? To what?

PETER: To the question of your loyalty to the Revolutionary
Government.

JOSEPH: That is perfectly clear, and requires no answer. In
respect of the Revolutionary Government, we are neither
for nor against it.

PETER: What absurdity is that? Can't you listen, the rest of
you, to what is being said? Can't you speak out, honestly,
against this kind of quibbling?

GEORGE: The unity of the party is necessary, Peter.

PETER: But not the unity of the government? Now, with an army marching in to destroy us?

MARK: You are asking for loyalty, as governments always ask for it. And there's always, haven't you noticed, an army at the gates? So never mind about terms, just be very obedient. But I see a greater danger than any army. That no sooner have we made our revolution, no sooner have we broken our chains, than we go out looking for chains, looking for authority: turning from this to that, weighing the chains in our hands, seeing which will serve. And I have to warn you of this. No revolutionary government will defeat that army. Only the people can defeat it.

PETER: Words again, just useless words. But it isn't words at the gates of the city, that disciplined army fighting its brutal way back to the throne and the whip. To stop them, now, needs immediate decision: for or against the Revolutionary Government.

JOSEPH: I have already explained this. We are neither for nor against you.

PETER: You have explained nothing. Your mind is not capable of it.

JOSEPH: In respect of the Revolutionary Government, we are neither for nor against it. We cannot be for it: its interests are not our interests. We cannot be against it: it is the first product of the Revolution. Thus we maintain our position, neither for nor against. Our business is to strengthen the people, and, in respect of the government, to make certain demands, in the name of the people.

PETER: But what right have you got to this name of the people? You are only a minority. The majority are with us and the other parties.

JOSEPH: We have been a minority from the very beginning. Nevertheless, we speak for the people.

PETER: Joseph, you're out of your depth. I'm even sorry for your party that it has no more capable spokesman. While you go on with this stupidity, you'll be simply swept aside. And in the judgement of history, you'll only be forgiven because you are wholly forgotten. History, at least, is still rational.

JOSEPH: Yes, it is. And have you anything more to say?

PETER: Not to you, Joseph. Not to a stupid boy, playing his game of Koba. When will Jordan be back?

MARK: A message has just come in. He's arrived in the city. The people met him at the station and cheered him. They're cheering him now through the streets.

PETER: That's much better news. Jordan at least is experienced and capable. Will he be coming here? I can wait and speak to him.

MARK: Yes, he's on his way here.

PETER: All right, then, I'll wait.

[JOSEPH *turns away, and walks to the window. He is silent for some moments, and then turns back and speaks.*]

JOSEPH: This is the headquarters of the Party. Will you show this man out?

MARK: I?

GEORGE: Joseph, be careful. He comes with the authority of the Revolutionary Government.

JOSEPH: I have issued an order, in the name of the Party. This man must go.

PETER: You are a fool, Joseph. A fool, no more.

JOSEPH: I have nothing to say to you.

[*He turns away again. The others hesitate, and then* MARK *goes across and opens the door and stands by it.* PETER *looks at* GEORGE, *and* GEORGE *turns away.* PETER *makes to speak, but then leaves angrily.* JOSEPH *waits, and then turns to the others.*]

JOSEPH: We have a draft to finish. We must get back to work.

MARK: But with Jordan in the city, Koba. He'll be here any minute.

JOSEPH: Then the draft must be ready. Come on.

[*There is a sound of cheering from outside, and then* JORDAN *enters, followed by* MAX.]

MARK: Jordan.

GEORGE: Jordan.

[*The cry is taken up again outside.* JORDAN'S *name is repeatedly shouted, while he waits impatiently.*]

JORDAN: This is no place to do business. Can't we have some quiet? Who's in charge here?

JOSEPH: I am in charge, Jordan.

JORDAN: Koba. Of course. And I'm glad to see you. Tell me what you've been doing. No, wait, don't tell me, let me tell you. You've been sitting in an office, Koba, making lists and drafting articles. Wonderful lists, I'm sure, but bad articles.

JOSEPH: Bad?

JORDAN: Look, I come to the capital of the revolution, and what do I find? A people needing leadership—a people confident of its power and waiting to be shown what to do. Then I look at your articles, Koba. Rudeness, yes. Neutrality, yes. Guarding the purity of the party, yes. But to the government, every attention; to the people, no attention, merely an old rhetoric. You address demands to the government, but don't you realise you are talking to dust, down on your knees talking to it, spitting at it, begging it to become a world? The fact is, Koba, we have only one demand to make of this government.

JOSEPH: Yes?

JORDAN: One demand: that it cut its throat and go.

JOSEPH: I see. Very well.

JORDAN: And this from you, Koba. You of all people. You, Koba, the man who cannot be mastered. And on your knees in the dust, drafting and redrafting demands. But it's time to get up, Koba.

GEORGE: This is madness, Jordan, and you know it. Taunt Joseph if you like; you can't hurt him. But when it comes to policy, try to use your intelligence. Yes, you've been cheered in the streets, but it's gone to your head. There will be no cheering, but only a people slaughtered by the army, unless all of us act, now, and together.

JORDAN: He calls you Joseph, Koba. He's still back twenty years, in the old situation. The reasonable liberal, calling on all good men to unite. But now, in this city, when we can seize full power.

JOSEPH: If the party's object is the attainment of power, certain steps must be taken to prepare for this attainment.

GEORGE: Is that all you can say, Joseph?

JOSEPH: It is all that needs to be said.

JORDAN: You see. I told you. He is not Joseph, but Koba.

GEORGE: And what has he said? That if we want to boil a kettle we must light a fire. Well, of course, but that isn't the question. What we want from you, Joseph, is an honest answer. Say, as you must, that there is no hope of power.

JOSEPH: I can only say that I have learned to wait.

MAX: Yes, perhaps. Because you don't understand power.

JOSEPH: For nearly twenty years I have been a member of the party. I have prepared the party to fight, and I have prepared myself to fight. But through all these years there has been another activity. Through all these years I have stood and listened to arguments like this one. Sometimes the arguments go this way, sometimes that. And that is right: it is the nature of arguments. But I, for my part, always wait for the argument to be finished. It is never the argument that matters. In argument, all policies are equal, but all are fruitless. A party lives by decisions, by conclusions, and by unity and energy in carrying them out. The correctness of a policy is determined by events. The test of men comes then.

MAX: This is the talk of a servant, not of a political leader.

JOSEPH: It is the talk of the people, not of those who climb to power on their backs.

JORDAN: You are both right, as you have both been before. While you are both with me, the party can know itself. But still we haven't much time. We must get this decision. You say I am mad, George, that my head's been turned by the excitement in the city. But Koba is right, events will decide what's correct. And I repeat it again: alone if necessary, mad if necessary, we have to break this government, and complete the revolution. For it can only be saved if we, at any cost, take power to save it.

GEORGE: At any cost. That is always the language of madness. And this is a day of madness, the eruption of a devil, destroying the earth. For it is defeat both ways, whether we win or lose. If we lose, the revolution is lost. If we win, what world, what power, shall we in fact inherit? If we strike now, we shall set fire to ourselves and set fire to the world. The fire will spread and rage, and we shall not see the end of it. No liberty, no dignity, no rights of man, no peaceful cities, will survive this fire. We shall make with our hands only ashes, blood, death, misery, hatred. So I ask you, while there is still time: wait, consider, before you set fire to the world.

MAX: The fire is here. We can only try to pass through it.

JORDAN: Yes, the fire is here. It is our business to control it.

JOSEPH: Ashes, blood, death, misery, hatred: these, in reality,

have been our history. This history can only be changed if
we are not afraid of them, if we even accept them.

JORDAN: And we will stake our lives on it.

JOSEPH: Yes.

MAX: Certainly.

MARK: Yes.

GEORGE: Your own lives, yes. But have you thought of the
lives of others? Of the millions who will die?

JORDAN: And of the millions beyond them who will live.
Certainly. That is the weight of our choice.

[JORDAN *puts out his hand.* MAX, MARK *and* JOSEPH *lay their
own hands on it.* GEORGE *moves away towards* RUTH, *who has
been sitting in silence, away from the men. He offers to take her
hand, but she gets up and moves towards* JOSEPH. *The stage
darkens.*]

SCENE VI

JORDAN, MAX, JOSEPH, MARK, GEORGE *stand facing outwards. It
is still half-dark, and they are cold and tired.*

JORDAN: It is what he said. Yet we have the power.

JOSEPH: This is all that matters. The past is past.

GEORGE: In a broken country. In death and weeping. In cold
and in famine.

JORDAN: But still with our lives, and with the future in our
hands. The grass will grow over the graves. The bruise of
weeping, the bruise of anger, will fade. New hands will
come to the plough, to the tractor, to the generator. We
will end the cold and the famine, and our people will live.

MAX: But alone, Jordan. Alone. Only we have come through.

MARK: And in coming through we have changed. We are not
a free people, alive and resilient. We are a hardened people,
with a bitter optimism. Hope and despair make the same
sound in our mouths.

JORDAN: That is where we began, Mark, while you were a
child. All the other ways had been tried: self-sacrifice,
charity, idealism, service. Generations had tried, in the
good ways: the best of humanity against the worst, and the
worst always won, and could laugh, contemptuously, at
each new young wave of dedication and hope. We began
at that point, and we wiped the laugh from their faces.

Because we watched power, watched its style and its habits, so that we could learn to destroy it. And then nobody could admire us, and nobody patronise us. We were not the good little people, easing the conscience of softness, the quick warm fellow-feeling. No friend or enemy could reach us, using our humanity as the way into compromise. When we were praised, we knew we were wrong. When we were seen as reasonable, we knew we were weak. But when they denounced us, as beyond humanity; when they went black with contempt and hating, as they described what we were: then, at last, we were honestly engaged; then, at last, we were a serious party. The innocents and the martyrs, in this final dialectic, lived again in our bodies, and lived as the world had shown them to live. Innocence and goodness had been tolerated in the world, on the clear understanding that they went down to defeat, to a noble and affecting defeat. But we were the change, Mark: the genetic change. Goodness and innocence passed through our minds into these altered forms; changed to survive and to grow, after the barren generations.

MARK: It is how the world sees us. But is it how we are? We have yet to prove that we too are not barren. Coldness and hatred have bred coldness and hatred, through the history of the world. Can we stand today and be sure that the chain is broken? What shall we create, as we now are?

JOSEPH: You are talking too soon. You are assuming a victory. But there is no victory yet. Do you think they will leave us alone, to create anything? With all the power and cunning they have they will come back and back. If we weaken for a moment, we shall be down with the innocents and the martyrs. We can only survive if we become even harder.

MAX: Hardness is nothing. There is the hardness of stone and the hardness of steel. Whatever we are, we can not survive on our own. And if we are to be helped from outside, if people are to see us as a revolution worth saving, then hardness alone will be nothing: just the empty gesture of the tyrant or the bureaucrat. We must be more than men, not less. We must be and become what men hope and imagine. Then in defending us they are defending their dreams.

JOSEPH: They would do better to wake, and to stop dreaming.

H*

Are we to be actors for this passive audience, flattering their stillness with our action? They sit and wonder, but we speak. They look round, embarrassed, while we act. And they will of course applaud, while we play the hero. They will applaud even louder when the last act comes, and the hero is dead, but has died nobly. But I have a different ambition, without a stage and without applause. The choice is the same as it has always been. With our own hands, with our own strength, without illusions and without concessions, we will become so strong, so strong as a people, that if the enemy comes, we can smash him; if a friend hesitates, we can push him aside; if a comrade weakens, we can go on without him.

GEORGE: This is lunacy, now, when we are not even strong.

JOSEPH: It was lunacy, then, as you told us, when we made the revolution.

MAX: You can seem hard, Koba, because you don't understand. Have you ever watched a procession to the law courts? Back in the middle, uncertain, unimpressive, are the actual judges: too close, too committed, to the real decisions, to have time for display. But in front, Koba, they send a sort of monkey, with the symbols of power. Too stupid to know what the judgement is about, but with a fine set face, set lips, a straight back. He probably thinks, as the procession advances, that he is the power, the intelligence, the reality of judgement. In fact, of course, he is the merest hanger-on: a monkey strutting to appear as a judge.

JORDAN: We've all seen this, Max. And it cuts both ways. I think Koba is right, that we have to be strong. But we can only become strong if we are very intelligent: subtle, flexible, ironic perhaps. That is our monkey, a clever monkey. But the judges, behind, are as Koba says: trusting nobody, without illusions, making no real concessions.

MARK: You too, Jordan?

JORDAN: Yes, Mark. Finally. Don't ever forget this.

[MARK *looks at* JORDAN, *but does not answer. Then he turns, quickly, and leaves.* GEORGE *looks from one to another, and then also goes out.* JORDAN, JOSEPH *and* MAX, *left together, stand watching each other. Then* JOSEPH *moves.*]

JOSEPH: I have a great deal to do, Jordan. I must go and make a start.

JORDAN: All right, Koba. Good luck.

[JOSEPH *leaves*.]

MAX: He needs the luck. But this can't last much longer. He is so stupid, he is already a hindrance. But you won't say this. You still temporise.

JORDAN: I have to temporise. Can't you see that, Max? Yes, we need intelligence, but that's so much more than a ready tongue, even a ready mind. Intelligence is construction: the contours of a society on the contours of a land. And I can only lead, only know, as I feel those contours.

MAX: We have been right so far.

JORDAN: Yes, Max, I think so. But this isn't the old geography. The land isn't still, it's moving and altering under our feet. To know the contours now is a matter of genius.

MAX: We have had this genius.

JORDAN: You say so, Max. You are probably right. But many millions of people, after many centuries of slavery. Who can know, in the end, what they will come to build? We have brought this plan to them. We have set them free to fulfil it. But what happens now, while this burns in our minds? What happens, Max, while the contours are moving?

MAX: It is God, surely? It is man as a god. To create from chaos, having first created himself.

JORDAN: To stay still for a moment. To stay still and look. But the land is moving beneath us, and we too have to move. Endlessly balancing, endlessly flexible, or we fall and destroy ourselves. I can see this figure of man the creator, the towering figure on the crest of the hill. But with the land moving, with the contours shifting, he can fall and break into a thousand fragments. So strong, so sure of himself, but he can fall like a statue, the fists clenched in stone and the arms rigid in dignity; unable, at last, even to reach out and save himself, reach out and break his fall.

MAX: Yes. That is just the danger. The hardness of stone, as I said to Koba.

JORDAN: You keep wanting to tell me what is wrong with Koba.

MAX: No, I want *you* to tell me. From you, at least, people will accept the truth.

JORDAN: But why are you so worried about him?

MAX: I'm not worried about him. He's so obviously mediocre, so pitifully second-rate.

JORDAN: But a second-rate man can make a second-rate revolution. Is that what's worrying you?

MAX: It could so easily go wrong. Men who cannot govern by intelligence and insight can nevertheless govern: by intrigue, by organisation, by the manipulation they find natural. Have we made this revolution for a gang of scheming officials?

JORDAN: We are all scheming officials. You and I too, Max. And we shall have to remain so until the people can govern themselves. That, after all, is the logic of what we have done.

MAX: I deny that entirely. Our logic was an idea.

JORDAN: And from the idea followed power, and from power followed the rest: intrigue, organisation, manipulation. What do you think I am, Max? The leader of a debating society?

MAX: While you are right you are the leader. This is what you have always said. And being right is the power of ideas. No other power is permissible.

JORDAN: And our army, Max?

MAX: An army built and led by an idea. Fighting and dying and overcoming for an idea.

JORDAN: Yet still an army. Still fighting with guns.

MAX: It is your own definition. And while the guns and the power simply serve the idea, we are within our logic. But can you be sure this will always be so?

JORDAN: No, I can't be sure. But we had no choice. We needed the guns.

MAX: And Koba?

JORDAN: Yes, can't you see? You don't have to tell me what Koba is like. He is strong and reliable, but also crude and limited. He is, precisely, the ambivalence of power.

MAX: But if ambivalent then dangerous. Will you at least not say this?

JORDAN: Yes, I will say it. But in my own way and in my own time.

MAX: It may be too late then. You may not even be heard.

JORDAN: I think I shall be heard, Max. And if I speak now, openly, the risks are too great. We have too little strength as it is; we can throw none away. I need you, I need Koba, I need a million others. The gesture would be easy, the arms rigid in dignity. But while the earth is still moving I need this flexible, this varying power. I have been through it all in my mind, and I have this doubting certainty. I have to govern a great country, but in chronic weakness and danger. I need every resource, Max: every kind of intelligence, every kind of power.

MAX: Yes, we must keep you well, Jordan. It's an immense burden.

JORDAN: Not a burden, Max. Not a dead weight. It is all creation and movement, and the setting of limits to make the movement possible. But it is what I wanted. It is what we have lived for. Sitting up late at night, in a generation's argument, and now the premises are men, the conclusions are men, and we are changing the history of the world.

MAX: Yes, we are changing the world.

JORDAN: Come on. No gestures. We have too much to do.

[MAX *and* JORDAN *go out.*]

SCENE VII

JOSEPH *enters, with* RUTH. *They settle down to work,* JOSEPH *writing and* RUTH *copying. There is a clear, absolute silence, then a loud rifle-shot, a pause, and a shout offstage. The shout is repeated, and* MARK *enters.*

MARK: Koba. Come quickly. He is dead.

[JOSEPH *looks up, but does not answer.*]

MARK: Can't you hear me, Koba? Can't you understand what's happened? He's dead.

[JOSEPH *stares, uncomprehending.* RUTH *gets up.*]

RUTH: Who is dead, Mark?

MARK: Jordan. Jordan is dead.

[JOSEPH *does not move. He still stares without focus.*]

MARK: Can't you say anything, Koba? Can't you speak at all? Did you hear what I told you? Jordan, Jordan, is dead.

RUTH: How did he die, Mark?

MARK: He was shot. Assassinated. As it used to happen. Except that he was not in a carriage, or in the dress of rank.

He was on the back of a lorry, in his own shabby clothes. He was addressing a meeting, and his face was pinched with the cold. Then the shot came, quite suddenly. They had just been cheering him, but this man at the window was loading his rifle. Jordan lifted his arm, to ask silence, and the shot came, as if he had given a signal. He was hit in the face, and the force of the shot spun him down. He died quickly, with us around him, on the back of the lorry.

RUTH: But that's terrible. Impossible. Who could have done it?

MARK: Any one of thousands. We can't count our enemies. For we are still at war, but now a war without Jordan, a revolution without Jordan. I still can't accept it, though I watched him die. For we lived in Jordan: in his spirit and in his genius. It felt, when he died, like the end of the world.

RUTH: Yes, Mark, that is just what it feels like.

MARK: A history and a future, in this vulnerable body, this body that has died. Can't you say anything, Koba? At a moment like this, at the death of Jordan, is there nothing you can say?

[JOSEPH *does not move, but still stares without focus.*]

MARK: Koba. Joseph. Answer.

[*He is shouting down into* JOSEPH'S *face.* JOSEPH *does not move, but at last looks up at him. There is the noise of movement outside, and then* GEORGE *and* MAX *enter, carrying the body of* JORDAN. *They lay the body down, in the centre of the group.* RUTH *kneels at* JORDAN'S *head, and weeps.*]

GEORGE: Yes. Ruth is right. We can only mourn.

MARK: We have led a revolution, we are the voices of the people, yet we can say nothing.

GEORGE: Whatever we have expected, the end is tragedy. He was the strongest man in the world, and now he is dead.

MARK: He came down like a god from the sky. We could not believe what he said we must do. We knew only our weakness, but he lived in another dimension. What he said was possible, we discovered to be possible. The miracle happened, like all miracles, just out in the street. And while he still lived with us, in our familiar streets, a new life was possible, incredibly possible. But now he is dead, and it is again incredible.

GEORGE: The circle is drawn, the inevitable circle. What strength could do, he has done. What genius could do, he has done. But strength and genius are only human, in the end. A bullet killed them, as it can kill anything. The human body dies, and with it its spirit.

MARK: History flared for a moment, in this vulnerable body. It has happened before, but so rarely, so briefly. The hunting animal, moving out across the plains, but itself in the end hunted and killed. The foodgrowing animal, working for harvest, and the harvest is cut and the seed is buried, and the labourer is buried with the seed. The machine is shaped and set running, and the power is certain, but the hand weakens, and withdraws its control. History is made, but the man dies.

MAX: We are all to blame. We failed to protect him. We set our lives to this risk, but he took the weight of the risk, he was the most exposed.

GEORGE: The end is tragedy, for this death was inevitable. Without his strength we could have done nothing. He was exposed without pity, for he had shown us a way beyond pity. His death was inevitable, in everything we have done.

MAX: Not inevitable. We could have protected him. We are all to blame.

[*They stand looking down at the body. There is a clear silence. Then* JOSEPH *comes forward, slowly. They all watch him, as he bends over* JORDAN. *When he rises he begins to turn away, but then turns back suddenly.*]

JOSEPH: The man who killed him is to blame. He will be taken and destroyed. Jordan is dead, and the loss is heavy. But Jordan is also alive, in our minds and hands. He has given us his strength, and we shall use his strength. There is no time for weakness, and no time for mourning. We commit to this man what this man was. We commit our promise to you, Jordan, as if you were still standing with us. The enemy who killed you will himself be killed. The enemy who opposed you will be opposed and broken. We promise this, Jordan. We promise this at your death. The future you fought for will go on being fought for, and it is a fight we will win. The people you spoke for will continue to speak, and more loudly, more clearly, in response to this death. We promise this, Jordan. Whoever may weaken, we shall not. Whoever may fear, we shall not. Whoever may hesitate, turn aside from his task, we shall not. We will become harder, in this rigour of your death. We have lost one man. We shall gain a million. We have fought hard before. We shall fight even harder. We promise this, Jordan. For we in this party are of a new flesh, a new blood. For the first time in history, human strength is sufficient. This is your strength, Jordan. This is the strength of our party. We promise this, Jordan. You are not dead. You can never die. In your fists clenched in death we see strength, power, an unbreakable power. We promise this, Jordan. We are a new flesh, a new blood.

[*He turns to the others.*]

We will bury this man as a hero, and make our whole people heroic. Take him up. Walk firmly. It is the future you are carrying.

ACT II

SCENE I

GEORGE *and* MARK *enter*

GEORGE: But every meeting now is the same. You can see the way it's all going.

MARK: Yes, of course. The pressures are terrible.

GEORGE: They are human pressures. Are you afraid to name them?

MARK: No, not afraid. But I've lived through these years. We argued this, you and I, in the very first days. The reality now, I remember you saying, is committees, white papers, administration, supplies. And you were right, I suppose. This is what we've become.

GEORGE: To make a society, we needed those things. To make the people free to direct their own lives. But that purpose, now, is completely forgotten. We are building a state, but not a society.

MARK: I said this too, at the beginning. That when we had thrown off the chains of an old tyranny, we hurried to find new chains: government, authority, discipline.

GEORGE: Then you are bound to oppose what is happening now.

MARK: No, I do not oppose it.

GEORGE: Then you are worse than anyone, because you see this evil and yet you support it.

MARK: I don't support it. I don't oppose it either. I have taken the weight of these years.

GEORGE: You're like Koba equivocating, in those early days. In a crisis like this, you must either support or oppose.

MARK: Yes. Even you, George, call him Koba. The boy Joseph is forgotten.

GEORGE: Does it matter what we call him? In any movement there are these conflicts of men. But this is different. This is a conflict of ideas, of history.

MARK: Of ideas and of history in men, and so, now, in Koba. I watched, as we all did, the same conflict in Jordan, and we know how it ended.

GEORGE: With a bullet, no more.

MARK: I mean before. In the whole action we've been living. The first struggle for power is in a man's own mind.

GEORGE: The struggle for an idea is in a man's mind. And then he seeks to live the idea, and to change his world. But there are other men, always, of a quite different sort. Power for them is a fact and an end in itself. They depose, first, so that they may impose, later. And they will use anything, Mark, any idea, any cause, any suffering of others, to achieve the power that is all they are after.

MARK: These are not different men, but the same men. The struggle for an idea begins in the mind, but it can also end there, and then the idea itself is defeated. When the idea has come clear, then a man knows power as a fact in itself. He deposes, first, so that he may impose, later. And he has no choice, if the idea is fact, if he has really achieved it.

GEORGE: While the idea lasts, we are right to seek power. But it is power for the idea, not power for ourselves.

MARK: There is no separation. While we live the idea, we are committed to power.

GEORGE: But we are not living it. We conceived the idea of freeing our people. But we have not freed them. We have merely changed their masters.

MARK: And the change of masters is of no importance? Can you really think that?

GEORGE: This is what men worked for, then? This, now, is what they worked and died for?

MARK: Yes, I think so.

GEORGE: Then you know nothing about it. That is your best excuse. For if you knew, in detail, the nobility of those men, if you knew even a little of their ideals, their faith, and their passion, you wouldn't dare to suppose this is what they fought for.

MARK: But I know what idealism is. I know what it means to have faith in my brothers. This, to me, was the real revolution. But the meaning I knew was denied at once, at the very beginning. Once Jordan spoke, we were on a different road.

GEORGE: Jordan was hard, certainly, but if he were living, now, he would be against what is happening. He never

sought power for its own sake. It was power for the
revolution.

MARK: For his idea of revolution, and that idea was the Party.
He sought power for the party; at any cost, you remember
him saying. And he warned me, directly, to have no
illusions, when the illusions I had were of immediate freedom, immediate dignity, immediate respect. But when we
seized power, back in those days, we took a different road.

GEORGE: That may or may not have been right. At the time I
was against it.

MARK: Yet you stayed with us, George.

GEORGE: Yes, I stayed. I could not oppose the revolution, even
when it took the wrong road. And I thought I could help
to keep us true to our principles, to speak for humanity even
in the worst times.

MARK: But you don't understand, you have never understood. Once that decision was taken, our only principle was
power. How could it be otherwise?

GEORGE: But power as a means. Never simply as an end.

MARK: There is no distinction. This is what I learned. And
when I look back now, I take the weight of the decision.
What I felt, at that time, was a new spirit in the world: a
liberation of spirit and a new stature in men. Every feeling
I had was of trust, acceptance, generosity, brotherhood.
And when I look back, I salute those feelings, I could not
live without them. Yet Jordan, clearly, spoke a different
language. Max and Koba, all the men with experience,
spoke a different language. They spoke the language of
power, and I felt ashamed and disgusted. But I listened. I
watched what happened. And at every crisis, I discovered
in detail, and against my will, that I had been wrong and
that they were right. You will have to face this yourself, in
the end, and I don't envy you. It is the hardest, the deepest
tragedy: this coming to terms with the world as it is, when
we have seen what it might be. But there is never a choice,
never a serious choice. We have to change the world in
the world's ways, or we shall not change it at all. We have to
fight the enemy with the enemy's weapons or we shall
simply be beaten, as the good have always been beaten.
Look anywhere in the world, and find an exception. There
is none, and can be none. This is what I learned. Yes, we

took power by force and fraud. Yes, we maintain power by force and fraud. But there is no alternative, anywhere. I stick to what I believe. I refuse to find names for force and fraud, that will conceal their reality. That is the business of hypocrites, and there are whole institutions devoted to training hypocrisy. I despise all that. I say force and fraud, but I say also, without them, there would be no revolution. A kinder revolution, a more open revolution: these are simple illusions and you know it. So in the end I make my choice, and it is a tragic choice. I accept force and fraud: not coldly, not willingly, but openly and honestly. I accept them because I have been shown, in detail, that the revolution requires them, and because the revolution is necessary, if man is ever to be free.

GEORGE: I must be mad or dead, hearing you say this. For I know you are good, Mark. I have never doubted that. And I would rather be mad, better be dead, than accept what you are saying as the words of a good man in a sane world. You speak of tragedy, but you have barely touched it. Can you think what it means to see the good destroyed, by their own conception of goodness? A struggle, yes, I accepted, and I accepted suffering where it could not be avoided. But I saw the struggle as between good and evil: that was always the framework, however the conflict might go. But now what I see is like the end of the world. I see your goodness changed into the acceptance of evil, and I might still oppose this, still fight it, but I don't know how. Because I also see, Mark, the change in myself: not the acceptance of evil, but the loss of a language in which I can speak to my friends. I can feel now, speaking to you, as I have felt before only in pain or delirium, in the long night, lying awake, without any human contact. Then the language of good and evil is madness, is death. The memory of normality, of the ordinary connection, is the worst kind of nightmare. For if we wake and speak we shall finally confirm our condition; that among men, in the world, we are mad or have died.

[MARK *hesitates, looking down, and then crosses to* GEORGE. *He kisses him, slowly, on each cheek. Then he puts his arm over* GEORGE's *shoulders, and leads him gently away. As they are just going out,* JOSEPH *enters.*]

JOSEPH: Mark. Is that you?

MARK: Yes.

JOSEPH: Wait just a minute, will you? I want to talk to you.
[MARK *hesitates, but* GEORGE *indicates that he can go on alone, and leaves.* MARK *walks back to* JOSEPH.]

JOSEPH: Was that George you were with?

MARK: Yes.

JOSEPH: Is he ill or something?

MARK: Not in the ordinary way. But he is almost broken. I feel sorry for him.

JOSEPH: Is that necessary? Surely he's sorry for himself, and one is enough.

MARK: Don't say things like that, Koba. Don't ever say things like that. I don't want to hate you.

JOSEPH: As you like, Mark. It isn't important. And my tongue's often rougher than I mean it to be.

MARK: That's common enough.

JOSEPH: Yes. Still, I like men to be men, you know. To give and take a hard knock, without a lot of sentiment and whimpering.

MARK: I also like men to be men, Koba.

JOSEPH: All right, we won't argue. There isn't time, for one thing. We have to recall the meeting.

MARK: Already?

JOSEPH: Yes, already. Not that I wanted it, but the opposition don't know when they're beaten. The decision was made, you were there and saw it. But already they're working against it: not just speaking, but acting. It's getting intolerable, and we must move at once.

MARK: But Max has left for the South.

JOSEPH: Has he?

MARK: Well he said he was going.

JOSEPH: Then that makes it easier. It's mainly Max we must deal with.
[MARK *hesitates, and does not answer.*]

JOSEPH: Well, isn't it? You were there, at the meeting. You heard his proposals. And you voted against them.

MARK: Yes, I voted against them. I thought he was wrong.

JOSEPH: Well then, what's the problem?

MARK: We can all be wrong, Koba. Now one, now another. And the party exists to make a decision.

JOSEPH: That's what I'm saying. The Party has made a decision. And can the Party tolerate men going straight from a meeting and acting against its decisions?

MARK: It's inevitable, surely. People have to go on doing what they think is right.

JOSEPH: Have to go on splitting the party, you mean? Putting their own interests above the Party's interests?

MARK: No, Koba. This is an old trick. What they are actually doing is perfectly clear: putting one version of the party's interests against another version. As they are bound to do, if they honestly disagree.

JOSEPH: Even when the Party has decided?

MARK: Decisions can always be changed. That is what the party is for.

JOSEPH: I remind you what Jordan said. The Party is not a debating society. We are governing a country, not settling an academic dispute.

MARK: Jordan said many things, Koba. You may find that to your cost.

JOSEPH: What things? What cost?

MARK: Well, it's common knowledge that he criticised you, criticised your methods in the party. This is just what he had in mind.

JOSEPH: Can you prove he said this?

MARK: I know that it's true, if that's what you're asking.

JOSEPH: Any slander can be used by the enemies of the Party.

MARK: Yes, Koba, but who are its enemies? Not its leaders, surely? Not its own trusted men?

JOSEPH: Trusted by whom? They are not trusted by the people.

MARK: We've left the people out of this pretty thoroughly already. This is no longer a struggle in the country. The people are tired, after all they have suffered. This is a struggle in the party. We can't call in the people to resolve it.

JOSEPH: That's where you're wrong, Mark. You don't know how wrong.

MARK: I don't understand you.

JOSEPH: The Party now is the people, the best of the people.

MARK: Yes, I accept this. But the party is arguing.

JOSEPH: The Party has decided. That is my whole point.

[MAX *enters, hurriedly.*]

MAX: Decided what, Koba? Have there been more decisions?

JOSEPH: You heard the decisions. They went against you.

MAX: But now you've recalled the meeting. As soon as you knew that I'd left for the South.

JOSEPH: But you've not left. You're here.

MAX: I was warned in time. I came back at once. You suppose you're cunning, but you're a fool, Koba. You haven't even the competence to conceive an intrigue, let alone carry it out. All your moves are so clumsy we see them a mile off. You're like a farm boy at a fair, clambering noisily into the ring and throwing his punches at his opponent's shadow.

JOSEPH: At his shadow, Max?

MAX: This is wasting time. Act your fantasies if you like, but don't look for me in the audience. You've recalled the meeting. All right, I accept this. If you want to push this to the final decision, all right, I'm ready. When the Party must choose, in any final way, I don't doubt the result.

JOSEPH: Nor do I. Why should I?

MAX: You think they'd choose you? Are you mad, Koba? I know you have this idea of yourself, as the efficient organiser . . .

JOSEPH: I have no such idea.

MAX: Then what, at all, if not that?

JOSEPH: I have no idea of myself. I am no more and no less than the will of the Party, the will of the people.

MAX: But this is megalomania. Do you know what you're saying?

JOSEPH: Certainly. And the same charge, the same slander, is familiar to the Party. We were called megalomaniacs when we reached for power in the revolution.

MAX: That was a party decision. What you're saying is different. You're saying that you, Koba, a single man, represent the will of the whole party. This is dangerous nonsense.

JOSEPH: It is simply the fact. Because I am nothing. I have no ambitions. I represent the Party as the Party represents the people. Other parties may flatter the people, and win their temporary support. Other men may flatter the Party, and deceive it for a time. But the will of the people, the will of the Party, cannot fail in the end to assert itself, in its final necessity. If it has been deceived before, the final assertion is necessarily severe.

MAX: Do you think you can threaten me, Koba? We are still rational men and a rational party. Only the argument, in the end, can decide.

JOSEPH: This is an old and common delusion. The decision will be made, not by the arguments, but by the facts.

MAX: I can't argue any more with a mind like this. Do you hear him, Mark? Can you see what this Koba is?

JOSEPH: He can see the facts, no doubt.

MAX: All right then, damn you. Let us appeal to the facts. Let us go to the meeting.

JOSEPH: Yes. Certainly.

[*They turn to go, but* MARK *hesitates.*]

MARK: Just one thing, Koba, to get my own mind clear. This is obviously a crisis, and the party is divided. Yet you speak, all the time, as if this is not so. Have you any reason for this?

JOSEPH: The Party is not divided. But the Party has not yet purged itself of those elements within it who are against the Party.

MAX: This is ludicrous doubletalk. You're just wasting your time, Mark.

MARK: I'm not sure, Max. I know Koba well. He's never this confident unless the facts are as he says.

MAX: What facts? That's the question. The facts are well known, to us all.

MARK: Koba is secretary of the party. And since Jordan's death there have been, we all know, many changes in the membership. There have been massive enrolments, and there have been expulsions.

MAX: Well? Go on.

MARK: We have all known this, in a general way. But Koba is secretary. He knows the details of these changes, far better than any of us, for he has been carrying them through.

MAX: I've watched this, of course. And I've watched his clumsy manoeuvring, to get his own men appointed to positions of influence. But it's all so childish and contemptible. We are an experienced party. We shall not be shifted like that.

JOSEPH: You speak of manoeuvres. That is another slander.
There have been no manoeuvres.

MARK: What do you call them, Koba?

JOSEPH: I stick to the facts. In every crisis of the revolution,
as we have all seen, certain men hold, certain men break.
The Party consists of the men who hold, and of new men,
from the people, who emerge from obscurity to reveal their
strength. As for those who have broken, the Party abandons
them. It also abandons, in the pressure of crisis, all those
who show signs that they are about to break, and so en-
danger the Party. This is nobody's will. It is the simple
logic of events.

MARK: In other words, you admit it. The party has been
reshaped, to a particular policy. Your policy, Koba.

JOSEPH: Not my policy. Simply the needs of the revolution,
the needs of the people.

MARK: Your conception of those needs.

JOSEPH: Not my conception. The Party's conception.

MAX: It is time to end this. We're not talking to a man any
more, but to a machine, an absurd machine with prefabricated answers.

MARK: A machine in a man, Max. That is much more for-
midable.

MAX: What is a machine in a man, against a human mind? I
tell you again, we are a rational party, an experienced
party. We have made a revolution. We have changed
human history. We shall not be deceived by prefabricated
men.

JOSEPH: I agree. We shall not. So shall we go to the meeting?

MAX: Yes. Yes.

[MAX *and* JOSEPH *go out.* MARK *hesitates, and then follows.*]

SCENE II

There is a long silence, and then JOSEPH *enters alone. He moves
slowly and quietly. When he stops, in centre stage, he holds his
shoulders against the cold. Then he turns and sits at his desk.*
RUTH *enters.*

RUTH: They told me you would be here. I've brought you
some food.

JOSEPH: Yes, thank you.

RUTH: You look very tired, Joseph.

JOSEPH: No, I am not tired.

RUTH: It's two days since you've been home. Whenever I've come, they've said not to disturb you, the meeting was still going on.

JOSEPH: Yes, Ruth, I'm sorry. It isn't much of a life for you. Though I told you how it would be, when I came to speak to your father.

RUTH: You mustn't apologise. The revolution still needs our strength.

JOSEPH: It is at least taking it, and still it is not enough. Every nerve, every muscle, cries out for rest. It is the end of the day, a long day, and the spirit fades with the light.

RUTH: You must try to rest, Joseph. You are more tired than anyone.

JOSEPH: No. Not tired.

RUTH: But how can you go on denying it? Your face is grey with tiredness, your whole body is aching.

JOSEPH: I can master my body. That is only the beginning. What I am feeling the whole people is feeling: the whole people, the whole world. So many years, Ruth, of struggle and suffering. The years of war, the years of famine and sickness, the years of absolute struggle, against all our enemies. Everywhere, now, the cry is for peace, for rest, for the easing of tensions. We feel the need of home, and our families, and the long evenings together. To sit back, like old men, and remember the past.

RUTH: Well, and we can remember. We have a victory to remember.

JOSEPH: Ashes, blood, death, misery, hatred. It is what they said it would be, when we made our decision.

RUTH: But there are other things, Joseph. Already, while we are tired, our children are growing. They are running to play in the streets and the fields where their fathers died, and as they play they shout, that hard beautiful shout, because the streets and the fields are the world they are young in. You must see these things, Joseph. They will warm you again.

JOSEPH: They would break me, Ruth. They would break my heart. If I look from the window, and see a child playing, I

unconsciously add ten years to his age, and I see him in
uniform, see him struggling in mud on our frontiers, and
the shout of the enemy as they come back to our country.

RUTH: Is this really so, Joseph? Is there no hope at all?

JOSEPH: Yes, there is hope, but I have to kill it. While there is
only hope, that child will be trampled. When I hear his
shout in the street, I hear through its happiness the shout
of the enemy, coming back to burn and destroy. And my
body is tired, Ruth. My soul is tired. Like millions all over
the world I want only to rest, to stay still. But we cannot
stay still. I have to master my body. I have to master my
soul. This is what it means, Ruth, to be in the party. In
every crisis I have known, as far back as I remember, the
moment has come when we are all tired, when every
instinct demands intermission, when relaxation and compromise seem the only qualities there are. And at every
such moment the party is tested, and because it is the party
it is not deceived, it cannot afford to be tired. All we have
done has depended on this. We have been weaker in
numbers, weaker in influence. Any common calculation
would have predicted defeat. But in that final moment we
have not only hung on, we have struck, we have taken the
initiative. In mastering ourselves we have mastered the
whole situation. We have been more than nature, and so
we have changed nature. And we have to do this once more,
and once more, and once more again.

RUTH: What is it, Joseph, you are planning to do?

JOSEPH: The people are tired, and they have to work harder.
The farmers have the land, and are satisfied, but millions
must leave it, to work in the factories, and those who are
left must grow much more food. After years of shortage,
we all want more for ourselves, yet we must learn to take
less than we already have. We cannot eat power stations,
we cannot wear mills and foundries, but we must give up
some of our food, give up hope of new clothes and furniture,
go back and get poorer till the power stations, the mills, the
foundries are built. Not ten or a hundred, while we keep
hope alive. But thousands and thousands again, in an endless series. There will be a whole generation without any
fruits of its labour that it can put in its mouth, but only the
tall chimneys, the great curves of the dams, the acres of

steel. And when we cry out, for rest or for comfort, we must choke the cry in the throat. The child must cry now, or in ten years he will be trampled and his children shot in the forest. And when the cry comes, when the body can stand no more, then still, here, the body must be mastered, the soul mastered. For to have pity, now, is to be without pity. [RUTH *is silent.* JOSEPH *hesitates, and then gets up and goes close to her, his hand over her shoulders.*]

JOSEPH: Ruth, this is not what I want to say, but I have to say it.

RUTH: If it is necessary, yes.

JOSEPH: There is no choice at all. Only our enemies want us weak, and they are using against us all our own best feelings. Can anyone think, for a moment, that we want life so hard? That we have any real choice?

RUTH: I can't be sure, Joseph. I have my own doubts.

JOSEPH: What doubts? I can show you the figures.

RUTH: It isn't the figures. I'm sure what you say is quite right. But it was your voice, Joseph, your voice as you spoke against pity.

JOSEPH: Not against pity.

RUTH: Against pity here and now, where we can actually feel it.

[JOSEPH *withdraws his arm, and moves a little away.*]

JOSEPH: Do you mean that my voice has changed?

RUTH: We have all changed, Joseph.

JOSEPH: I have aged but not changed, Ruth. My voice, now, is my voice in prison and exile. My voice is Jordan's voice, in those last days, when we had to take the decision. It is not my own voice. It has never been that. It is the voice of the party, which can never be broken. It is the voice of the people, which can never be mastered.

RUTH: Koba.

JOSEPH: Koba is my work, but I am still Joseph.

RUTH: Koba.

JOSEPH: It is a party decision. It is not my decision.

RUTH: You have remade the party. The party is Koba.

JOSEPH: The decision was made. The party made it. It is still Jordan's party.

RUTH: Jordan is dead.

JOSEPH: But his party lives, his revolution lives.

RUTH: And his people, Joseph?

JOSEPH: Lives.

RUTH: Take him up. Walk firmly. It is the future you are carrying.

JOSEPH: Lives. Lives.

[*He walks slowly out, and* RUTH *follows him.*]

SCENE III

MARK *enters, carrying papers.* GEORGE *is following him*

GEORGE: You must listen to me, Mark. A whole people is dying. They are actually choosing to die.

MARK: That is always their privilege. A fool's privilege.

GEORGE: I won't let you provoke me. I know the style you have got used to in power. The guards are there at the door. The generals come for their orders. And you, the political leaders, drive through the streets, in your closed cars. The speed is intoxicating, and the efficiency confirms you. You have only to reach back your hand and a secretary is ready, putting your papers between your fingers. At the long table the papers are turned, but the voices are low, there is no excitement. A man draws up his chair, and a province, a division, is drawn up with him. A paper is turned, and thousands of men move at once into action. You sit very still, at your centre of power. In your young middle age you have achieved your style. You are without emotion, but you have your ideas. You are clean, spare, dedicated men. Each face gives you back the same image of the world. You speak your own language, clipped and dry, for you have absolute power, in the turn of a paper, and the untidy language of men is forgotten, shut out, beyond the guards at the door.

MARK: Not shut out altogether, since you have come in.

GEORGE: You can let me in because I am not important. I can speak but nobody listens. Even the young don't listen. All over the country, all over the world, young men still powerless are rehearsing your language, reproducing your gestures, asking nothing more than that they should become as you are: hard, professional, spare. And when

you listen now, when I tell you of death, you are not to be
moved, for you have your world. Every door you open
gives the same answer. Men. Men with power. Men as
they should be. All the voices are the same.

MARK: You can still make speeches. That is the old world.

GEORGE: Yes, rhetoric, tub thumping, the old kind of wind-
bag. I know how you see me, and the guards will agree, you
have only to call them. The old kind, the speechifiers,
parading their emotions in public, their messy emotions.
The old ranters, still parading the streets, with their mob
slogans, their over-excitement, their endless simplifying,
their absurd and vain self-exposure. So call the guards,
Mark. They're quite certain to agree. Exhibitionists are
not men, not professional men. So what will you do with
us? We are inconvenient.

MARK: Not inconvenient, George. You are simply irrelevant.
Whatever you think of us, we have to get things done, we
have to take decisions. Only the facts count then.

[*A guard enters.* GEORGE *and* MARK *turn to look at him, and then
at each other. But the guard stands quite still, and* JOSEPH
and the SECRETARY *enter behind him. The guard goes out.*]

SECRETARY: Have you business with Koba?

GEORGE: Yes.

SECRETARY: But I made no appointment. I don't think I
know you.

JOSEPH: I know him. Leave us.

[*The* SECRETARY *goes.*]

GEORGE: Thank you, Joseph.

JOSEPH: There is no need to thank me.

GEORGE: I feel I can speak to you. To these others I am crazy.
But I've known you from the beginning. I can still
remember the boy, so shy and yet so determined, who
came to us from the college.

JOSEPH: That was in another world.

GEORGE: Yes, those men are happy, who plan revolutions.
They can look suffering in the face, because they have an
answer to it.

JOSEPH: I can still look suffering in the face.

GEORGE: Can you? You think you can, from the window of
your office. But I have been out in the country. I have seen
men and women settling down like animals to die, and their

children too hungry to cry, only their eyes staring without understanding. I have seen famine before. It is always terrible. But this is not the terror of nature, the drought or the storm. This is the act of men, of you as men. You have forced a meaning on them, your own meaning, and you are so sure it is right you continue to force it, to the point of their death. Perhaps your meaning is right. I can't argue that. There has been misery before, in the great changes, and we translate it as birth pangs, the blood and pain of new life. But to see this blood on your hands, to know this pain in your own body's movements, willed, determined, executed: this, Joseph, is what you have to answer.

JOSEPH: Yes, I answer for it.

GEORGE: Do you know what you are saying? Has it gone so far? I expected you to plead that you were too far away, that you didn't know what's been happening.

JOSEPH: I do not plead. I know what is happening.

GEORGE: Yet your agents lie about it. Every official word is a lie.

JOSEPH: In a campaign of this kind, we don't inform and encourage our enemies.

GEORGE: But who are your enemies? These ordinary suffering people?

JOSEPH: Our enemies, first, are beyond our frontiers. In a matter of years they will come back and try to destroy us. Our enemies, second, are all those here, who from pity or fear or from conscious design, try to stop us paying the price of the future, the heavy but necessary price. Our enemies, third, are ourselves, all wanting the easy way out: the bland way we can call humanity; the popular way we can call responsible: all the familiar hypocrites we can quietly become, who change countries in their heads and are ashamed of work and dirt on their hands. All these are our enemies.

GEORGE: And if we are our own enemies, must we even lie to ourselves?

JOSEPH: There is no lying here.

GEORGE: Not even the lie about Max? You weren't content to defeat him at the meeting. You had to drive him from the country and now you call him a traitor.

JOSEPH: He has left the country, and so of course he is a

traitor. By his own choice, he became our enemy. But there are other enemies still here. They come to this room, and present their arguments.

GEORGE: That is another lie. I am not your enemy.

JOSEPH: Then are you serious at all? What sort of man are you? You have sought us out to denounce us. You have spoken very clearly and with genuine feeling. Or was it not genuine? Do you not really oppose us?

GEORGE: It was genuine and I oppose you, but I am not your enemy. I am not an enemy of the people.

JOSEPH: It is a familiar pattern. You are all of a piece. In any revolution, you support the idea but oppose the practice. In the same way, now, you oppose us openly, yet say you are not our enemy.

GEORGE: I oppose a policy. Can you never see this?

JOSEPH: A policy may be wrong. We have in fact pressed too hard. We shall slow our pace.

GEORGE: But on the same road. With the same ends.

JOSEPH: Yes. Of course. They are the correct ends.

GEORGE: Then I continue to oppose you. This is no real change.

JOSEPH: Then you become our enemy. This is no change either.

GEORGE: You are trying to drive me to this. Why, Joseph?

JOSEPH: It is perfectly clear. It is your own decision.

GEORGE: Very well. Then I take my decision. I oppose you openly, in the name of the people.

JOSEPH: You have no people. You have broken with that.

GEORGE: I have broken with you. You are not the people.

JOSEPH: These are matters of fact. There is no point in arguing.

GEORGE: Not with you, Joseph. Not with you, Koba. But there are others, many others, millions of others.

[JOSEPH *turns his back.* GEORGE *looks at* MARK, *who quietly shakes his head.* GEORGE *hesitates, making to speak to* JOSEPH *again, but then turns and goes.* JOSEPH *waits for some time, before turning back.*]

JOSEPH: He must be arrested tonight, before he leaves the capital. Will you give the instructions?

MARK: You're not serious, Koba?

JOSEPH: I was never more serious. There is not much time.

MARK: But he isn't dangerous. He could never be dangerous. We've known him for years, we know what he's like.

JOSEPH: He says what I hear, in my own mind. I have mastered my own weakness. I will master his.

MARK: But arrest? On what charge?

JOSEPH: The charge can come later. The crime is already a fact.

MARK: But what crime? Do you know what you are saying?

JOSEPH: He has become an enemy. In political life, that is the only crime.

MARK: And you are asking me to arrange his arrest?

JOSEPH: Yes, Mark, I am asking you.

MARK: You ask with a reason. What is it?

JOSEPH: I have said it already. We must begin with ourselves, with mastering ourselves.

[*The* SECRETARY *enters, hurriedly.*]

SECRETARY: Koba, forgive me . . .

JOSEPH: Yes?

SECRETARY: It's your wife, Koba. She insists on seeing you. She came here and into my room. She seems ill.

[JOSEPH *looks at* MARK, *and is silent for a moment. Then he turns to the* SECRETARY.]

JOSEPH: Ill? Do you know what it is? Can she come this far?

SECRETARY: She wants to come here, sir. She especially said this.

JOSEPH: Then ask her to come.

[*The* SECRETARY *goes out.* MARK *moves uneasily, and then turns towards* JOSEPH. JOSEPH *looks at him, abruptly, and then turns his back.*]

JOSEPH: What are you waiting for? You have your duty.

MARK: There are people waiting to see me. I'd perhaps better go.

JOSEPH: Not people waiting. The arrest.

MARK: But we'd not finished discussing it. You must listen to me, Koba.

JOSEPH: There is no time. You can see there is no time.

[MARK *hesitates. The* SECRETARY *enters, supporting* RUTH's *arm. They stop and look across, towards* JOSEPH, *who keeps his back turned.* MARK *hesitates, and then goes quickly out.* RUTH *frees her arm, and nods to the* SECRETARY, *who also leaves.*]

I

RUTH: Well, Joseph, won't you turn and look at me?

[JOSEPH *turns, slowly. When he sees her face he comes quickly across to her.*]

RUTH: No, don't touch me. I want you to stay where you're bound to look at me.

JOSEPH: You're so pale, Ruth. Shall I send for help?

RUTH: There is no need, Joseph. There is no time. I came to help you, not myself.

JOSEPH: Won't you at least sit down?

RUTH: No, I must stand. You mustn't see me as weak. I have always believed there is only tenderness in loving, only touch and kindness, all the good of the world. But now I know this is false, for I have known you, Joseph. You have grown to a man in my arms, to the strength of a man, and you have taken that strength and used it, the strength of your hands to hold down a whole people, to destroy other lives.

[*She covers her face.* JOSEPH *remains quite still.*]

RUTH: I haven't much time, but I must make you know this. If I hadn't loved you, it would be so much easier. I wouldn't now have to die.

JOSEPH: You mustn't speak about dying.

RUTH: But I am dying, Joseph. When I came in I was dying. When the message came, that I could come in and see you, I took the poison, I had it ready in my bag.

JOSEPH: Poison. What poison?

RUTH: It doesn't matter. It's too late for you to stop it. But I had to tell you like this, so that you would know the truth, and not be able to forget it. I have lived with you, Joseph, in this light of the revolution, where every feeling is clarified, where every feeling is lived. I give my life, willingly, in this same light.

JOSEPH: But why, Ruth, why? There is no need for you to die.

RUTH: There was no need for the others to die, but they are already dead and forgotten. You will not be able to forget me.

JOSEPH: I'll take you now, and we'll get to the hospital. They'll be able to save you. I'll make them save you.

RUTH: But I want to die. I have chosen death. Just as they chose death, when they slaughtered their cattle, and sat down to die. You have a terrible power, Joseph, but you must know its limits. When we choose death, we are passing beyond you, and you can no longer touch us.

JOSEPH: But what good can this do? What possible good?

RUTH: Come closer to me. I can't talk much longer. We have loved in our bodies, and a new life has grown there. But there is another growth in the body, that we don't understand. There is the twisting of life into a growth that destroys us: all the energy of living, the growing delight of the body, into a wrong pattern, a killing pattern, and the growth kills us.

JOSEPH: We shall master this also. We shall have to master it.

RUTH: There is no mastery, where I am living, Joseph. I see in myself all the others who are dying, and I choose to be with them, and you cannot prevent me. You have forced your meanings to the limits of life, but you cannot pass those limits, only we can pass them.

JOSEPH: Who has been speaking to you? Who has been lying to you?

RUTH: No-one has been lying, Joseph. The deaths are so many, they make their own truth.

JOSEPH: Was it George? That old fool. Has he been coming lying to you?

RUTH: Nobody has lied to me. Even you can't, Joseph. And your wife chooses death, beyond any lying.

[*She sinks down. He kneels in front of her.*]

JOSEPH: Ruth, listen. If you could only understand.

RUTH: I have blessed our marriage. I still want to bless it. But you have made me curse it, with a public curse. I am dying for this, Joseph. I am dying with the others, but it is my curse you are hearing.

JOSEPH: You will not die. I won't let you die.

RUTH: You are Koba, my husband. You are the man who cannot be mastered. I have loved you, Koba, and my love has grown into death, just as you, who were Joseph, have grown into death.

[*She falls back.* JOSEPH *kneels over her, supporting her head.*]

JOSEPH: You must wait. You must listen. In all the world, Ruth, only you have touched me. I have served my people, and I have learned only hardness. Only you, always, have been able to touch me. You are all I have left of pity and tenderness, so you must not die. You must live and teach

me, you must live and keep me alive. Don't you see, Ruth, you must live, you must live.
[*He looks down into her face. She has died while he has been holding her. He feels her face and her hands, and collapses over her body. Then he recovers and gets up, slowly. Standing above her, he lifts his voice to a shout.*]
JOSEPH: Guard! Guard!

SCENE IV

The SECRETARY *enters, and lays papers on the table. As he sets them ready,* MARK *enters.*
MARK: He is not here, then?
SECRETARY: He is expected shortly.
MARK: He always does this now, making us wait for him, making us ask 'when will he come, when will Koba come?'
SECRETARY: We choose to ask this.
MARK: What do you know of choice? You are always the servant, watching in corridors, having the papers ready. In yourself you are nothing.
SECRETARY: It is what he says, of his own duty.
MARK: Yes, in himself he is nothing. The voice of the party, and the party is the voice of the people. Do you believe that any more?
SECRETARY: I have never disbelieved it.
MARK: Yes, that's quite true. Neither belief nor disbelief: they are not in your world.
SECRETARY: It's easy to talk, but I know my duty. In the world we are making there are no masters or servants: there are only the facts, of our place in the world. Other people can afford gestures. I have heard them drunk, late at night, or in the false excitement of meetings: ruled by ideas, arguing about principles, passionately declaring their beliefs and their doubts. But the rest of us watch, and we know one thing quite well: the worst thing that could happen would be the delivery of human destiny into the hands of such men. The people know this with an instinctive wisdom. Talkers, sentimentalists, every kind of emotional crank: the people reject them, for they know their irrelevance.

When it comes to living, and to actual business, there are
quite different men, on whom the real burden falls.

MARK: Yes. I know what you mean. But tell me one thing:
does it ever worry you that you are serving a revolution;
that you, in detail, administer a revolutionary change?

SECRETARY: Worry me? Do you really not understand?
History has produced our revolutionary society. Would
you have me go back, and serve different ends?

MARK: I just wondered, that's all. Would there be a man like
you in every society? At every elbow, accepting every
order? Would you have been there administering the
inquisition, or a feudal court, or a mining company?
Would you have counted the slaves on to the ships of the
traders? Would you have stood at the door, into every
destiny, and called out the names, in your efficient voice,
and made up the lists and ordered the records? Is there a
family of you, in the whole record of man: always correct,
always efficient, always sure of your duty?

SECRETARY: These questions are childish. You should know
better than to ask them.

MARK: Yet I do ask them. Can you do better than answer?

SECRETARY: I said childish, but that was wrong. Children are
realists, knowing their parents, knowing their home, as
grown men come to know where they actually live. But
there is a stage between these, and many are fixed in it. The
questions you ask are adolescent questions: neither the
habit of children, nor the conscious acceptance of men, but
a familiar chaos, disorganised, rootless; ridden by fantasies
and without self-knowledge; a pointless enthusiasm and
pointless destruction; romantics, anarchists, every kind
of bohemian; the perpetual delinquents, in every society.

MARK: You haven't answered my question, though you've
relieved your feelings.

SECRETARY: It is so stupid a question there is no need to
answer it. Would I have stood by a slave ship, or in a
feudal court? But where are these things? They are not in
my world. History has destroyed them, and there is no
arguing with history. Your questions are fantasies, as your
thoughts are fantasies. You can never know when a thing
is finished; when history has moved on, and posed new real
questions. While men like myself deal with the facts of the

world, you shout in our ears about things that are over and
done with. You have no observation, you have only
nostalgia. You live on the cross because you have seen it
painted, or in the poor man's hovel because you have read
an affecting story, or on the barricades because you still
have dreams of a slogan and a flag. Can you never live
where you are? Can you never see the actual facts, and the
actual measures that must be taken to deal with them? You
are lost in dreams and ideas because you have no nerve,
ever, to face things as they are. And the practical men,
bound by actual disciplines—empirical as they must be,
with the facts on their tables—you think you can sneer at,
to raise the laughs of your friends. You call us bureaucrats,
mediocre officials, men bound by routine. But you live
through us, you depend on us. You are the romantics that
we who are realists have to carry on our backs.

MARK: I was a romantic. I am not one now. Would you care to
look at me, at this fact by your table?

[*The* SECRETARY *looks, and pauses. He moves the papers
nervously.*]

SECRETARY: I was speaking generally. You must understand
this.

MARK: Yes, I do understand it.

SECRETARY: I have heard so much irresponsible criticism. I
get carried away, by the sheer illogic of it.

MARK: Yes, I had noticed. You spoke quite passionately,
when you spoke against passion.

SECRETARY: I got carried away. I don't often speak out. But
it's always the same, when you get to arguing with them.
They drag you down, into their own messy world. You'll
understand this, with your own responsibilities. It's more
than a man can easily take, when he's worked to the limit
with actual things. I usually manage to control myself,
when I hear them shouting and arguing. I come back here,
where I know where I am.

MARK: Yes, I know. And I come back here. We both come,
and we wait for Koba.

SECRETARY: It's good when he comes, because then at last
things are clear. That extraordinary power of decision, and
without any gestures. I have seen foreigners come here,
people who have read of our revolution. They seem to

expect some wild revolutionary figure, some man from a poem. And I watch them as they come in here, and the room is quiet, and there are no interruptions, and the whole tone is businesslike: just a man at his desk, carrying the weight of a world, but never raising his voice, listening calmly and answering calmly. It isn't what they expect, but they quickly appreciate it. There is some hope of sanity when men are like this.

[*There is a sound at the door.* JOSEPH *enters, followed closely by the* WARDER. *He nods to* MARK, *and goes across to his desk. The* WARDER *waits.*]

JOSEPH: I'll sign these later. I have other things to settle.

SECRETARY: Yes, of course. As you wish. But this top one is urgent.

JOSEPH: What is it?

SECRETARY: Confirmation of the administrative arrangements arising from yesterday's decision of the court.

MARK: So quickly, is it? There was talk of an appeal.

JOSEPH: There is no appeal, in such cases. The law is perfectly clear.

MARK: He has asked to see you, you know.

JOSEPH: There are more than twenty of them. Can I see them all?

MARK: But he is rather different. Since you've known him so long.

JOSEPH: He should have thought of that before he became a criminal.

MARK: A political criminal.

JOSEPH: That is what I said.

[*He turns to the* SECRETARY.]

JOSEPH: Is it here I sign?

SECRETARY: Yes, there where the cross is. And just over the page, if you would.

[JOSEPH *begins to sign.*]

MARK: No.

[JOSEPH *does not look up, but finishes signing.*]

MARK: No, Koba, no. I won't let you do this.

[JOSEPH *does not look at him, but hands the paper to the* SECRETARY, *who turns to leave.* MARK *crosses to prevent him.*]

SECRETARY: If you would excuse me. I have a great deal to do.

MARK: Twenty-four men. Twenty-four human beings who worked for the revolution before you had even heard of it. And you will carry your paper and they will be shot in the back of the neck.

[*The* SECRETARY *looks round at* JOSEPH, *who does not even look up. The* SECRETARY *looks across at the* WARDER, *who at once steps forward.*]

WARDER: Shall I take the paper?

MARK: No.

WARDER: Now look, sir, he has his job to do, like we all have.

MARK: Who are you? I don't know you.

JOSEPH: Mark.

MARK: Yes.

JOSEPH: He is the man you sent to arrest George. Do you really not know him?

MARK: I've never seen him before.

JOSEPH: You've been lucky, Mark. For you it all happens on paper.

WARDER: You just leave it to us, sir. We know our own job.

MARK: Yes, but do I know mine? Was it really you who arrested George?

WARDER: Him and the others. I don't remember all the names.

MARK: Will anyone remember them, when you get that paper?

JOSEPH: Yes, Mark, the people will remember them. They will remember the criminals who endangered their country. They will remember the gang who conspired against them.

MARK: It is what you will say. You have plenty of paper. Because for you, too, it is all on paper. Would you go down yourself, to that filthy prison, and wake up George and the others, and take them out and shoot them?

JOSEPH: Yes, of course. They are enemies of the people.

MARK: Then why don't you do it? Why still use these agents? Stand up, Koba, and draw your own gun.

[JOSEPH *unlocks the drawer of his desk, and then slowly stands up, holding a revolver pointing at* MARK.]

JOSEPH: Was this what you asked for?

MARK: Stop playing, Koba. This is the final lunacy. Yesterday it was the court, but today only the gun.

JOSEPH: It is what you asked for. You didn't want it only on
  paper.

MARK: That is not what I meant, and you know it.

JOSEPH: I wonder, Mark, if you know at all what you mean.
  Look, I'll put down the gun. Do you see? Now just look
  behind you. Do you see what has happened?

  [*The* WARDER *has drawn his own gun, and is covering* MARK.]

MARK: What does this prove? That you have trained him
  well? That he is your performing animal?

JOSEPH: It proves the nature of power. That is all I am saying.

MARK: Yes, but what power? Power in what name? This is
  what you must prove.

JOSEPH: You have never accepted it. You have always lied to
  yourself.

MARK: I have called facts by their names.

JOSEPH: Except this fact, Mark. Do you remember that day,
  when we stood in the capital, and had to take the decision?
  We put our hands together, to complete the revolution.
  But that wasn't rhetoric, Mark. It was taking the gun, as
  the decisive fact.

MARK: We had reason then, Koba. We were freeing the people.
  The army stood at the gates, to destroy our freedom.

JOSEPH: The army is still there, only a little further back.
  We've very little time, before they cross the frontier and
  march through to burn and destroy us.

MARK: Then we must hold to each other, be strong with each
  other. This is the way we have offered the world.

JOSEPH: And the world has rejected it: that is the fact we must
  live with. Do you suppose for a moment that I prefer the
  gun? You and the others can win verbal victories, without
  the least difficulty. The people hate war, the people hate
  violence. In some quiet place, away from the danger, even
  the idea is incredible; only evil men have it. From the
  beginning of my life I have heard good men, honest men,
  despising violence. They dismiss the gun as the toy of the
  militarist or the whip of the tyrant. But have you watched
  what happens, in a besieged city, when the use of the gun is
  questioned? Men and women run from their homes,
  ordinary peaceloving men and women, and they tear to
  pieces the man who stands up and refuses to fight. And
  they have no choice; it is their own lives at stake. And if a

I*

man steals water, or cheats on his rations, or dodges his share of the work, the people turn and destroy him, for they know he is betraying them. Yes, we all hate war. We all hate hardship and shortage. But who is the friend of the people, when these things come? The liberal, the pacifist, can offer only his fantasy: saying how things ought to be, not how they are. And he is the man who makes war more likely, by showing his weakness, his willingness to compromise. We are fighting, Mark, to keep all the things that we value. At the first sign of panic, the first sign of betrayal, even the first sign of fantasy, diminishing the danger, weakening our will to resist, then the gun must be drawn, even within the city, for it is life itself we defend.

MARK: That remains to be seen. I can say no more.

JOSEPH: You have interfered with an order. Will you now stand back?

MARK: No, Koba, I cannot stand back. I am defending a life.

JOSEPH: This is your last chance, Mark. You are my friend and comrade, but don't imagine I shall hesitate.

MARK: I know that, Koba. That is part of the choice.

JOSEPH: Well then?

MARK: All I know is this: that you are killing my friend and my former comrade. One by one, Koba, you have forced us to this, and you will soon be alone. Of the men who were there, when we made the decision, all are dead or in exile; only we two are left. And your wife has died, in the same action, and the rigour of death, once again, becomes your own more powerful rigour. Only think, Koba: yourself alone, only these two serving you, as they would serve your enemies if the power shifted. Is that, in the end, what you want?

JOSEPH: What I want doesn't matter. It has never mattered. But don't be stupid, Mark. Don't slip away into fantasy. I, Koba, alone? You count yourself, Mark, but you don't count the others. You could go to that window and shout and a people would answer you. Millions of voices, Mark, and the same answer. Could we govern this country alone? Could we plough and start the machines, over thousands of miles? Could we do anything, if we were not the people?

MARK: Yes but that, don't you see, is the final betrayal? From the beginning you made the distinction: what is right for the people and what the people themselves may say. Through all the years, of preparation and exile, you lived by this: that you were the people, the best and the future, even when they rejected you. And you were right, Koba. We were all right.

JOSEPH: It is the same situation. I have never changed. But the people now have a voice of their own.

MARK: Are you sure, Koba? Shall I go to that window, and shout what is happening? Shall I go to the streets, and tell the people the truth?

JOSEPH: You can go to the window. Go on, open it.

MARK: Yes, then the order passes.

[JOSEPH *does not answer.* MARK *hesitates, and then resigns himself. He speaks to the* WARDER.]

MARK: Do you intend to arrest me?

WARDER: I don't look for trouble, sir. Just whatever's necessary.

MARK: Then take me. Look, I hold out my hands. You are too late to arrest me, for I have arrested myself. When I gave the order, for the arrest of the others, I turned my own key. So take me. Accept this submission. What I started myself I will complete myself. And so it will be, Koba, in an endless process. What we write in blood we shall write in our own blood. Even you, Koba, will learn this in the end.

[JOSEPH *nods, and the* WARDER *at once takes* MARK'S *arm, holding the revolver against his back. The* SECRETARY *turns, and when* JOSEPH *nods again goes out with the order.* JOSEPH *sits to his desk, and looks down at his papers. The* WARDER *leads* MARK *out.*]

SCENE V

JOSEPH *is sitting alone. Beyond the window of his room the sky is alight with fires, and there is a long, almost continuous barrage of artillery.* JOSEPH *gets up, and crosses to look from the window.* LUKE *enters, and stands watching him. There is silence in the room for some moments, and then* LUKE *moves.* JOSEPH *at once swings round.*

JOSEPH: Who's there? Answer. Who are you?

LUKE: Don't you know me, Koba?

JOSEPH: No, I don't know you. I've never seen you before.

LUKE: I was watching as you stood at the window. It is how I remember you.

JOSEPH: You remember nothing. You are deceiving yourself.

LUKE: The darkness flowers. Do you remember, Koba? The darkness flowers, in its own season.

JOSEPH: Get back. Keep away from me. I don't know you.

LUKE: I am much older, Koba, and you are older. But what we saw is now fact.

JOSEPH: We saw nothing. I don't know you. I have never seen you before.

LUKE: You are frightened, Koba. That isn't like you. All over the city people are watching this window, and taking what comfort they can from their knowledge of Koba. That he, at least, will never be frightened.

JOSEPH: I am not frightened. This is nonsense you're talking.

LUKE: The man who cannot be mastered. It is how they think of you, Koba. It is how you think of yourself.

JOSEPH: Those are enemy guns, at the gates of the city, and I am still here. And I will take those guns, take their noise and flame, and I will burn and deafen the men who have brought them. I will burn the city that sent them, and leave it in rubble and ashes.

LUKE: I believe you, Koba. I have always believed this.

JOSEPH: Yet you can still insult me? Still say I am frightened?

LUKE: It isn't of that you are frightened, Joseph.

JOSEPH: Then what? Say it. Don't waste my time.

LUKE: There are so many voices. My own is the least of them.

JOSEPH: I don't understand you. What are you?

LUKE: Do you still not know me? Do you not remember my voice?

JOSEPH: Why should I remember your voice?

LUKE: The child at the breast becomes the man at the plough, gives the earth his blood and gives others his harvest. The girl screams on the bed of straw, in new blood, in new hands, and still the harvest is taken. War and tyranny and fever and ignorance, generation on generation, taking and destroying our children.

JOSEPH: Those are my own words. You are repeating my own words.

LUKE: They have become my words, for I am nothing. I am only a voice, speaking the words of many.

JOSEPH: What are you? Say what you are.

LUKE: No liberty, no dignity, no rights of man, no peaceful cities.

JOSEPH: Answer me. Answer.

LUKE: What we write in blood we shall write in our own blood. Even you, Koba.

JOSEPH: I don't know who you are. I don't know how you dare to approach and defy me.

LUKE: I have loved you, Joseph, and my love has grown into death.

JOSEPH: No.

LUKE: I am dying with the others, but it is my curse you are hearing.

[JOSEPH *steps away, hiding his eyes.*]

LUKE: You have a terrible power, Joseph, but you must know its limits. When we choose death, we are passing beyond you, and you can no longer touch us.

[JOSEPH *looks up slowly, and stands quite still. Then he moves decisively.*]

JOSEPH: You are the last enemy, the private enemy, but you can still not make me afraid. With an army at the gates, am I to be frightened by echoes?

LUKE: My voice is never an echo. It is a human passing of words, and it cannot be killed.

JOSEPH: Look around this room. It is the centre of power. Men have come to this room, powerful men, and been taken away, with only death in front of them.

LUKE: Yes.

JOSEPH: I have drawn my gun in this room, as I am drawing it now.

LUKE: Yes, Joseph.

JOSEPH: Are you not afraid? Do you think I would hesitate?

LUKE: You have already hesitated.

JOSEPH: What are you? I don't know you.

LUKE: In myself I am nothing. I have no name.

JOSEPH: You were with me in exile. There, in the north, where we shared a hut.

LUKE: He spoke and he was killed. He is many men.

JOSEPH: You were learning to write, while I stood by the window.

LUKE: Not an echo, Joseph. A voice.

[JOSEPH *crosses and looks from the window.*]

JOSEPH: What do you want with me?

[LUKE *does not answer.*]

JOSEPH: Say what you want. There's no need to be afraid. Look, I've put away the gun. You can say what you want. You can speak quite freely.

LUKE: I have said what I came to say.

JOSEPH: But it is nothing. Only words, echoes, fragments of voices from the past.

LUKE: Voices speaking now.

[JOSEPH *turns and looks into* LUKE's *face.*]

JOSEPH: You are only a man. Don't think you can frighten me.

LUKE: What else would frighten you, Joseph?

JOSEPH: You are not even a man. You say nothing for yourself.

LUKE: Yes, Joseph. We have met on that.

JOSEPH: I don't understand you. I don't know what you are saying.

LUKE: The darkness flowers, in its own season. The darkness flowers, passing beyond its source. In this far instant, when the darkness flowers, there is a new country, between earth and sun.

JOSEPH: I don't understand. I don't know what is happening. But I want to kneel to you.

LUKE: Not to me, Joseph.

JOSEPH: You have no name, and I am only Koba. You are a voice I know, and have almost forgotten. I want to kneel, not to you but to the voice.

[LUKE *stands watching him.* JOSEPH *prepares to kneel. There is a clear silence, as the distant gunfire ceases. Then there is a sudden salvo of guns, directly outside, and the sound of cheering.*]

JOSEPH: What is it? You hear the shouting out there. And the guns, so close.

LUKE: It sounds like victory, Joseph.

JOSEPH: Victory? Or the beginning of victory. Is it really true? Yes, of course it is. It is what I predicted. I had almost forgotten.

[*The* SECRETARY *enters. The light of the room increases.*]

SECRETARY: Can't you hear then, Koba? They're calling for you. The battle is won, the enemy has retreated. Everyone's calling out Koba. Koba and victory are the same words.

[JOSEPH *looks at the* SECRETARY, *then at* LUKE. *He smiles, slaps his side, and crosses quickly to the desk.*]

JOSEPH: It is what I said it would be. They all disbelieved me. They said I was wrong, through all those years. One after another they turned against me, but now they are dead, and this is the victory.

LUKE: Not your victory, Koba. Not only yours.

JOSEPH: What are you? I don't know you. You are just the latest in line. One after the other they have spoken against me, convinced they were right, that their feelings were right. But who is right now? Do you hear that shouting? They're calling for me, for Koba, because I am right, because Koba is right. It is what Jordan said, about a man who can lead. He leads because he is right. The others may seem right, their ideas better, their feelings better. But the man who is right holds on, whatever it costs him. You heard me say, years ago, that the enemy would come. You heard me say what to do, to get ready to beat him. And now he has come, and we have beaten him. All the weak voices, all the confused ideas: where are they now, on the day of the victory?

LUKE: And the men, Koba? The men who have died?

JOSEPH: They have died for their country. They have died for this victory.

LUKE: I mean the men who were killed, in their own country, by their own country.

JOSEPH: So that their country could live. They were wrong. The party was right. The people were right. And this is only the beginning. I have said before, we will take those guns, take their noise and flame, and we will burn and deafen the men who brought them. We will burn the city that sent them, and leave it in ashes and rubble.

LUKE: Ashes, blood, death, misery, hatred.

JOSEPH: It is not our choice. It is the choice of history. We accept its decision, as we accepted it before.

SECRETARY: Will you come now, Koba? The people are waiting to see you.

JOSEPH: There's no need to hurry. Let them ask when Koba will come.

LUKE: Do you know what will actually come?

[JOSEPH *looks at* LUKE, *and then turns his back.*]

JOSEPH: How did this man get in here? I don't know him.

SECRETARY: I don't know, sir. I simply assumed . . .

JOSEPH: Assume nothing. There are many impostors, with persuasive voices. But it isn't the voice that decides history. You can hear the decision, outside, in the streets.

LUKE: Very well. I'll go. But I'll see you again.

JOSEPH: No.

LUKE: Inevitably, Koba.

JOSEPH: Do I have to repeat myself? No.

[*The* SECRETARY *steps forward, and shows* LUKE *out.*]

SCENE VI

The DOCTOR *stands by the window, looking out. The* SECRETARY *enters.*

SECRETARY: Doctor.

DOCTOR: Yes.

SECRETARY: He is in great pain. Will you not go in to him?

DOCTOR: Do I have to repeat myself? No.

SECRETARY: But you have sworn an oath, to relieve suffering. Can you dare to break this?

DOCTOR: I have already told you.

SECRETARY: I don't understand you. He's not only a man, and in pain. He's also a leader, the leader of a people. In turning from him, you are turning from everyone.

DOCTOR: He will understand that. He has taught us too well.

SECRETARY: I don't understand you. Don't you know this is Koba?

DOCTOR: Yes, I know this is Koba.

SECRETARY: Have you ever seen him? Have you ever spoken to him? Do you know at all what he's like?

DOCTOR: I've seen him from a distance, on the saluting platform. I've seen the face at the window of the car, driving fast and closed through the city. Would you call this knowing him?

SECRETARY: Of course not. All you've seen is the image, the sign of the leader. But what you forget, Doctor, is that there is a man behind this: a man like ourselves, a human being who is now in pain

DOCTOR: It was not a man who arrested my brother. It couldn't have been. My brother was quiet and gentle. He only thought of his work. But he went the way of the others: the sudden arrest, the camp in the north. He died there last year: a prisoner but still also a doctor, giving his life willingly for his patients, in the epidemic which in the end killed him. When you talk of a man, remember I have this idea of a man: of what a man is at his best.

SECRETARY: An idea, however, which you deny in yourself.

DOCTOR: There have been tyrannies before. It is a normal history. But this, with us, is unique. Other systems have exploited the worst in man: his aggression, his greed, his capacity to be cruel. Our system is different. What is exploited in us is the best in man: loyalty, comradeship, self-sacrifice, the future. We have given all these beyond measure, and Koba has taken them; taken and killed.

SECRETARY: He has had to be hard. There has been terrible danger. But he has brought us through it.

DOCTOR: Do you think I am not hard? We are all hard. We have learned to be hard, in a hard history. I'm not an idealist, you must understand that. All the comfortable people outside, they forget their own history. Its blood has faded and is now never seen, under their nice modern light. We have had cruel enemies, and we have had to be hard. But still something has happened, that we're beginning to recognise. Something has broken, in what once seemed necessary. Enemy, now, has lost its meaning: there is no such distinction. We are our own enemies, and we are destroying ourselves. Our own best people have become our enemies: the bravest, the clearest; the most articulate and the most humane. For them, as we are, destruction is certain. Death homes on them, now, with a fine logic. And the rest of us see this, and draw our conclusions. We kill all these things in ourselves, commit the suicide of the heart, so that it will not betray us, not involve us. And then the process runs faster, and we are all become Koba.

[JOSEPH *has entered. He stands, listening, holding himself up by the door.*]

JOSEPH: We have mastered ourselves, and we have become Koba.

[*The* SECRETARY *and the* DOCTOR *watch him, but do not speak.*]

JOSEPH: Will you not come near me? Have you nothing to say to me?

SECRETARY: Koba.

JOSEPH: You are only an echo. You can say nothing.

SECRETARY: This is the doctor, Koba.

JOSEPH: He has come too late. He can only watch me die.

DOCTOR: I have watched others die.

JOSEPH: Yes, of course. It is not significant. The death of one man is a normal business.

SECRETARY: But Koba . . .

JOSEPH: It is not Koba dying, it is Joseph dying.

SECRETARY: Yet a single death can be the death of a people. You are our father, Koba.

JOSEPH: The people is Koba, and cannot die. In myself I am nothing. I have mastered myself.

DOCTOR: You have mastered a people.

JOSEPH: And they have become Koba: a people who cannot be mastered. A people strong and absolute, with a place and a future. What does Joseph matter? They can forget him or set him aside. But the power is real, and it is the power of life. I see this figure of man the creator, the towering figure on the crest of the hill.

[*The* SECRETARY *and the* DOCTOR *are silent, watching* JOSEPH *as he struggles to hold himself up.* LUKE *enters, but* JOSEPH *does not notice him.*]

SECRETARY: Will you not help him, doctor? You can see how he needs you.

DOCTOR: No. He has spoken the truth. I can do nothing for him.

[LUKE *crosses to* JOSEPH, *who does not recognise him.*]

LUKE: You have lived by death, Joseph. I will kneel to your death.

JOSEPH: You must not kneel. Men have kneeled enough. We must learn to stand, in our own strength.

LUKE: I kneel to your death, Joseph.

JOSEPH: Only strength matters. Does any man living deny this? We have learned to be strong, and we have become strong. We have the strength of life. We give this strength to others, and we are strong in ourselves.

LUKE: I kneel to your death, Joseph.

[*He kneels and lowers his head.*]

JOSEPH: I will not die. I am Koba. I will master death.

[LUKE *does not move.* JOSEPH *tries to speak again, but the power to speak has left him, though he still holds himself upright.*]

DOCTOR: Do you see his face?

SECRETARY: Is he dying?

DOCTOR: Not yet, not just yet. He is mastering himself.

SECRETARY: But he cannot speak. He is trying to speak, and no words will come.

DOCTOR: Yes, he has waited for the argument to end. Only the facts count now.

SECRETARY: Have you no pity at all?

DOCTOR: Did he have pity?

SECRETARY: That man kneeling has pity.

DOCTOR: But he is only a voice. He will not alter the facts.

[JOSEPH *tries to speak again, but can make no sound. In his effort he loses his grip on the door, and almost stumbles, but succeeds in recovering himself.* MARK *enters, with the* WARDER *following.*]

MARK: Have I come in time?

SECRETARY: He is as you see him. He can no longer speak.

MARK: Who is that kneeling?

SECRETARY: A man. I don't know him.

MARK: I was released this morning. Did he give the order?

SECRETARY: Koba? No.

[MARK *turns to the* WARDER.]

MARK: Who gave the order?

WARDER: It came. I don't question my orders.

[MARK *turns to the* SECRETARY.]

MARK: Did you give the order?

SECRETARY: I am only the Secretary. I give no orders.

MARK: Are we all silent? Can none of us speak any more? Is there anyone responsible? Can nobody speak?

[JOSEPH *again tries to speak, and* MARK *goes across to him.*]

MARK: Can you hear me, Koba? Do you know who I am?

[JOSEPH *stands quite still.*]

MARK: You can still see, though you cannot speak. Do you not see how we are? Do you not see what has happened?

[JOSEPH *looks around him, and again tries to speak. When the words do not come, he tightens his grip on the door.*]

MARK: Can't you understand me, Koba? Can't you hear what

I'm saying? Is there nothing you can say, at this last moment? Can you say nothing? Can you do nothing? [LUKE *rises and turns to* MARK. *He takes his arm and leads him away from* JOSEPH. *They turn, and stand watching.* JOSEPH *takes his hands from the door, slowly, and stands upright, facing them. Then he falls, stiffly, face down, and lies still.*

SCENE VII

The body of JOSEPH *is laid in state at the back of the stage, on a raised platform.* MARK *is sitting at the desk, and* LUKE *stands facing him. The* SECRETARY *and the* WARDER *are to the right, guarded.* JOSEPH *stands near the window, in shadow.*

MARK: There is so much to do. Even before the funeral, I have given the order. There will be no more killing.

LUKE: Except for these two.

MARK: They were Koba's agents. To stop the killing, we must punish the killers.

LUKE: Or when the master is dead, you will shoot the dogs.

MARK: I know what you mean, Luke, but this is a political world. Do you understand, even yet, the scale of this killing? You have seen the leaders, shot and imprisoned. But with every leader went a thousand others, and their wives and their children. There is no counting the killing. The mind breaks at its numbers. But now we must end it, and be seen to end it. Yet will anyone believe us, if its agents go free? I wish it could be different, but we are bound to punish all those responsible, for this crime that has weighed on our lives.

LUKE: You mean we must punish ourselves?

MARK: Take care what you say, to a victim.

LUKE: I am also a victim, but I know my own guilt. And because I accept that, I want an end to the killing.

MARK: No, you're not guilty. You're less guilty than I am. When Koba broke, we were all victims.

LUKE: When Koba broke? But then who was Koba?

MARK: Do you need to ask? He is lying in death and in state. We have all seen him, and we have seen him change. At the time of the famine, when Ruth took poison, we saw him break. He had been hard before, but it was a hardness

of policy. We all saw it change to a thing in itself. He simply
went mad, a rigid madness, from which no-one was safe.
He arrested and killed in a separate logic. Whoever
opposed him, or might oppose him, he merely destroyed.

LUKE: We have all done this, Mark. We are all implicated.

MARK: That is simply a lie. We have not all killed.

LUKE: But we have accepted a state that was built by killing.

MARK: How far will you go? Will you go back on everything?
Will you go back to the beginning, to the revolution itself,
and repudiate that?

LUKE: The revolution was not the beginning. It seemed like
an end. But yes, I go back to it, and I see its killing. I go
back to the state the revolution destroyed, and I see its
killing also. I see other countries, now ordered and peaceful, and every one of them has been built by killing, at one
time or another. All of us, Mark, are involved. We can't
hide in time or in a change of name. We have killed and
accepted the subsequent order, or others have killed and
we have inherited.

MARK: Yet when we change our lives we change the inheritance.

LUKE: When we change, yes. But it's too easy a word. It's
more than forgetting, or the easy decision that we needn't
kill any more, because the situation is different. There's
still the inheritance, the real inheritance. That we need not
kill may be just our luck.

MARK: But the change has happened. I know how people are
feeling.

LUKE: We are feeling easier, of course. More secure, better
furnished. And we don't want to kill; we have room to live
and let live. We don't need to kill; we have become strong.

MARK: Yes, certainly. This is the change.

LUKE: It is no change at all. It isn't even our luck. Luck or
madness, these are simple disguises. What we have really
to face is how all this happened, how we became strong.

MARK: It was not only Koba. In many ways he made us
weaker.

LUKE: But in other ways stronger. Do you really deny that?

MARK: Of the beginning, no, I do not deny it.

LUKE: But which was the beginning, and which the end?
There was the same feeling, always. He was always Koba.

Once the world seized him, that old dark world, he was no longer Joseph and he was always Koba.

MARK: He was Koba and he changed. We have all seen this. But it is more than his history. It is the history of need. When the need arises, the absolute need, most men will kill. This is the history of the world. You ask us to be guilty, because it is so, but guilt is irrelevant, and we have to reject it. If we want to change, we must learn to look at the need. If we want to end killing, we must change the world in which killing is normal. Neither guilt nor pity will help us in that, but only knowing the need and meeting the need.

LUKE: Koba killed beyond need. Isn't that what you're saying?

MARK: The need broke him, the genuine need. In any man this can happen, and he can become a killer.

LUKE: It was our need. It was not only his.

MARK: The need has changed. He became irrelevant. While he served the need, the genuine need, he was changing the world, and that is what we remember. The tragedy of Koba is that the need broke him, and in the end destroyed him. What he made has condemned him. This is where we now are.

LUKE: It is all very easy, while that body lies there. You can point to Koba, and he is your guilt. You can condemn him and excuse yourselves.

[MARK *gets up.*]

MARK: Yes, this is so, and it must be so. Unless this is so, there will be no change. Koba is dead, and his world dies with him. This is what life demands, and it is a tragic justice.

LUKE: All the guilt on to him. Is that how it will be?

MARK: Yes, that is how it must be.

LUKE: Then why kill these others?

MARK: Because they are part of him. Because they are Koba.

LUKE: We are all Koba. You are arguing like him.

MARK: No, Koba is dead, and that is an end.

[LUKE *turns and walks to stand by* JOSEPH's *body. He looks back at* MARK, *and then walks to the* SECRETARY *and the* WARDER.]

LUKE: You admit that you killed?

SECRETARY: It's completely absurd. I've killed nobody. I've never so much as touched a gun.

LUKE: But you carried the orders to kill.

SECRETARY: They were Koba's orders. I had to transmit them. It was my duty as secretary.

LUKE: And you, Warder, you admit that you killed?

WARDER: Yes, sir.

LUKE: And must be killed in your turn?

WARDER: It's what they say, sir. But I don't see it myself. After all it was orders. It was to look after the country. Every decent man must do that.

LUKE: This is where it all starts. You're quite right.

WARDER: Or take these others, sir, now their luck's turned. They'll do what I did, what suits them, like anyone else.

LUKE: What they think right, don't you mean?

WARDER: That's what I said, sir. Any decent man.

[LUKE *turns to* MARK.]

LUKE: I face these men, who face death,
    And I see in their shadowed faces,
    Not the agents I know, but brothers,
    Men of my own kind, men sharing my breath,
    Men who have lived in ordinary places,
    And have killed and forgotten their kind.
    The evil cannot be shifted, from them or from others,
    But the judgement dies, the habit of anger dies,
    For over the untold dead I cannot be blind
    To the neighbour's look in these men's eyes.

[MARK *turns away.*]

MARK: They are not my brothers.

LUKE: Then we shall go on killing, until we are brothers?

WARDER: You're quite right, sir, and he'd do well to listen.

SECRETARY: It is what we worked for, that men should be brothers.

[MARK *turns back.*]

MARK: You see how it is, Luke. Any feeling can be used.

LUKE: And given. And given again.

[MARK *stands, stiffly.* LUKE *waits, and then crosses to kneel by the body of* JOSEPH.]

LUKE: I can say no more. I can only kneel. I kneel to this life and this death, for it has been our history and it is still our tragedy. The darkness flowered, in its own season. The darkness flowered, passing beyond its source.

[MARK *looks across at the* SECRETARY *and the* WARDER. *He lifts his hand for them to be taken away.*]

MARK: You can take them away.

[JOSEPH *steps forward.*]

JOSEPH: No.

MARK: Who are you? What are you?

JOSEPH: My name is Joseph. I'm a student.

MARK: Joseph? Come closer. Here, in the light, where I can see you.

JOSEPH: No. I stay here. Come closer yourself if you like.

MARK: What's that you're carrying?

JOSEPH: This? It's a book. Why?

MARK: I'm sorry. I have to be careful.

JOSEPH: Because there are books the party accepts and books it rejects? Is that why you're worried?

MARK: We'd be fools to take risks, after so much danger.

JOSEPH: He's dead, isn't he?

MARK: Is that all you can say?

JOSEPH: It's all that needs to be said. He's dead and it's over.

MARK: You can see for yourself that it isn't over. You can see his agents, still here.

JOSEPH: Which are they?

MARK: The men guarded.

JOSEPH: It's as well to know. Will you dismiss the guards?

MARK: I will certainly not dismiss them.

JOSEPH: Then they will have to take me.

[MARK *hesitates. He looks from* JOSEPH *to the body in state.* JOSEPH *comes forward and speaks to the guards.*]

JOSEPH: You can release these men.

[*The guards hesitate, and look across to* MARK. *He turns away from them.*]

JOSEPH: I asked you, friends, to release them.

[*The guards again hesitate, and then release the* SECRETARY *and* WARDER.]

JOSEPH: The guards can go.

[*The guards leave.* JOSEPH *moves very close to the* SECRETARY *and the* WARDER.]

JOSEPH: I wanted to look at you. But now you must go. Without office you are nothing. Go away and live as you can.

[*The* SECRETARY *and the* WARDER *wait, as if for an order.*]

JOSEPH: You heard us. Go.

[*The* SECRETARY *and the* WARDER *leave, looking back.*]

JOSEPH: All right. Now I'm here in the light. You can look if you want.

MARK: And your name is Joseph?

JOSEPH: You're afraid because he is lying there. But who is that kneeling? Why should he kneel?

MARK: He has seen it all through. He is a good man.

JOSEPH: Then he should not kneel. You are all so afraid of the dead.

MARK: There have been so many.

JOSEPH: Take him up. Walk firmly. It is the future you are carrying.

MARK: Those were Koba's words, at the death of Jordan.

JOSEPH: They were terrible words. There was death in them. As there is death, now, in this room.

MARK: We are older than you. We have seen more death.

JOSEPH: All right, if you're tired. Let the days pass. People will quickly forget.

MARK: And that is enough?

JOSEPH: It may be enough. You'll pay your respects and have a drink after the funeral. You'll grudge the expense of the monument, but you'll still put it up. The dead have to stand, overlooking the city.

MARK: Then what would be enough?

JOSEPH: You should take this body and burn it. You should tell the truth and then scatter the ashes, to the sun and the winds. You should fight this man dead, since you failed to fight him alive.

MARK: That's easy to say but not easy to do. People respect the dead.

JOSEPH: They must respect the living.

MARK: By insulting the dead?

JOSEPH: We have to master our fear of them. They were men like ourselves.

MARK: You are talking like Koba. Those were Koba's words.

JOSEPH: Not exactly his words, but he is not Koba. He is Joseph and dead.

MARK: And you are Joseph and living. But then who was Koba?

[LUKE *rises, and turns to* JOSEPH.]

LUKE: I think Koba still lives.

JOSEPH: Yes, he still lives.

LUKE: He is the name of our fear. A name born out of darkness.

JOSEPH: He is the name of our strength. A name born into light.

LUKE: It is a hated name, since he has used it. Even to say Koba is to say killing.

JOSEPH: To say Koba is to say that men will not be mastered.

[MARK *crosses and stands by* JOSEPH'*s body, looking down.*]

MARK: I am still afraid. I am afraid of the word. I am afraid of mastery. I have seen what the will can do, what power can do, against flesh and blood. . . . When I met this man, I believed in love and in freedom. He offered to show me their world, and he taught me to kill. He taught me the method of power, the excitement of mastering life. I don't know any more. I am afraid of strength.

[*He turns to* JOSEPH.]

And now you have come, and I hear your voice, a young voice, and the echo disturbs me. You speak of not being mastered, and the echo disturbs me. I have seen too many die, with those words in their faces. You say I am afraid, and I admit I am afraid. I am afraid of that man who lies dead, and of you who reject him, with the same hardness and confidence. I am even afraid because your name is Joseph.

LUKE: Yes, Joseph. Now that you have come I have seen the circle of tragedy. The man dies but the spirit lives. It will always be so, in the world. There is always Joseph, there will always be Koba. But I am certain of this, that I will go on witnessing. I will say tragedy when others say life. I will say tragedy when others say Koba. I haven't the last word, but I have my own word.

[JOSEPH *turns away, and seems to be going. But he turns back, and crosses to look down into* JOSEPH'*s face.*]

JOSEPH: He is Joseph again. Only the action is Koba. And I am Joseph because he was Joseph, and the action has changed us. We have completed the circle, and so now we can break it. We have fought and changed. We shall mourn and change. Take him up, walk firmly, it is the past we are carrying. The action is ended, and we can make a beginning.

[MARK *and* JOSEPH *take up the body, and carry it out.* LUKE *watches them, as the curtain falls.*]

INDEX

INDEX

(*a*) Authors   (*b*) Works   (*c*) Ideas